LEAVING CERTIF

GW01091143

LESS STRESS MORE SUCCESS

Business Revision

John F. O'Sullivan

g GILL EDUCATION

Gill Education
Hume Avenue
Park West
Dublin 12
www.gilleducation.ie

Gill Education is an imprint of M. H. Gill & Co.

© John F. O'Sullivan 2018

978 07171 8357 9

Design by Liz White Designs
Artwork and print origination by Síofra Murphy

For permission to reproduce photographs, the author and publisher gratefully acknowledge the following:

© Alamy: 19, 24, 150, 189, 195, 210, 223T, 224, 237, 260, 264T, 284, 316, 335; Courtesy of ASTI: 26R; Courtesy of Construction Industry Federation: 4C; © E+/Getty Premium: 4B; Courtesy of Energia: 323; © Getty Images: 47, 136, 250; Courtesy of Irish Congress of Trade Unions: 4T; Courtesy of INTO: 26C; © iStock/Getty Premium: 75, 98, 174, 241, 264B, 296, 325, 347; © Photocall: 223B, 252; Courtesy of TUI: 26L; Courtesy of VHI: 117.

The authors and publisher have made every effort to trace all copyright holders, but if any have been inadvertently overlooked we would be pleased to make the necessary arrangement at the first opportunity.

The paper used in this book is made from the wood pulp of managed forests. For every tree felled, at least one tree is planted, thereby renewing natural resources.

CONTENTS

Introduction

General Examination Advice: Higher Level

> **HL** *Note:* Material that is to be studied only by those taking Higher Level is indicated in the text.

Section 1 Short answer questions

HL

1. Short answer questions only have four lines of space for writing answers, so keep your answers short and to the point.
2. Write two points of information for each answer (unless told otherwise in the question). The first point should be a definition; then you can use an advantage/disadvantage or an explained example as a second point.
3. Answer all ten short questions if you have time. The examiner will mark you on your eight best answers.

Section 2 Applied Business Question (ABQ)

1. The Applied Business Question describes a business situation facing a company or business person.
2. It usually contains three paragraphs of text with three questions based on the information given.
3. It is a compulsory question and carries 20% of the total marks. You must answer all three questions in the ABQ. There is no choice.
4. The ABQ each year is based on three different units of the course.

Advice for answering the Applied Business Question

1. Read the questions first. This will tell you what to look out for when you read the paragraphs of text.
2. Read the information in the ABQ paragraphs. Highlight or underline relevant points as you read the text.
3. Answer each of the three questions as follows:

(A) State the point – give a heading.
(B) Explain and develop the point – theory/textbook knowledge.
If the question says 'describe', 'analyse' or 'evaluate', you must give more detailed information. 'Evaluate' means you must give your opinion on the topic. ('I think it is good (or bad) because . . .') Give a reason why (maybe advantage or disadvantage).

– Always write a heading evaluation in the answer.

– Give an opinion or judgement on the issues covered in the answer.

(C) Quote from the text to back up your point.

You must quote from the text for every point you make in your answer even if not asked to do so in the question. Use a red pen to highlight your quotes.

Section 3 – Long answer questions

1. Answer the required number of questions from Part 1 and Part 2.

2. Read the questions carefully and ensure you give the required information in your answers.

3. Divide the marks by 5 to see approximately how many points you are expected to make in your answer.

4. Answer in point form (no essays).

    Number each point clearly. For each point in your answer:

    - State the point
    - Explain and develop the point
    - Give an explained example, if possible.

> **exam focus**
>
> - In answering the questions on the ABQ, candidates **must** make use of relevant knowledge/theory (and understanding) gained in the subject while studying the course, in addition to the relevant links from the ABQ.
> - In relation to the links given, they **must** be a direct, relevant quote/phrase/statement from the ABQ indicating that candidates clearly understand the point(s) of theory presented.
> - No marks are awarded for links without relevant business theory.
> - Separate links are required in each section.
> - No marks are awarded for business theory unless theory is relevant to the ABQ.

Mini ABQ questions

These are appearing frequently in recent years.

Each question contains a short piece of text about a business and then asks questions about it. When answering the questions, you must quote or reference the text in each part of your answer.

Key verbs in the questions that regularly appear at Higher Level

- **Analyse:**
    - State the point
    - Explain the point
    - Make a comment on it, state an advantage or disadvantage.
- **Apply:** Use knowledge or skill for a particular purpose.
- **Compare:** Examine two or more things so as to discover their similarities or differences.
- **Calculate:** Find out or ascertain by using numerical data.

- **Contrast/differentiate/distinguish:**
  - Show the differences between the two things mentioned in the question
  - If the differences are obvious, you could use the word 'whereas' to link the differences; otherwise you can show the differences by stating a number of points about each topic.
- **Define:**
  - State the precise meaning of the topic
  - Give at least two points of information.
- **Describe:** Give an account of person, event, institution, etc.
- **Discuss:** Give a detailed explanation, debating both sides of the issue.
- **Draft:** Draw up whatever document is requested – business letter, report, memo, agenda, business plan – or sketch a diagram or chart.
- **Evaluate:**
  - State the point
  - Explain and develop the point
  - Evaluate: Give your opinion on the topic (assess or judge something). State whether it is a good thing or a bad thing and back it up with a reason (advantage or disadvantage).
- **Explain:** Make clear in a detailed manner.
- **Identify:** Show that you recognise something.
- **Illustrate:**
  - State the point
  - Explain and develop the point
  - Give an example for each point (make clear by means of examples, charts, diagrams, graphs, etc.).
- **List:** Write down a number of names or things that have something in common.
- **Outline:** Give a short summary of the chief elements, omitting details.

Legislation on the course

The following are the nine laws in the course:

- Sale of Goods and Supply of Services Act 1980
- Consumer Protection Act 2007
- Competition and Consumer Protection Act 2014
- Industrial Relations Act 1990
- Workplace Relations Act 2015
- Employment Equality Act 1998 to 2015
- Unfair Dismissals Acts 1977 to 2015
- Data Protection Act 2018, incorporating the General Data Protection Regulation (GDPR)
- Companies Act 2014 (as it relates to the formation of private companies only)

Practise calculation-type questions

- Ratio analysis (profitability, liquidity, debt–equity ratio)
- Tax calculation
- Average clause (insurance)
- Balance of trade/balance of payments
- Break-even point/margin of safety
- Analyse a cash flow forecast

Practise essential diagrams

- Maslow's hierarchy of needs
- Break-even chart
- Bar chart, pie chart
- Product life cycle
- Organisational chart (functional/matrix)
- Span of control
- Channels of distribution

Drafting documents

- Business letter
- Business report
- Notice, agenda and minutes of meeting
- Memorandum (memo)
- Business plan

Higher Level examination layout – 400 marks – 3 hours (180 minutes)

Section	Questions	Answer	Marks (%)	Areas covered	Timing
1	Ten short answer questions.	Eight questions.	80/400 (20%)	All parts of course.	30 minutes (approx. 4 minutes per question).
2	Applied Business Question (ABQ).	All three parts (compulsory question).	80/400 (20%)	The ABQ each year is based on three different units of the course as follows: 2019 – Units 1, 2, 3 2020 – Units 2, 3, 4 2021 – Units 3, 4, 5 2022 – Units 4, 5, 6 2023 – Units 5, 6, 7 2024 – Units 1, 2, 3 2025 – Units 2, 3, 4 2026 – Units 3, 4, 5 2027 – Units 4, 5, 6 2028 – Units 5, 6, 7	40 minutes.
3	Seven questions. Part 1 contains **three** questions. Part 2 contains **four** questions.	Four questions Part 1: Answer **one** question. Part 2: Answer **two** questions. Answer fourth question from either Part 1 or Part 2.	240/400 (60%) Each question is worth 60 marks.	Part 1 questions are taken from units 1, 6, 7. Part 2 questions are taken from units 2, 3, 4, 5.	100 minutes (approx. 25 minutes per question).

Timing above allows five minutes for reading the examination paper and selecting questions, and five minutes for reading over your answers and checking your work at the end of the exam.

Section 3 past exam paper analysis Higher Level

	2018	2017	2016	2015	2014	2013	2012	2011	2010	2009	2008	2007	2006	2005
Unit 1														
Relationships in Business	Q1(A)	Q1(A)	Q1(B)	Q1(AB)	Q1(B)	Q1(C)	Q1(B)	Q1(A)	Q1(C)	Q1(AB)	Q1(A)	Q1(C)	Q1(AC)	Q1(AB)
Consumer/Retailer		Q1(C)	Q1(C)		Q1(C)	Q1(B)	Q1(C)	Q1(B)	Q1(B)		Q1(B)	Q1(B)		Q1(C)
Employer/Employee	Q1(BC)	Q1(B)	Q1(A)	Q1(C)	Q1(A)	Q1(A)	Q1(A)	Q1(C)	Q1(A)	Q1(C)	Q1(C)	Q1(A)	Q1(B)	
Unit 2														
Enterprise	Q3(C)	Q4(A)	Q4(A)			Q4(A)		Q4(A)			Q4(A)	Q4(A)	Q4(C)	
Unit 3														
Management														
Leading, Motivating	Q6(B) Q3(B)				Q4(C)		Q4(C)	Q4(B)		Q4(AB)			Q4(AB)	Q4(C)
Communication		Q4(BC)		Q4(A)	Q4(AB)		Q4(AB)			Q4(C)6(A)	Q4(B)	Q4(BC)		Q4(AB)
Planning, Organising, Controlling	Q3(A)		Q4(BC)	Q4(BC)		Q4(BC)		Q4(C)	Q4(ABC)		Q4(C)			

	2018	2017	2016	2015	2014	2013	2012	2011	2010	2009	2008	2007	2006	2005
Unit 4														
Household and Business: Finance				Q6(C)	Q6(BC)	Q5(C)				Q6(C)	Q6(A)	Q6(B)		
Household and Business: Insurance	Q5(B)			Q6(A)	Q5(C)			Q5(C)			Q6(B)		Q5(A)	
Household and Business: Taxation	Q6(C)					Q5(A)		Q5(B)			Q6(A)	Q5(AB)		
Human Resource Management	Q6(A)	Q6(A)	Q5(A)	Q6(B)	Q5(A)	Q5(B)		Q5(A)	Q5(A)		Q5(AB)			
Changing Role of Management			Q5(BC)				Q6(A)			Q6(B)	Q5 (C) 6 (C)	Q5(C)		Q6(A)
Monitoring the Business		Q6(BC)			Q5(B)		Q5(B)		Q5(BC)	Q5(C)		Q6(C)	Q5(B)	
Unit 5														
Identifying Opportunities		Q5(A)	Q6(A) Q7(A)			Q6(A) Q7(A)	Q6(B)	Q6(C)	Q7(A)	Q7(A)	Q7(C)			Q6(A)
Marketing	Q7(ABC)	Q5(B) Q7(BC)	Q6(BC) Q7(BC)	Q5(AB) Q7(ABC)	Q7(AB)	Q7(BC)	Q7(AB)	Q7(BC)	Q7(BC)	Q7(BC)	Q7(B)	Q6 (A) Q7(ABC)	Q7 (ABC)	Q6 (B) Q7(ABC)
Getting Started	Q5(C)	Q5(C) Q7(C)		Q5(C)	Q6(A) Q7(C)		Q6(C)	Q7A	Q6(BC)		Q7(A)		Q6(A)	Q5(A)
Business Expansion	Q5(A)					Q6(BC)	Q7(C)	Q6(AB)	Q6(A)	Q5(AB)			Q6(B)	Q5(BC)

	2018	2017	2016	2015	2014	2013	2012	2011	2010	2009	2008	2007	2006	2005
Unit 6														
Categories of Industry		Q2(A)				Q2(C)						Q2(A)	Q2(A)	
Type of Business Organisations	Q2(A) Q2(C)		Q2(B) Q2(A)	Q2(A)	Q2(B)	Q2(A)	Q2(A)	Q2(B)	Q2(B)	Q2(A)				Q2(A)
Community Development								Q2(C)						Q2(B)
Business and the Economy	Q2(B)			Q2(B)				Q2(A)				Q2(B)	Q2(B)	
Government and Business		Q2(C)	Q2(A)		Q2(AC)	Q2(B)	Q2(B)		Q2(C)	Q2(C)	Q2(C)			
Social Responsibility of Business		Q2(B)	Q2(C)	Q2(C)			Q2(C)		Q2(A)	Q2(B)	Q2(B)	Q2(C)	Q2(C)	Q2(C)
Unit 7														
International Trading	Q3(C)	Q3(A)	Q3(C)			Q3(AB)	Q3(B)	Q3(A)	Q3(AB)			Q3(A)	Q3(C)	
European Union	Q3(B)	Q3(C)	Q2(C)	Q3(C)	Q3(BC)	Q3(C)	Q3(C)	Q3(C)	Q3(C)	Q3(A)	Q3 (ABC)	Q3(C)	Q3(AB)	Q3(AB)
Interionational Business	Q3(A)	Q3(B)	Q3(B)	Q3(AB)	Q3(A)		Q3(A)	Q3(B)		Q3(B)	Q2(A)	Q3(B)		Q3(C)

General Examination Advice: Ordinary Level

Section 1 Short answer questions

1. Short answer questions have only four lines of space for writing answers, so keep your answer short and to the point.
   Write two points of information for each answer (unless told otherwise in the question).
2. Answer all 15 short questions if you have time. The examiner will mark you on your 10 best answers.

Section 2 Long answer questions

1. Answer the required number of questions from Part 1 and Part 2.
2. Read the questions carefully and ensure you give the required information in your answers.
3. Divide the marks by five to see approximately how many points you are expected to make in your answer.
4. Answer in point form.

Number each point clearly. For each point in your answers:

- State the point
- Explain the point
- Give an example, if possible.

Key verbs in the questions that regularly appear at Ordinary Level

- **Calculate:** Find out or ascertain by using numerical data.
- **Define:** State the precise meaning of.
- **Describe:** Give an account of.
- **Discuss:** Give a detailed explanation.
- **Distinguish:** Show the differences.
- **Draft:** Draw up – document, letter, sketch, diagram.
- **Explain:** Make clear in a detailed manner.
- **Identify:** Show that you recognise something.
- **Illustrate:** Make clear by means of examples, charts, diagrams, graphs, etc.
- **List:** Write down a number of things that have something in common.
- **Outline:** Give a short summary, omitting detail.

Ordinary Level examination layout – 400 marks – 2½ hours (150 minutes)

Section	Questions	Answer	Marks (%)	Areas covered	Timing
1	15 short answer questions.	10 questions.	100/400 (25%)	All parts of course.	32 minutes (approx. 3 minutes per question).
2	Eight questions. Part 1 contains **three** questions. Part 2 contains **five** questions.	Four questions. Part 1 answer **one** question. Part 2 answer **two** questions. Answer the fourth question from either Part 1 or Part 2.	300/400 (75%) Each question is worth 75 marks.	Part 1 questions are taken from units 1, 6, 7. Part 2 questions are taken from units 2, 3, 4, 5.	108 minutes (approx. 27 minutes per question).

Timing above allows five minutes for reading the examination paper and selecting questions, and five minutes for reading over your answers and checking your work at the end of exam.

UNIT 1

Introduction to People in Business

Business is primarily concerned with people and their relationships. This section introduces the main parties in business and their roles, and it examines how they work successfully together. It also looks at areas where their interests may not coincide and ways of resolving such situations of conflict.

Objective
To enable pupils to understand the form and the dynamic nature of the relationships between the different parties in business.

- **Chapter 1:** People and Their Relationships in Business
- **Chapter 2:** Conflict Resolution 1: Consumer and Retailer
- **Chapter 3:** Conflict Resolution 2: Employer and Employee

People and Their Relationships in Business

Main parties and people in business

Business – business is about producing and supplying goods and services.

Stakeholder – anyone or any group of people that has an interest/involvement in or is directly affected by how a business is run.

People in business – business is concerned with people and their relationships.

Entrepreneurs

- Individuals or a group who undertake the **risk of establishing and running a business.**
- They follow through on **ideas** and take the chance of failure.
- They **see an opportunity** and set out to exploit that opportunity.
- They take the risk of **organising all the resources** necessary to provide a product or service.

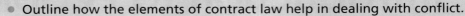

Parties in business include:
- Entrepreneurs
- Service providers
- Investors
- Employers
- Producers/suppliers
- Employees
- Consumers
- Interest groups

Investors

- Investors provide capital/finance/grants needed for businesses/entrepreneurs.
- **Investors risk money in a project** that may or may not make a profit for them in the future.
- The money is used to **purchase assets and finance the enterprise.**
  Examples:
  (i) Shareholders – with a view to profit/dividend
  (ii) Owner's capital – with a view to profit
  (iii) Lenders (banks) – provide loan capital, which must be repaid with interest
  (iv) Government grants – repayment not required but conditions attached.

Producers/suppliers

- These are the **manufacturers and suppliers** of goods and services.
- Producers make goods that satisfy consumers' needs and wants.
- Producers want high prices and profit.

Consumers

- Are the **users** or purchasers of goods and services for personal use.
- They want **quality** and **service** at reasonable **prices**.

Service providers

- These provide a **range of services** for the efficient operation of business (e.g. banking, insurance, transport).

Employers

- An employer is a person or business that hires employees/staff to produce goods or provide services and pays them agreed wages/salaries for their work.
- Employers want an **honest and reliable workforce** and good quality work.

Responsibilities of an employer

- (i) to provide a safe and healthy working environment
- (ii) to pay the agreed wage for the work done (at least minimum wage rate)
- (iii) to adhere to legislation, e.g. Employment Equality, Unfair Dismissal
- (iv) to provide a contract of employment
- (v) to keep appropriate records for income tax and PRSI returns
- (vi) to provide appropriate annual leave as per legislation.

Employees

- Employees **work for employers**, producing goods or supplying services.
- Their **rights** include reasonable pay, safe working conditions and a contract of employment.
- Their **responsibilities** include honest work, compliance with their contract of employment and compliance with reasonable instructions from their employer.

Interest groups

- An interest group is an organisation which **represents the common viewpoint**, objectives and goals of a particular group.
- Interest groups seek to **influence** decisions and policy affecting their members through negotiation, lobbying, boycotting and possibly legal action.
- Lobbying is the deliberate effort to influence the decision-making process by promoting a particular point of view with government or MEPs or with other organisations.
- Interest groups may or may not succeed in achieving their desired objectives.

Examples

- **Business Associations**:
  - Irish Business and Employers Confederation (IBEC)
    - Represents employers on industrial relations matters
    - Negotiates with government and ICTU on wage agreements
    - Advises members on the effects of new EU legislation, etc.
  - The Irish Congress of Trade Unions (ICTU)
    - Represents almost all trade unions in Ireland
    - Represents and advances the economic and social interests of working people
    - Negotiates national agreements with government and employers
    - Regulates relations between unions and rules on inter-union disputes, etc.

  - The Construction Industry Federation (CIF) represents businesses in all areas of the construction industry.
  - The Irish Farmers' Association (IFA)
    - The IFA lobbies government to initiate pro-farming policies that would improve and consolidate farm incomes.

- **Trade Associations**:
  - The Society of the Irish Motor Industry (SIMI) represents members in the motor industry.
  - The Irish Travel Agents Association (ITAA) represents travel agents.

Relationships between parties in business

People in business can either co-operate with each other and help one another or can compete with each other.

- A **co-operative relationship** exists where stakeholders work together towards a common objective to everyone's benefit.
- A **competitive relationship** exists where stakeholders pursue individual objectives and seek to achieve their objectives at the expense of each other.

1. Relationship between entrepreneur and investor

Entrepreneurs are risk-takers: they exercise initiative and take a risk in starting up a business with the hope of making a profit.

Investors invest finance in an enterprise; investors can be banks or other financial institutions or private individuals with money who wish to invest. If the investor feels that the venture is a good risk when compared to the possible return in the future, then a decision will be made to invest.

Co-operative relationship

When an entrepreneur seeks finance for a new project, they build a strong relationship with an investor. The relationship between the entrepreneur and the investor must be one of co-operation to ensure that both of them gain.

The relationship will remain co-operative as long as the entrepreneur presents a strong business plan with a projected cash flow forecast, profit and loss account and balance sheet.

Investors will also want to see the plans for the repayment of the funds to minimise the risks involved.

Competitive relationship

A competitive relationship will arise if the investor refuses to advance the funds required to establish a new business.

It will also exist if the entrepreneur – having received finance – is not living up to the commitments entered into and is defaulting on repayments.

2. Relationship between producers and interest groups

Producers manufacture goods or supply services that satisfy consumers' needs.

Interest groups are groups that wish to influence the decision-making process but are not part of the accepted political structure.

Interest groups may affect producer interests.

Co-operative relationship

Producers may have their own interest group, which lobbies government on their behalf to change laws relating to taxation or the operation of their industry.

Competitive relationship

Interest groups can affect producer interests.

They can cause bad publicity for a business or cause the image of a business to be damaged (e.g. a fall-off in demand for its products).

This can increase costs as more advertising is needed to counter the bad publicity.

Security may have to be increased because of protest meetings, possible picketing at premises, etc.

3. Relationship between producers and consumers

Producers are the manufacturers and suppliers of goods and services.

Producers are interested in making profit, but they can do so only if they make goods that satisfy consumers' needs and wants.

Consumers are the purchasers or users of goods and services supplied by firms.

Consumers try to satisfy their wants by buying products and services that are of good quality, reasonably priced and come with good after-sale service.

Co-operative relationship

Producers co-operate with consumers and the relationship is good when:

- Producers provide the products/services demanded by the consumer
- Products are top quality and reasonably priced
- Consumers are satisfied with the product

Competitive relationship

The interests of consumers and producers are sometimes in conflict because the consumer wants low prices and high quality, while producers want high prices and profit.

A competitive relationship between producers is beneficial for the consumer as every business must work hard to satisfy consumer needs.

Producers will compete on prices of goods and services, quality, sales, etc.

Consumers will benefit from:

- Improved quality
- Improved customer services
- Better choice of products
- Better value for money

4. Relationship between producers in the same line of business

Co-operative relationship

A co-operative relationship exists where joint action or effort is required so that producers work together to everyone's benefit toward a common objective.

Example

Producers in the same line of business sometimes co-operate with each other to:

- Protect their industry against an outside threat
- Encourage economic development and to create jobs for the benefit of the community
- Lobby the government in order to solve problems of mutual interest, such as achieving a change in legislation or a reduction in VAT
- Agree on a common scale of discounts for their customers

Competitive relationship

A competitive relationship between producers in the same line of business means each is pursuing individual objectives and seeks to achieve these objective at the expense of each other. This is beneficial for the consumer as every business must satisfy consumer needs.

Example

Producers in the same line of business may compete on:

- Prices of goods and services
- Quality
- Sales

5. Relationship between employer and employees

Employers aim to:

- Keep production costs low so that the firm will remain competitive
- Increase profits so that retained earnings can be built up to give a good return on the capital invested for the owners

Employees want:

- Reasonable wages, good working conditions and a good standard of living
- Job security and promotion

A good relationship between employers and employees is vital for the success of the business.

Co-operative relationship

When employers and employees have a co-operative relationship the business can be successful.

Employers and employees co-operate when:

- Agreeing pay and working conditions
- Producing goods and services for consumers
- Consulting each other and making decisions together
- Coming to agreement in relation to issues such as profit-sharing, granting share options, maintaining productivity, etc.

Competitive relationship

Employees may want higher pay, while the employer wants costs kept to a minimum. Employers want increased profits and cost reductions, which may lead to redundancies, while employees want job security.

A competitive relationship occurs when employees are faced with a wage cut or the threat of losing their jobs.

6. Relationship between an enterprise and its stakeholders

Co-operative relationship

A co-operative relationship exists where an enterprise and its stakeholders work together for their mutual benefit.

This requires joint action or effort and can occur between:

- **People within an organisation** (e.g. employees helping each other in a spirit of teamwork to achieve a certain level of sales or profit), or
- **Organisations** (e.g. one business co-operating with another business in the marketing or distribution of each other's products or services)

Competitive relationship

An enterprise and its stakeholders can pursue different objectives to each other or attempt to achieve particular objectives at the expense of each other.

This can involve people within the enterprise and outside interests which impact on the enterprise.

For example, a competitive relationship **within the organisation** might be where sales people compete with each other for orders or employees compete for promotion. **Outside an organisation** competitive issues can relate to prices, quality, sales, the recruitment of employees, etc.

Make sure that you can explain the co-operative and competitive relationship between people in business and are able to give examples. This is examined almost every year.

(i) Explain the term **co-operative relationship** between stakeholders in a business.

(ii) Describe **one** example of a co-operative relationship which could arise between **each** of the following pairs of stakeholders:

- Employer and employee
- Investor and manager of a business
- Producer and consumer

(20 marks)

Source: 2017 Higher Level Section 3

Suggested solution

(i) A co-operative relationship is where an enterprise and its stakeholders work together for their mutual benefit.

(ii) **Employer and employee**

A fair wage, which reflects work being done and qualifications and skills of employees, is offered by the employer and a fair day's work is provided by the employee.

Wages/good pay and conditions of work

- Employee benefits from being rewarded with good pay and conditions for their work if they meet agreed targets.
- Employer benefits from increased productivity/staff motivation/higher profits caused by employees working harder/job satisfaction.

Safe and healthy work environment

The employer provides a better and healthy working environment, meeting the legal and moral requirements and the employee feels safe, leading to a productive environment.

Investor and manager

The financial resources provided by investors are not wasted but are used productively by management to generate a fair return on investment for the investor.

Transparent financial information

All financial information provided by the manager to the investor is accurate and up to date. The manager uses the investment appropriately.

- Investor will benefit from seeing that their investment is safe.
- Manager will find it easier to acquire the necessary finance to fund new projects.

Producer and consumer

Brand loyalty: Where the consumer repeatedly purchases the product.

- Producer maintains the quality of the product.
- Consumer benefits from certainty in the quality that they purchase, leading to repeat purchase and brand loyalty.

Agreed terms of sale (fair price, profit margin).

- Producer provides a quality product at a reasonable price.
- Consumer pays a reasonable price for the product based on its quality/value for money.

The producer has an open and fair complaints procedure and consumer complaints are dealt with in a fair manner.

Marking scheme

(i) 5 marks (2 + 3)

(ii) Three points @ 5 marks each (2 + 3)

Benefit to each stakeholder required.

HL Describe **one** example of a co-operative relationship and **one** example of a source of conflict that could arise between the following stakeholders:

  (i) Investor and entrepreneur

  (ii) Supplier and purchasing manager

          (20 marks)

Source: 2015 Higher Level Section 3

Suggested solution

(i) A co-operative situation would arise when the entrepreneur gives open, transparent and honest information to the investor, e.g. accurate business plans and cash flow forecasts and, in return, the investor provides a reasonable rate or return, etc.

    A possible source of conflict could arise if the entrepreneur gives false information to the investor/defaults on loan repayments/does not give an adequate return to the investor/re-invests profits rather than giving a return to the investor. Investor may want immediate returns and is not prepared to wait/may want greater returns out of profits rather than retaining funds in the business for further expansion.

    Where there is a downturn in business, the entrepreneur may request more time to repay the loan, while the investor may insist on repayments as per the agreed schedule.

(ii) A co-operative situation would arise when the supplier provides good quality raw materials, components and finished goods to the purchasing manager, who pays on time and offers a fair price.

    A possible conflict situation could arise if poor quality materials are provided or poor after-sales service is offered by the supplier. Or if the purchasing manager fails to pay for goods purchased on credit, creating a bad debt for the supplier.

    There may be conflict between the two sides as to their perceptions of what is a fair price and as to what the optimum quality is.

Marking scheme

(i) Co-operative relationship: 5 marks (3 + 2)

    Source of conflict: 5 marks (3 + 2)

(ii) Co-operative relationship: 5 marks (3 + 2)

    Source of conflict: 5 marks (3 + 2)

Describe using examples, one co-operative and one competitive relationship that may exist either between or within organisations.

(20 marks)

Suggested solution

Co-operative relationship
A co-operative relationship exists where joint action or effort is required so that people can work together to everyone's benefit. (5 marks)

Example
One business co-operating with another business in the marketing or distribution of each other's products or services. (5 marks)

Competitive relationship
This is where parties compete with each other and are pursuing different objectives. These objectives may be achieved by one party at the expense of the other. (5 marks)

Example
Business enterprises competing with each other for market share on areas like price, quality and service. (5 marks)

Marking scheme
Co-operative relationship – 10 marks
(Explanation 5 marks, example 5 marks)
Competitive relationship – 10 marks
(Explanation 5 marks, example 5 marks)

Law of contract

Introduction

A contract is a formal agreement between two or more people that is enforceable by law. When you buy goods or services, you enter into a contract with the seller. Certain elements must be present for a contract to be legally binding. Contracts are made up of terms; some of which can be implied terms.

key point

A contract is a legally binding agreement between two or more parties that can be enforced by law, e.g. a contract for the sale of a house.

Contracts may be written or oral. It is easier to know what the terms are in a written contract but an oral contract is also enforceable in law. Terms in consumer contracts must always be fair and clear to the consumer.

Elements of a valid contract

1. Agreement

For agreement to exist, there must be a clear, complete and unconditional offer and acceptance of that offer.

Offer

An offer is a promise to be bound, provided the terms of the offer are accepted.

The offer can be made orally, in writing, or by conduct and is a clear indication of the offeror's willingness to enter into an agreement under specified terms.

Example: the price of the car was €30,000; John (the buyer) offered €30,000 for the car.

Invitation to treat

An invitation to treat is an invitation to someone to make an offer which can be accepted or rejected.

For example, goods on display in a shop window are only inviting customers to enter the shop and make an offer. They can do so by bringing the goods to the checkout and offering to buy them.

Acceptance

The party answering the offer agrees to the terms of the offer orally, in writing, or by conduct.

The offer must be accepted and taken up by the other party as it stands, without any conditions. Example: WMB motors (the seller) accepts John's offer of €30,000 for the car.

2. Consideration

Each party in a contract must give something of value to the other party. Something of value must be exchanged.

Consideration is usually some monetary payment, but it could also be something valuable exchanged as part of the contract.

Example: John pays WMB Motors €30,000 and receives the car.

3. Intention to contract

There must be an intention by the parties to create a contract.

With business agreements, it is presumed that a legal contract is intended.

With social and personal agreements (e.g. an agreement to go to the cinema), it is presumed that the parties do not intend that a legal contract should exist.

Example: The agreement between WMB Motors and John is a business agreement and therefore assumed to be legally binding.

4. Capacity to contract

The parties to a contract must have the capacity to make a contract.

All natural persons and corporate bodies (such as companies) have the legal right to enter into a contract.

The contractual capacity of a company comes from its Certificate of Incorporation (separate legal entity). If the company acts beyond its legal powers it is said to be acting *'Ultra Vires'*.

The following generally do not have capacity to contract:

- Infants, that is, persons under the age of 18 (except in certain cases, e.g. necessities)
- Persons under the influence of drink or drugs
- Insane persons
- Bankrupt persons

These people are deemed to be incapable of making valid contracts because it is presumed that they do not fully understand what they are doing. If they enter into a contract, the contract is void.

Example: John is over 18, so he has the legal capacity to enter a contract.

5. Legality of form

Certain contracts, to be considered legal, must be drawn up in a particular manner. Some contracts must be in writing if they are to be legally valid.

These include:

- Insurance policies
- Hire purchase agreements
- The sale of property or land
- Share transactions
- Consumer credit and bank loans.

Example: If John was buying the car on hire purchase, he would have to get a written contract.

6. Consent to contract

Real consent must exist between the parties to a contract.

Both parties in a contract must enter into a contract of their own free will – under no undue pressure or duress.

Example: WMB Motors advertised the car for the agreed price and the salesperson and John signed all the relevant documentation.

7. Legality of purpose

The court will not allow action to be taken on illegal contracts such as those which break the law of the land. These include, for example, contracts to:

- Commit a crime
- Evade tax
- Interfere with the court of justice

If an illegal contract exists, no action can be brought for its breach.

Termination of a contract

1. Performance

Both parties to the contract fulfill their obligation and the contract is completed. Both parties have done what they agreed to do.

Example: Once the car is delivered and the guarantee period expires, the contract between WMB Motors and John is performed.

2. Breach

If one of the parties does not perform his/her side of the bargain/ contractual obligation, i.e. does not honour the promises made,

> **A contract can be terminated by:**
> - Performance
> - Breach
> - Agreement
> - Frustration

the contract is said to have been repudiated. The party is in breach of a condition/ essential element agreed. The second party has the right of compensation/action in the courts against the first party who caused the breach.

Breach of a **condition** (a clause that is vital and goes to the heart of the contract) entitles the injured party to treat the contract as terminated and sue for damages for loss suffered. Breach of a **warranty** (a less important clause) allows the injured party to sue for damages only.

Example: A condition of the contract states that the car is to be black metallic. When it is delivered it is red, non-metallic. This is a fundamental breach of a condition of the contract and the buyer is entitled to seek redress (i.e. rescind, seek damages, seek specific performance).

3. Agreement

The parties to the contract may agree to end/cancel a contract by mutual consent whether or not the purpose of the contract has been achieved.

Example: If WMB Motors had difficulty getting delivery of a black metallic car from the manufacturers, then both WMB Motors and John could agree to cancel the contract.

4. Frustration

An unforeseen event prevents the contract from being completed. Something happens which makes it impossible to complete the contract.

Example: The death or bankruptcy of one of the parties to the contract.

Remedies for a breach of contract

When there is breach of contract, the courts can award the following remedies.

1. Damages

A sum of money is awarded as compensation for any damage or loss caused to the injured party as a result of the breach of contract.

This should put the injured party in the same financial position they would have been in if the contract was not broken.

2. Specific performance

The party in breach of a contract would be ordered by a court to carry out its agreed contractual obligations, i.e. to do what had been promised in the contract.
This would not be awarded by the courts if an amount of money would have been a remedy.

Example: Specific performance may be used as a remedy in a contract for the sale or lease of land or for the sale of a unique item, such as a work of art/completion of construction of a property, etc.

3. Rescinding the contract

This means that the innocent party (the party that has not breached the contract) has the right to have the contract set aside and to be restored to the position they were in before the contract began.

A legal contract can be terminated by **performance**, whereby parties to the conflict fulfil their obligations as agreed. Outline **three** other methods for terminating a legal contract. (20 marks)

Source: 2016 Higher Level Section 3

HL

Suggested solution

Frustration – an unforeseen event makes it impossible to complete the contract.
Concert is cancelled as singer is taken ill and unable to perform/death or bankruptcy of one of the parties to the contract.

Breach – one party in the contract fails to fulfil his/her contractual obligation. The party is in breach of an essential condition of a contract. The other party may have the right of action in the courts and may sue for damages.
Professional footballer does not turn up for training session and has thereby breached his contract with the club.

Agreement – both parties agree to end the contract whether or not the purpose of the contract has been achieved.
Employee hired for nine-month contract but completes project in six months. Both employer and employee agree to end the contract.
A contract of employment may be ended by agreement if it includes a clause stating the contract can be terminated if, say, for example, one month's notice is given.

Marking scheme

8 marks (State 4 marks, explain 4 marks)
6 marks (State 3 marks, explain 3 marks)
6 marks (State 3 marks, explain 3 marks)

Be able to:

- Outline non-legislative ways of resolving conflict between retailer and consumer.
- Outline how legislation helps in dealing with conflict between retailer and consumer.
- **HL** Describe a possible business conflict and show how the law could be used to solve it.

Conflict

Conflict occurs where people are in dispute. The pursuit of their goal may result in some damage to the other party with whom they are in conflict.

key point

There are two methods of resolving conflict:

- Non-legislative
- Legislative

Methods of resolving conflict

Non-legislative

A non-legislative method of solving a business conflict means that the parties involved don't use a law, or an office or organisation set up under law, to assist in solving their conflict.

Legislative

A legislative method of solving a business conflict is to use the law to solve the conflict, or to use an office or organisation set up as a consequence of a law, to help in finding a resolution to the conflict.

Conflict resolution between consumer and retailer

Non-legislative methods of solving conflict between consumer and retailer

1. Contact retailer

The consumer should contact the retailer giving details of the complaint. Putting things in writing means the problem is taken more seriously.

2. Talk

Discuss the problem to clarify any difficulties

3. Negotiation

This involves parties explaining their position and bargaining to try to reach a mutually acceptable solution.

If negotiations fail, the involvement of a third party may be necessary to resolve the conflict.

4. Third parties

Third parties are independent outside agencies that may be involved in negotiations to help parties resolve their differences.

A. Ombudsman for public services

The Office of the Ombudsman investigates complaints about the activities of government, local authorities, the Health Service Executive and An Post.

The Ombudsman only investigates complaints after the person has tried to solve the problem with the public body involved and all other avenues for solving the problem have been exhausted.

Complaints must be made within one year of the complaint event. After reviewing the complaint, the Ombudsman decides if it is justified. If it is, the Ombudsman makes a recommendation to the public body in order to resolve the problem.

Recommendations of the Ombudsman are not legally binding on the parties involved with the complaint.

B. Financial Services Ombudsman

Investigates claims from consumers about financial service providers, including banks, building societies and insurance companies.

C. Consumers' Association of Ireland

It is a voluntary association which gives information and advice to consumers about goods, services and consumer law.

It was set up to protect the interest of consumers in Ireland.

It helps consumers to solve complaints.

D. Trade associations

Set standards for their own members which ensure that customers get the best possible service.

Consumers can complain to the relevant association (such as the Society of the Irish Motor Industry [SIMI] and the Irish Travel Agents Association [ITAA]) if standards are not being met.

exam focus

Evaluation of the Ombudsman Service

The Ombudsman service is effective because:

- The Ombudsman is impartial and the service is free
- The Office of the Ombudsman deals with about 3,000 complaints per annum and has, over the years, advised and guided many others with valid complaints.

Legislative methods of solving conflict between consumer and retailer

If consumers and retailers cannot reach a satisfactory agreement in a non-legislative manner, a legislative approach will have to be pursued. Consumers are entitled to have their rights and interests protected by law. Irish consumer protection law, which is based on Irish and European legislation, is a distinct area of the law that addresses the general protection and promotion of consumer rights and interests.

Consumer law aims to ensure that consumers have enough information about prices and quality of products and services to make suitable choices on what to buy. Consumer law also aims to ensure that goods are safe and are manufactured to an acceptable standard. Consumer contracts are protected by the Sale of Goods and Supply of Services Act, 1980.

key point

The consumer can insist on their legal rights as set out in the following acts:

- Sale of Goods and Supply of Services Act 1980
- Consumer Protection Act 2007

Sale of Goods and Supply of Services Act 1980

1. Rights of buyer in relation to goods sold

Merchantable quality

Goods must be of reasonable standard and quality, taking into account what they are meant to do, their durability and their price (e.g. a new car that breaks down immediately is deemed not to be of merchantable quality).

Fit for purpose

Goods must be reasonably fit for the particular purpose indicated by the buyer (e.g. washing machines should wash clothes).

Sale by description

Goods must be as described by the seller in advertisements and brochures or as stated by a sales person and must match the description given on the packaging.

Sale by sample

If the sale is by sample, then the bulk of the goods must correspond to the sample.

Ownership and quiet possession

The buyer of the goods has a right of ownership and possession of the goods. This means the following:

- The seller has the right to sell the goods
- The buyer should enjoy quiet possession and be able to use the goods as they wish.

2. Rights of the buyer in relation to services

If you have a contract with a supplier of a service, you can expect that:

- The supplier has the necessary skill to provide the service
- The service will be provided with proper skill and diligence
- The materials used will be sound and fit for their purpose
- Any goods supplied as part of the service will be of merchantable quality.

key point

A seller's responsibility is not limited when they display signs with messages such as:

- No money refunded
- No liability accepted for faulty goods
- Credit notes only

3. The retailer/seller is responsible

The seller or the service provider is responsible for putting right defective goods or services. The manufacturer may be at fault, but the contract is with the seller and the duty to put things right lies with the seller.

4. Signs limiting consumer rights

Consumers' rights under the Act cannot be taken away or limited by signs such as 'Credit Notes Only', 'No Cash Refunds', 'No exchange', etc.

These signs are illegal and do not affect your statutory consumer rights. A credit note is not a refund as it restricts you to shopping in that shop.

It is an offence for the retailer to display signs that give the consumer the impression that they have no legal rights.

5. Guarantees

Guarantees are seen as additional protection given to the consumer and they cannot limit the consumer's rights under consumer law. The guarantee must clearly show what goods are covered, the timeframe involved and the procedure for making claims. The customer can choose to have the goods fixed by the manufacturer or they can insist that the retailer deals with the complaint. The contract is between the seller and the buyer.

6. Unsolicited goods

These are goods that are sent to someone without having received an order. The consumer has the right to keep the goods without payment after 30 days if the consumer has sent written notice to the sender and informed him where they can be collected. S/he has the right to keep the goods after six months if the sender has not collected them and the consumer has not prevented the firm from collecting them.

Redress available to consumers for breaches of the Act

The form of redress is dependent on **how serious the fault is**, the time it occurred **and how soon after the purchase the complaint was made**. If the complaint is valid, the consumer is entitled to one of the three Rs – refund, replacement and repair.

- **Full refund or replacement**

  If a consumer purchases a **faulty good and complains promptly,** then he/she is entitled to a full refund of money paid. A replacement may also be provided, e.g. a new model of the same or similar quality given in its place.

- **Partial refund or repair**

  When the consumer has used the product, when there is a **delay between the purchase date and the actual complaint, or when the fault is of a minor nature**, then the consumer may only be entitled to only a partial refund or repair.

EVALUATION OF THE SALE OF GOODS AND SUPPLY OF SERVICES ACT 1980

The law is effective in protecting consumers because:

- It ensures that consumers receive a refund if they purchase a faulty product or a product that is not up to standard.
- By banning illegal signs (such as 'Credit notes only'), consumers are protected because they do not have to accept a credit note and can insist on a full refund.

(i) Outline the rights of consumers under the terms of the Sale of Goods and Supply of Services Act 1980.

(ii) Illustrate two forms of redress available to consumers for breach of the Act.

(30 marks)

Source: 2017 Higher Level Section 3

Suggested solution

(i) Goods

<u>Goods should be of merchantable quality</u>. – They should be of reasonable standard/quality taking into account what they are supposed to do, their durability and their price.

<u>Goods must be fit for the purpose intended</u>. – This means that the goods must be able to do what they are meant to do and what they were designed for (i.e. **fit for the particular purpose for which the buyer intends to use them**).

For example, a waterproof jacket and leggings should keep the rain out. A combined fridge-freezer must be capable of freezing food.

<u>Goods sold must be as described</u> by the sales person, catalogue/package or sample. For example, if a consumer orders blue, floral wallpaper from a catalogue, then it can't be gold, plain wallpaper when delivered.

Services

<u>Services</u> must be provided with **due care and attention** – a car is left at a garage for a full service, but the garage failed to change the oil.

A service provider must have the necessary competence and skill set. In addition, any materials used in the delivery of the service must be of merchantable quality.

Other Provisions

<u>Unsolicited Goods/Inertia Selling</u>

It is illegal for a supplier to demand payment for unsolicited goods. These are goods that are sent to someone without having received an order. If a company sends you something you didn't order and doesn't provide for return post, it cannot invoice you for the product, e.g. Book Club. This demand is an illegal act and the consumer has specific rights. The right to keep the goods without payment after thirty days if the consumer has sent a written notice to the sender and informed him/her where the goods can be collected.

Consumers' rights under the Act **cannot be taken away** or limited by signs such as 'Credit Notes Only', 'No Cash Refunds', 'No Exchange', etc. These signs do not affect your statutory consumer rights. A credit note is not a refund as it restricts you to shopping in that shop.

Guarantees are seen as something extra (additional protection) that are given to the consumer and they cannot limit the consumer's rights under consumer law. The guarantee must clearly show what goods are covered, the time frame involved and the procedure for making claims.

(ii) The form of redress is dependent on **how serious the fault is**, the time it occurred **and how soon after the purchase the complaint was made**. If the complaint is valid the consumer is entitled to one of the three Rs – refund, replacement and repair.

If a consumer purchases a faulty good and complains promptly then he/she is entitled to a full cash refund or replacement. For example, if a consumer purchases a microwave oven and the minute timer doesn't work (i.e. it is not of merchantable quality), then he/she is entitled to a full refund of money paid. A replacement may also be provided, e.g. a new model of the same or similar quality given in its place.

When the consumer has used the product, when there is a delay between the purchase date and the actual complaint, or when the fault is of a minor nature, then the consumer may only be entitled to a partial refund or repair.

The consumer's rights lessen the longer he/she puts off making the complaint.

Marking scheme

(i) Four points @ 5 marks (State 2 marks, explain 3 marks)

(ii) Two points @ 5 marks (State 2 marks, explain 3 marks)

Consumer Protection Act 2007

The Consumer Protection Act 2007 provides protection to the consumer through a variety of measures. The Act protects consumers from misleading, aggressive or prohibited practices.

Misleading practices

A misleading practice involves providing false, misleading and deceptive information. Misleading practices are banned if they would be likely to impair the average consumer's ability to make an informed choice in relation to a product and would cause the average consumer to make a decision about a transaction that they would not otherwise make.

Misleading claims

Under the Act, it is a criminal offence for any retailer to make a false or misleading claim about goods, services and prices. It is also an offence to sell goods which bear a false or misleading description. Misleading advertising, misleading information and withholding material information are considered misleading practices.

Aggressive practices

The Act prohibits traders from engaging in aggressive practices, such as harassment, coercion, or exercising undue influence. Examples of harassment are pressurising, intimidating and taking advantage of vulnerable consumers.

Price display regulations

The Act provides that prices of certain products must be displayed inclusive of charges, fees and taxes.

Enforcement of the Act

The Act is enforced through the Competition and Consumer Protection Commission (CCPC). The Central Bank of Ireland has a role in enforcing the provisions of the Consumer Protection Act 2007 in the financial services area.

Competition and Consumer Protection Act 2014

The Competition and Consumer Protection Act 2014 provided for the establishment of the Competition and Consumer Protection Commission. This agency replaced, and took over the functions of, the National Consumer Agency and the Competition Authority. It has a general function of promoting consumer welfare and is responsible for investigating, enforcing and encouraging compliance with consumer law.

The Competition and Consumer Protection Commission [CCPC]

The Competition and Consumer Protection Commission (CCPC) is the statutory office with responsibility for providing advice and information to consumers on their rights. The CCPC is responsible for the enforcement of a wide range of consumer protection laws. The CCPC does not intervene or become involved in individual issues or disputes between consumers and sellers of goods or service providers. The CCPC can advise you if you have a particular consumer problem. The CCPC has a dual competition and consumer protection mandate.

Role and Functions of the Competition and Consumer Protection Commission

The statutory functions of the CCPC in relation to consumer law include:

Promoting and protecting the interests and welfare of consumers

The CCPC informs consumers of their rights by providing them with the information they need. The CCPC also develops public awareness campaigns and uses various media to communicate its messages.

Carrying out investigations into suspected breaches of consumer protection law

The CCPC has the power to enter business premises, accompanied by Gardaí, to gather evidence.

Enforcing consumer protection law

The CCPC enforces a wide range of consumer protection legislation. It has a variety of enforcement tools to tackle unacceptable business practices.

Encouraging compliance with consumer protection law

The CCPC aims to create a culture of compliance by helping businesses to actively comply with the law.

Small Claims court

This deals with consumer claims and business claims in relation to goods and services purchased for private use. Claims can be made for faulty goods, bad workmanship and minor damage to privately owned property. Maximum damages that can be claimed are €2,000.

A claim is made on a special application form and is lodged with the Small Claims Registrar of the District Court with a fee of €25.

How does the Small Claims court operate?

- Both sides make their case and are encouraged to reach a settlement.
- A decision made by the Registrar of the court is not legally binding, but it is usually accepted.
- Appeals can be made through the District Court and heard before a judge.

EVALUATION OF THE SMALL CLAIMS COURT

The Small Claims court is very effective because of the following:

- It is a fast, informal and easy way for consumers to resolve disputes.
- It is an inexpensive method of solving disputes. (A fee of €25 is payable to the District Court when the claim is lodged. No solicitors are required.)
- Consumers receive an unbiased and fair judgment.
- The process can be carried out online.
- It has a very high success rate.

Read the information supplied and answer the questions that follow.

Samsung Electronics abandoned its Galaxy Note 7 smartphone after customers reported that phone batteries were prone to catching fire.

Source: adapted from Irish Independent, *October 2016*

(i) Name the Act which protects consumers who purchased the Samsung Galaxy Note 7.

(ii) Outline three provisions of the Act regarding a consumer's statutory (legal) rights in relation to the Samsung Galaxy Note 7. (20 marks)

Source: 2017 Higher Level Section 3

Suggested solution

(i) The Sale of Goods and Supply of Services Act 1980.

(ii) **Goods should be of merchantable quality.**

Goods should be of **reasonable standard**/quality **taking into account what they are supposed to do, their durability and their price**. The mobile phone is a high-price commodity, and, therefore, should be of a high standard.

Goods must be fit for the purpose intended.

This means that the goods must be able to do what they are supposed to do and what they were designed for (i.e. fit for the particular purpose for which the buyer intends to use them).

Goods sold must be as described by the sales person

If a phone is purchased following a demonstration by a salesperson, the actual phone purchased should correspond with the demonstration.

Redress

If the complaint is valid, the consumer is entitled to one of the three Rs – refund, replacement or repair. If a consumer purchases a faulty phone and complains promptly then he/she is entitled to a full cash refund or replacement. The form of redress is **dependent on how serious the fault is, the time it occurred and how soon after the purchase the complaint was made.**

The retailer is legally responsible under the Act.

The consumer's legal right is against the retailer under the Act rather than the manufacturer.

Guarantees

The guarantee is only an additional right whereby the consumer can have the product fixed under the manufacturer's guarantee.

Marking scheme

(i) 2 marks

(ii) 3 points @ 6 marks (3 + 3)

(Name the provision and explain the provision. Merchantable quality is a compulsory point.)

 Be able to:

- Outline non-legislative ways of resolving conflict between employer and employee.
- Outline how legislation helps in dealing with conflict between employer and employee.
- Describe a possible business conflict and show how the law could be used to solve it.

Industrial relations

Industrial relations refers to the relationship that exists between management and employees in an organisation and how they co-operate and communicate with each other.

Good industrial relations will have high staff motivation and morale and high productivity. **Poor** industrial relations will have poor motivation, high labour turnover and low productivity.

Employees may join a trade union to strengthen their bargaining power with management.

Trade unions – introduction

A trade union is an organisation representing employees in negotiations with employers. A shop steward is elected as their official union representative in the workplace.

Employees have a constitutional right to join a trade union. It can be made a condition of employment that you must join a particular union upon accepting a job offer and remain in that union while you remain an employee in that job. There is a view that this may not be constitutional, but this has not been tested in the courts yet. If you are already in the job without being a union member and are at a later stage required to join a union by your employer, you can refuse, as such a requirement is unconstitutional.

Complaints of dismissal or victimisation due to membership of a union are heard by the Workplace Relations Commission.

Irish National Teachers' Organisation
Cumann Múinteoirí Éireann

A century of service

The functions/benefits of trade union membership to employees

A trade union:

- Protects workers rights
- Seeks better pay and working conditions for members and tries to prevent pay cuts
- Represents members in negotiations with employers/government
- Negotiates with the employer on behalf of its members in a trade dispute
- Provides services for members, such as credit unions and insurance schemes
- Protects the job security of its members in the event of threatened layoffs
- Negotiates redundancy packages if jobs cannot be saved.

Shop steward

A shop steward is an elected representative of union members in a workplace. He/she acts as a communication link between members and their union.

Collective bargaining

Negotiations between employer and employee representatives in a particular firm or industry to determine rates of pay and conditions of employment, etc.

National agreements

Agreements negotiated between government, employers represented by IBEC and employees represented by ICTU (social partners).

This relationship is called 'social partnership' and covers pay and other issues such as tax reform, job creation and other social issues.

Industrial disputes

Causes of industrial relations disputes

1. **Pay/disputes over pay:** Workers may launch a variety of different pay or pension claims, e.g. cost of living claim, comparability claim or relativity claim. If the employer resists or rejects these pay claims, it could lead to industrial disputes.

2. **Disputes over working conditions/duties:** Safety is a fundamental need for employees. Failure by management to provide safe working conditions, safe equipment, proper hygiene and adequate heating can lead to industrial disputes. Changes to working conditions may also cause a dispute.

3. **New work practices/new technology:** Workers may resist the introduction of new technology if they believe that the employer has not provided adequate training or financial reward for their increased productivity.

4. **Redundancies:** Selection for redundancy/redundancy package. If workers feel that unfair procedures for selection are being used or if redundancy payments are not adequate, e.g. employers may wish to 'cherry pick' employees for redundancy, while a trade union representing the employees may prefer a LIFO (last in, first out) system.

5. **Democratic issues:** Differences in pay and conditions of work between similar groups of workers.
6. **Promotion procedures:** May arise if agreed procedures on promotion are not followed.
7. **Discrimination:** Some employees treated less favourably than others.
8. **Unfair dismissal:** Dismissal without adequate reasons.

Types of official industrial action a trade union can undertake as part of a trade dispute

Industrial action

An industrial action is any action which may affect the terms of a contract which is taken by workers acting together to compel their employer 'to accept or not to accept terms or conditions of or affecting employment.' Examples of industrial action include a picket, a work-to-rule, an overtime ban or a strike.

1. **Official strike:** Complete withdrawal of labour. This involves workers picketing outside the premises of their employer to highlight the industrial dispute taking place. Employees hold a secret ballot, receive union approval and give their employer one week's notice of strike action. Secondary picketing occurs where employees picket another premises, if that other business is assisting their employer to complete work, thereby frustrating the industrial action.
2. **Work-to-rule/go-slow:** Where employees do their work as per their employment contract and will not complete any extra duties outside of those stated in the contract. A go-slow is an action in which employees protest against an employer by doing their job as per the contract, but doing it at such a slow pace that it frustrates the employer.
3. **Overtime ban:** Where workers refuse to do overtime. This can cause major disruption, leading to lost orders and lost sales, especially at peak trading times, e.g. an airline during summer holiday season.
4. **Token stoppage:** This involves a brief stoppage of work to highlight the employees' frustration. It is intended to carry the threat of further more serious action if agreement is not reached.

Types of unofficial industrial action a trade union can undertake as part of a trade dispute

Unofficial industrial action/unofficial strike

- Workers go on strike without a secret ballot, without giving the employer a week's notice and without the approval of the trade union and ICTU.
- Organisers of unofficial strikes do not have legal protection against being sued by their employer.

Conflict resolution – employer and employee

Non-legislative methods

1. Meet and talk

Parties should discuss the situation and clarify any difficulties; negotiation may be required.

2. Negotiation

Negotiation is a process of bargaining to try to come up with a mutually acceptable solution. Employees are represented by their union. The employer is represented by management.

Each party sets out its position, issues are discussed, points of difference are identified and the parties try to reach a solution acceptable to both. This might involve compromise, with both parties giving up something in order to reach agreement.

3. Third parties

If negotiations fail, it can be useful to seek the services of third parties to solve the conflict.

Third parties can help solve conflict through conciliation and arbitration.

Conciliation

This is where a **third party/conciliator** assists the parties in dispute to resolve their differences themselves through continued negotiation.

The conciliation process gets the two sides to listen to each other's point of view, discuss the issues, and negotiate an agreed settlement before the dispute grows into a serious one. An agreement, if reached, is **not legally binding**, but the aim is to resolve the dispute without strike action.

Mediation

The mediator presents his/her own proposals/recommendations to resolve the conflict. It is a useful form of intervention if both parties are not prepared to listen to each other any longer. However, the parties themselves must solve the dispute.

Arbitration

Arbitration is where the settlement of a dispute is sent before a neutral third party (arbitrator) for adjudication.

The arbitrator listens to both sides of the dispute and makes a recommendation for settlement. The decision is usually **binding** on both parties. (The parties agree in advance to the arbitration process and that the arbitration decision will be binding on them.)

The main types of disputes dealt with by arbitration are ones that concern employees, trade unions and employers.

Legislative methods

Industrial Relations Act 1990

1. Trade dispute

Most of the law on trade disputes and industrial action is contained in the Industrial Relations Act 1990.

A trade dispute is defined as 'any dispute between employers and workers that is concerned with employment or non-employment, or the terms or conditions of the employment of any person'.

A **legitimate trade dispute** can arise from any of the following issues:

- Pay and conditions of employment – rates of pay, overtime, holidays
- Physical conditions of work – safety, heating, canteen
- Employee dismissal
- Employment policy of employer – methods of recruitment, etc.
- Trade union recognition in the workplace
- Range of duties required of employees

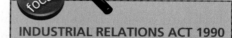

exam focus

INDUSTRIAL RELATIONS ACT 1990

The main provisions of the Industrial Relations Act 1990 are:

- Definition of a trade dispute
- Trade union immunity from prosecution
- Picketing
- Balloting

2. Trade union immunity from prosecution

Trade unions and workers cannot be sued for damages (or losses) suffered by the employer arising from a trade dispute – provided it is an official trade dispute – if the correct procedures have been followed, that is, if the union held a secret ballot and gave one week's notice to the employer.

3. Picketing

It is lawful for workers to assemble at the entrance of a workplace and carry placards giving information about their dispute or strike.

Pickets can only be placed at a workplace and picketing must be peaceful. There must be no obstruction caused.

Placards communicate information to the public and other workers regarding the trade dispute.

Types of picketing

- **Primary Picketing:**
  - Picketing the business premises of the employer involved in the dispute.
- **Secondary Picketing:**
  - Picketing another employer not involved in the dispute, e.g. where another employer undertakes the delivery of goods normally delivered by the employer involved in the dispute.

- This is lawful only if the workers believe that the second employer was acting to frustrate the industrial action by directly assisting their employer.

4. Balloting

A secret ballot must be held before industrial action can take place.

A majority of votes must be cast in favour of industrial action.

One week's notice must be given to the employer involved in a dispute.

If the correct procedures are followed, an employer cannot sue unions or workers for damages.

Workplace Relations Act 2015

The Workplace Relations Act 2015 came into effect on 1st October 2015. It saw the existing five employment rights bodies merged into two bodies:

- The Workplace Relations Commission will deal with all cases at first instance

The WRC is the body to which all industrial relations disputes and all disputes and complaints about employment law is presented.

- The Labour Court will deal with all cases on appeal

The Labour Court is now the single appeal body for all workplace relations appeals against decisions of WRC Adjudication Officers. Labour Court decisions can be appealed to the High Court, but only on a point of law.

Workplace Relations Commission

The Workplace Relations Commission provides information on industrial relations and rights and obligations under Irish employment and equality legislation.

The Workplace Relations Commission (WRC) has responsibility for:

- Promoting the improvement of workplace relations and the maintenance of good workplace relations
- Promoting and encouraging compliance with relevant laws
- Providing information to members of the public in relation to employment.

The establishment of the Workplace Relations Act 2015 has resulted in amendments to the Industrial Relations Act 1990, the Employment Equality Acts 1998–2015 and the Unfair Dismissals Acts 1977–2015. Most appeals under the above three Acts are adjudicated by the Workplace Relations Commission in the first instance. All appeals are adjudicated by the Labour Court.

Complaints in relation to contraventions of employment, equality and equal status legislation may be presented/referred to the Workplace Relations Commission.

The Workplace Relations Commission provides the following services:

Advisory Service

The Workplace Relations Commission's Advisory Service promotes good practice in the workplace by assisting and advising organisations in all aspects of industrial relations in the workplace. It engages with employers, employees and their representatives to help them to develop effective industrial relations practices, procedures and structures. Such assistance could include reviewing or developing effective workplace procedures in areas such as grievance, discipline, communications and consultation.

Conciliation

Conciliation is a voluntary process in which the parties to a dispute agree to avail of a neutral and impartial third party to assist them in resolving their industrial relations differences. The Workplace Relations Commission provides a conciliation service by making available Industrial Relations Officers (IRO or Conciliation Officer) of the Commission to chair 'conciliation conferences'. Conciliation conferences are basically an extension of the process of direct negotiations, with an independent chairperson present to steer the discussions and explore possible avenues of settlement.

Participation in the conciliation process is voluntary, and so too are the outcomes. Solutions are reached only by consensus, whether by negotiation and agreements facilitated between the parties themselves, or by the parties agreeing to settlement terms proposed by the Conciliation Officer.

The conciliation process is informal in its practice. The parties are free to represent themselves or be represented by trade unions or by employer organisations. The Commission does not believe that the nature of the process requires legal representation of either party at conciliation meetings.

Mediation

Mediation seeks to arrive at a solution through an agreement between the parties, rather than through an investigation or hearing or formal decision. The WRC offers a mediation service in certain cases to facilitate the resolution of complaints/disputes where possible at an early stage and without recourse to adjudication.

The Mediation Officer empowers the parties to negotiate their own agreement on a clear and informed basis. The process is voluntary and either party may terminate it at any stage.

Where an attempt at mediation has been successful, the Mediation Officer will record the terms of the agreement in writing. If each of the parties are satisfied that the record accurately represents the terms of the resolution, they will sign the record.

Where an attempt at mediation has proven unsuccessful, the Mediation Officer will notify the Director General of the WRC and each of the parties in writing of that fact. The complaint or dispute will be referred for adjudication by an Adjudication Officer.

Adjudication

Adjudication Officers of the WRC are statutorily independent in their decision-making duties. The Adjudication Officer's role is to hold a hearing where both parties are given an opportunity to be heard by the Adjudication Officer and to present any evidence relevant to the complaint. The Adjudication Officer will not attempt to mediate or conciliate the case. Parties may be accompanied and represented at hearings by a trade union official, a practising barrister or practising solicitor, for example.

The Adjudication Officer will then decide the matter and give a written decision in relation to the complaint.

A party to a complaint may appeal to the Labour Court against a decision of an Adjudication Officer.

Compliance/Inspection Service

Inspectors visit places of employment and carry out investigations on behalf of the WRC in order to ensure compliance with equality- and employment-related legislation. Such investigations involve examining books, records and documents related to the employment and conducting interviews with current and former employees and employers. Where breaches of legislation have been found, an inspector may issue either a Compliance Notice or a Fixed Payment Notice to an employer.

Enforcement of Decisions

If an employer fails to carry out a decision of an Adjudication Officer of the Workplace Relations Commission, or a decision of the Labour Court arising from an appeal of an Adjudication Officer's decision, within the prescribed time, an application may be made to the District Court for an order directing the employer to carry out the decision.

The Labour Court

The Labour Court is an independent workplace dispute resolution body providing a comprehensive service for the resolution of disputes concerning industrial relations and employment rights.

The Labour Court deals with two distinct types of cases.

1. Industrial relations disputes

In industrial relations disputes, it operates as a tribunal which hears both sides to a dispute and issues a written recommendation setting out its opinion on how the particular dispute should be resolved. The parties to the dispute are expected to give serious consideration to the Court's recommendation.

The primary role of the Labour Court in industrial relations disputes is to make recommendations for the resolution of disputes when other efforts have failed to resolve the dispute. Workers and employers are required to first effectively utilise direct means of resolution and other machinery of the State, e.g. the WRC Conciliation Service or the WRC Mediation/Adjudication Service. Where every effort to resolve the dispute has been made at the WRC and the dispute remains unresolved, the matter may then be referred to the Labour Court.

2. Employment rights cases

In employment rights cases, the Court hears cases under all of the various employment law statutes where an individual worker makes a complaint alleging a breach of their statutory employment rights by their employer. These cases concern the statutory entitlements of workers, therefore, the Labour Court issues written decisions which are legally binding and enforceable on the parties. Decisions can be referred to the High Court on the basis of an appeal on a point of law.

In employment rights cases, the worker must first refer their case to the WRC for adjudication. Where either party is dissatisfied with the decision of the Adjudication Officer, that decision can be appealed to the Labour Court. It is important to note that a case on appeal before the Labour Court is heard afresh in its entirety as though the first stage had not occurred. No new claims can be introduced at the appeal stage.

EVALUATION OF THE LABOUR COURT

The Labour Court has, since its establishment, played a very important role in Irish industrial relations.

It has enjoyed a high profile, often resolving disputes of great public interest. Overall, it has carried out its dispute-resolution functions with great success. The Labour Court has intervened and solved very difficult disputes – e.g. public transport disputes.

The Labour Court has the respect and confidence of all parties in industrial relations. Its recommendations are not binding on either parties, but in the majority of cases they will be accepted by the parties.

Employment Equality Acts 1998–2015

The Employment Equality Acts 1998–2015 outlaw discrimination in a wide range of employment and employment-related areas. These include recruitment and promotion; equal pay; working conditions; training or experience; dismissal and harassment, including sexual harassment.

What is discrimination?

Discrimination is defined as less favourable treatment. An employee is said to be discriminated against if they are treated less favourably than another is, has been or would be treated in a comparable situation on any of the following grounds:

- Gender: this means man, woman or transgender person
- Civil status: includes single, married, separated, divorced, widowed people, civil partners and former civil partners
- Family status: this refers to the parent of a person under 18 years
- Sexual orientation: includes gay, lesbian, bisexual and heterosexual
- Religion: means religious beliefs, background, outlook or none
- Age: this does not apply to a person aged under 16
- Disability
- Race: includes race, skin colour, nationality or ethnic origin
- Membership of the Traveller community.

Specific situations covered by employment equality legislation

Disability: Employers are obliged to make reasonable accommodations for staff with disabilities. This includes providing access to employment, enabling people with disabilities to participate in employment, including promotion and training.

Pregnancy: Pregnancy-related discrimination is discrimination on the grounds of gender and includes recruitment, promotion and general conditions of employment.

Equal Pay: Employment equality legislation provides for equal pay for like work. Like work is defined as work that is the same, similar or work of equal value. It is one of the terms that must be part of the contract of employment.

Harassment (including sexual harassment) that is based on any of the nine grounds is a form of discrimination in relation to conditions of employment. Bullying at work, which is linked to one of the nine discriminatory grounds above, comes under employment equality legislation.

Victimisation: Under employment equality legislation you are protected against victimisation if you bring a claim or are involved in a complaint of unlawful discrimination against your employer. This means that your employer may not penalise you by dismissal, unfair treatment or unfavourable change in your conditions of employment.

Enforcing your rights

The Workplace Relations Commission is the place to bring a discrimination claim under the Employment Equality Acts 1998–2015.

The two methods of handling equality or discrimination disputes are mediation and adjudication.

Mediation

Mediation is an attempt to get agreement between the parties. At the end of mediation both sides sign an agreement, which is legally binding, so that both sides must keep to the terms of the decision. If agreement is not reached through mediation, the case will be referred to an Adjudication Officer.

Adjudication

If mediation is not used or is not successful, the complaint or dispute is referred to an Adjudication Officer who will conduct an inquiry and issue a legally binding decision. Remedies will include one or more of the following: compensation, an order for equal pay or equal treatment, and/or an order that somebody take a specific action.

EVALUATION OF THE EMPLOYMENT EQUALITY ACTS 1998–2015

The Acts are effective in protecting employees because:

- They set out nine grounds under which discrimination is outlawed so that all workers must be treated equally.
- The Workplace Relations Commission hears cases of discrimination and issues legally-binding decisions.

Unfair Dismissals Acts, 1977 to 2015

1. Purpose of the Acts

The purpose of the Acts is to protect employees from being unfairly dismissed from their jobs.

2. Who is covered?

In general, the Acts apply to any person working under a contract of employment. The Acts do not apply to a person who has been in the continuous service of the employer for less than one year. However, the one-year continuous service criterion does not apply where dismissal results from **certain types of leave**, including **maternity, adoptive, parental** or **carer's leave** and/or **trade union membership** or to **rights under the Minimum Wage Act 2000**.

The scope of the legislation has been broadened to include part-time workers who work less than eight hours per week.

3. Burden of proof *w/ employer*

In general, the Acts provide that every dismissal of an employee will be presumed to have been unfair unless the employer can show substantial grounds justifying the dismissal.

4. Grounds for fair dismissal

To justify a dismissal, an employer must show that it either resulted from one or more of the following causes:

- **Incompetence on the part of the employee.** The employee lacks ability to carry out required duties satisfactorily (poor work performance; failure to meet set targets and standard of work expected).

- **Qualifications (misrepresentation by the employee).** Lack of formal technical or professional qualifications as appropriate for the work the employee was employed to do; misleading employer in relation to qualifications.

- **Conduct of the employee.** Improper/unacceptable behaviour by the employee (e.g. theft, substance abuse, violence at work, refusal to obey reasonable orders, breach of employer's rules, causing physical injury).

- **Redundancy.** Due to closure, competition, decline in demand, cutbacks (fair procedures applied).

- **Incapability.** Employee is incapable of carrying out the work he/she was employed to do. (Incapability refers to employee's attendance, i.e. persistent lateness, absenteeism or extended sick leave, illness.)

- **Legal reasons.** If continuation of the job was to break the law in some way (e.g. if an employee's work visa expired, etc.).

5. Unfair dismissals

Dismissals will be unfair under the Acts where it is shown that they resulted from any of the following:

(a) an employee's trade union membership or activities, either outside working hours or at those times during working hours when permitted by the employer

(b) religious or political opinions

(c) race or colour or sexual orientation

(d) the age of an employee; dismissals on the grounds of age, other than being under 16 or reaching the normal retiring age for that particular employment, is deemed to be unfair

(e) an employee's membership of the Travelling community

(f) legal proceedings against an employer where an employee is a party or a witness

(g) unfair selection for redundancy

(h) an employee's pregnancy, or any matters connected therewith

(i) the exercise or proposed exercise by the employee of the right to maternity, adoptive, parental, carer's leave or paternity leave.

Employees claiming dismissal due to (a), (h), (i) may bring an unfair dismissal claim **even though they do not have one year's continuous service with their employer**.

Constructive dismissal

- Constructive dismissal arises where **the employee terminates their contract of employment**, with or without prior notice, **due to the conduct of their employer**.

- Even though the employee has not actually been dismissed, he/she can claim unfair dismissal against his employer, under the terms of the Unfair Dismissals Acts 1977–2015.

- In a constructive dismissal situation it is up to the **employee** to prove that the resignation was justified.

- The employer's conduct, however, must be such that it would have been reasonable for the employee to terminate their contract without giving notice.

6. Claim for unfair dismissal and time limits

In order to **qualify to bring a claim for unfair dismissal** under the legislation the following requirements must be met:

Time limit

The time limit for beginning a claim for unfair dismissal is six months from the date of the dismissal.

Service

Normally the employee must have at least 12 months' continuous service with their employer in order to bring a claim for unfair dismissal. However, there are important exceptions to this general rule as outlined above.

Employment status

The person must be an employee, working under a contract of service. The essential element of such a contract is that the relationship is one of employer/employee.

The fact of dismissal

The person must have been dismissed in order to bring a claim. The one exception to this is the concept of constructive dismissal, where the person resigned but claimed that the employer's conduct towards them forced their resignation.

If the employer disputes that a dismissal actually took place, the employee will have to establish that it did. Only then will the claim continue to the next stage of deciding whether the dismissal was fair, which is a matter for the employer to prove.

Excluded categories

The Acts do not apply to the following:

(a) an employee who is under 16, or who has reached normal retiring age

(b) a person working for a close relative in a private house or farm, provided both also live in the same house or farm

(c) a member of the Defence Forces

(d) a member of the Garda Síochana

(e) a person undergoing full-time training or an apprenticeship.

How to apply

The employee should make their complaint to the **Workplace Relations Commission**. Complaints will be referred to an **Adjudication Officer** for hearing.

All decisions of an Adjudication Officer can be **appealed to the Labour Court**.

7. Redress under the Unfair Dismissals Acts

Where an employee has been unfairly dismissed, he/she can, under the Acts, be awarded either:

(i) **Re-instatement** – Employee is treated as if he/she had never been dismissed. Employee is entitled to loss of earnings from the date of the dismissal to the date of the hearing, and is also entitled to any favourable changes in the terms of employment during that period, for example, pay rises.

(ii) **Re-engagement** – The employee will be given his or her job back, but only from a particular date, for example, the date of the decision. This means that the employee will not be entitled to compensation for any loss of earnings. Often this remedy is used where it is felt that the employee contributed to the dismissal, even though the actual dismissal was unfair.

(iii) **Compensation** – Compensation is only rewarded in respect of financial loss. Generally, the maximum compensation is two years' pay.

EVALUATION OF THE UNFAIR DISMISSALS ACTS, 1977–2015

The Acts are very effective in protecting employees because:

- The employer has to prove that he/she has substantial grounds justifying the dismissal.
- If an employee is unfairly dismissed, they can take their case to the Workplace Relations Commission and, if they win their case, they are entitled to their job back or financial compensation.

Procedures an employer should follow before dismissing an employee:

All dismissals are presumed to be unfair unless the employer can prove otherwise. The burden of proof lies with the employer. The employer must show that there were substantial grounds for justifying the dismissal, e.g. misconduct such as theft or assault caught on CCTV.

Counselling/Advice

Counselling (i.e. advice on how to improve) is given by supervisor and recorded on the employee's personal record. The employer outlines what the employee needs to do to rectify the situation. The employee is made aware of the consequences.

Formal verbal warning

The employer has to inform the employee of the reasons for the possible dismissal. The evidence for the dismissal must be made known to the employee. This is given in the presence of the employee's representative. The employee is given the opportunity to respond fully to any such allegations or complaints. The warning is recorded on the employee's personal record.

First written warning

If there is no change to the situation, a formal written warning follows the oral warning. A copy will be given to the employee's representative.

This may be followed by a final written warning, suspension without pay, transfer to another task or section of the enterprise, demotion, some other appropriate disciplinary action short of dismissal and, finally, dismissal.

Employee's Rights of Appeal

The employee has the right to a fair and impartial determination of the issues concerned, taking into account any representations made by, or on behalf of, the employee and any other relevant or appropriate evidence, factors or circumstances.

Employer Duties/Responsibilities

The employer must recognise the employee's right to representation at a hearing into the dismissal and the hearing itself must be impartial. The employer is required to give the Procedure for Dismissal (i.e. Handbook for Employees) to all employees. A written copy of the reasons for dismissal must be forwarded to the employee within 14 days of the dismissal.

(i) Outline two reasons for fair dismissal, as set out under the Unfair Dismissal Acts 1977–2007. (12 marks)

Source: 2016 Higher Level Section 3

Suggested solution

Incompetence on the part of the employee. The employee lacks the ability to carry out required duties (poor work performance; failure to meet set targets).

Qualifications (misrepresentation by the employee): Lack of formal technical or professional qualifications as appropriate for the work the employee was employed to do/misleading employer in relation to qualifications.

Misconduct by the employee: Improper/unacceptable behaviour by the employee e.g. theft, substance abuse, violence at work.

Redundancy: Due to closure, competition, decline in demand, cutbacks (fair procedures applied).

Incapability: refers to employee's attendance, i.e. persistent lateness, absenteeism, or extended sick leave, etc.

Legal reasons: If continuation of the job was to break the law in some way, e.g. if an employee's work visa expired, etc.

(ii) Explain the term 'constructive dismissal', providing an example to support your answer. (8 marks)

Constructive dismissal refers to a situation where an **employer makes it so difficult for an employee**/the **employee feels they have no other option but to resign their position**, with or without notice. E.g. an employee is constantly being harassed by her manager, who blames the employee for all problems in the business. The employee feels she has no option but to resign her position.

Marking scheme

(i) 2 × 6 marks (State 3 marks, explain 3 marks)

(ii) 8 marks (4 marks (2 + 2) + 4 marks for example)

UNIT 2

Enterprise

Enterprise is the source of all business. Innovation is central to business development. This section looks at the nature of enterprise, characteristics of enterprising people and associated skills. Unit 2 also examines the application of enterprise in other areas of life.

Objective
To enable pupils to understand the importance of enterprise in business and community life.

- **Chapter 4:** Introduction to Enterprise, Characteristics of Entrepreneurs and Enterprise Skills

4 Introduction to Enterprise, Characteristics of Entrepreneurs and Enterprise Skills

 Be able to:

- Define enterprise.
- Identify the importance of enterprise skills in areas such as the home, school, community, government departments and business start-ups.
- Explain the basic enterprise skills.
- Identify the characteristics of enterprising people.
- Analyse the importance of enterprise in business and in the community.
- Identify enterprise skills, opportunities, risks and rewards from information given.

Enterprise

- Enterprise is being innovative and creative while taking personal/financial risk to achieve one's goal.
- Enterprise is when an individual (or group of people) takes the initiative/starts something new.
- Enterprise involves the risk of organising all the resources necessary to provide a product or service while exploiting an opportunity for a possible reward called profit.

Entrepreneur

An entrepreneur is an individual who undertakes the risk of establishing and running a business (alone or with others).

Entrepreneurs use their initiative in seeking out opportunities and turning them into businesses.

The entrepreneur organises all the resources necessary (financial and human) in setting up the business in the hope of making a profit.

Examples of **well-known entrepreneurs**:

- Sir Richard Branson – a British billionaire who has built his company (Virgin) into one of the world's biggest brands
- Patrick and John Collinson – set up Stripe, a company which enables websites to accept credit and debit card payments

- Mary Ann O'Brien – founder of Lily O'Brien's Chocolates
- Brody Sweeney – founder of O'Briens Irish Sandwich Bars
- Eamonn Fallon – founder of Daft.ie, Irelands largest property website.

Entrepreneurship

An entrepreneur is an individual who undertakes the risk of establishing a business. Entrepreneurship is the process of taking the initiatives and carrying the risk of organising all the resources necessary to provide a product or service.

The entrepreneur not only sees an opportunity (e.g. a new product or service) but also sets out to exploit that opportunity.

Profit is the reward entrepreneurs get for their efforts.

Intrapreneur

Intrapreneurs are employees who work within an organisation in an entrepreneurial capacity, creating innovative new products and turning them into profitable activities.

An intrapreneur comes up with new ideas, ways of saving money and new ways of solving problems (e.g. new work methods or new production processes) **within the business** in which he/she is employed. An intrapreneur would therefore work for an organisation such as a transnational company or a government department. Intrapreneurs need the freedom and resources (human and capital) to pursue their ideas.

For example, Intel has a tradition of encouraging intrapreneurship. It gives its employees the freedom to create their own projects and funds their development.

Intrapreneurship

- Intrapreneurship involves entrepreneurial activity **within the business/employees** come up with **new ideas/take personal responsibility** which may turn into profitable activities.
- Intrapreneurs are inventive, creative and innovative; they are constantly looking for ways of growing/expanding the business and improving business processes/ product without the financial risk.

Methods of promoting intrapreneurship

- **Empowerment** – employee participation encourages creativity as it allows employees greater freedom to do their job by placing real power, responsibility and authority in the hands of employees.
- Create a **culture** within the organisation where it's **OK to make mistakes.**
- **Financial rewards for effort and creativity.** These rewards could involve a mixture of pay, incentives and benefits. For example, a bonus or profit-sharing scheme or shared ownership scheme.
- **Teamwork** encourages creativity among employees as it facilitates brainstorming sessions as part of the product development process.

- **Resource provider** – makes resources available to help employees to pursue their ideas (e.g. finance, time).
- **Training programmes** for employees and management, training them on the implementation of an intrapreneurial culture within a business.

Characteristics of entrepreneurs

1. Innovative/Creative

Entrepreneurs are good at coming up with new ideas and ways of improving what they do. Entrepreneurs show imagination, initiative, resourcefulness and readiness to undertake new projects. They think outside the box to develop new products or new versions of existing products.

2. Risk-taker

Being an entrepreneur involves both personal and financial risk in pursuit of a business idea. Successful entrepreneurs are not afraid of taking risks. They are realistic risk-takers.

3. Resilient/Confident

Entrepreneurs are not put off by failure. Entrepreneurs have a strong sense of self-belief and conviction about their own business ideas.

They see failure as an opportunity to learn. Having ambition and having a strong desire for success or achievement is central to being an entrepreneur.

4. Reality perception/Realistic

An entrepreneur sees things/situations for what they are and not as he/she would like them to be. Entrepreneurs must be realistic with their ideas and plans and be realistic about what they can achieve in a specific timescale/reality perception.

5. Customer focus/Future focus

Entrepreneurs are very aware of customer needs and are willing to change their business model to meet those needs.

Customer satisfaction is the key to any successful business, so a customer focus is required.

6. Networking/Persuasive abilities/Human relations

Entrepreneurs recognise the importance of a wide range of contacts to provide guidance and support.

Entrepreneurs need to be able to persuade others.

Human relations skills – the ability to relate well with people. Good human relations are vital. They will also be dealing with customers and potential customers.

7. Initiative/Exploiting opportunity

Uses initiative – sees an opportunity and uses initiative to set up the business/has the drive or 'get up and go' to take action.

8. Decisive/Decision-making

The ability to make quick and effective decisions is essential for enterprising people. Entrepreneurs must be able to assess situations, identify opinions and weigh up the pros and cons before making decisions.

9. Proactive

This is the ability to act in advance of a future situation, rather than just reacting; the need to take total control and make things happen rather than waiting for something to happen.

10. Flexible

The ability to change as circumstances change. The business environment is very dynamic, so everything may not go exactly to plan. There is a need to be flexible and adapt to the changing circumstances.

Enterprise skills

1. Planning and goal-setting

Entrepreneurs must be able to set short-term and long-term goals. Plans must be drawn up to achieve these goals. When planning, entrepreneurs will carry out a SWOT analysis.

2. Assessing and managing risk

Entrepreneurs must estimate the level of risk involved in a project and compare it with the likely return before a decision is made to proceed with the project.

3. Time management

The ability to use time effectively to ensure that all necessary tasks are completed is an important skill for an entrepreneur to have. This skill also involves taking appropriate action at the appropriate time and prioritising or ranking tasks in order of importance.

4. Decision-making/Decisive

Entrepreneurs must be good decision-makers. When making a decision, they must choose the best option for the business from many different possible alternatives.

5. Human relations

This is the skill of being able to get on well with people, to develop good working relationships with them and to be able to organise them into teams.
This requires good interpersonal skills and good communication skills.

6. Reality perception

Seeing things as they really are is important for entrepreneurs. They must be able to realise when things are going wrong. They should recognise their own limitations and be able to seek advice when the need arises.

7. Inner control

Entrepreneurs want to control their own situation, and not to be controlled or influenced by others. They want to make things happen themselves.

8. Innovation/Creativity

This is the skill of coming up with new ideas and better ways of doing things. Entrepreneurs who are innovative try to solve problems by finding new solutions.

9. Leadership/Delegation

Leadership involves directing and assisting people in order to ensure work is done effectively so that objectives can be met.

10. Communication/Feedback

Speaking, listening and writing to communicate with stakeholders.

Enterprise in different situations

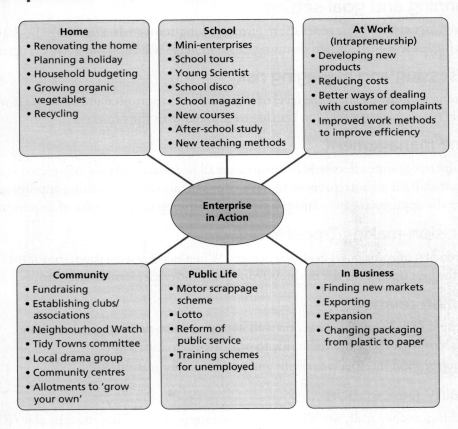

Home
- Renovating the home
- Planning a holiday
- Household budgeting
- Growing organic vegetables
- Recycling

School
- Mini-enterprises
- School tours
- Young Scientist
- School disco
- School magazine
- New courses
- After-school study
- New teaching methods

At Work
(Intrapreneurship)
- Developing new products
- Reducing costs
- Better ways of dealing with customer complaints
- Improved work methods to improve efficiency

Enterprise in Action

Community
- Fundraising
- Establishing clubs/associations
- Neighbourhood Watch
- Tidy Towns committee
- Local drama group
- Community centres
- Allotments to 'grow your own'

Public Life
- Motor scrappage scheme
- Lotto
- Reform of public service
- Training schemes for unemployed

In Business
- Finding new markets
- Exporting
- Expansion
- Changing packaging from plastic to paper

Importance of enterprise in business and in the local community

1. Employment creation

Enterprise creates new businesses, which in turn create employment.

2. Increased local business

Workers spend money in the local shops, restaurants, etc. This helps local businesses to survive and expand.

3. Attracts new business

Enterprise attracts entrepreneurs and new business to the area.

4. Government revenue

Increased government revenue results from the success of businesses through PAYE and business taxation.

5. Improved infrastructure

New houses and roads are built and the telecommunications infrastructure in the local area is improved.

Read the information supplied and answer the question which follows.

Stripe, the fast-growing online payments business, was established by Limerick brothers Patrick and John Collison when they were aged just 22 and 19. Stripe enables websites to accept credit and debit card payments. It employs over 600 people globally and is worth more than $9bn.

Source: adapted from www.siliconrepublic.com and The Irish Times

(A) Outline the characteristics/skills that you would associate with entrepreneurs.

(20 marks)

Source: 2017 Higher Level Section 3

Suggested solution

● **Risk-taking**

An entrepreneur takes a personal and financial risk in setting up a new business with no guarantee of success. If the product is successful in the market place, the risk pays off and the entrepreneur makes a profit.

● **Decision-making**

An entrepreneur has to be able to make decisions for the benefit of the business, often in pressurised situations. They must be able to analyse the intended and unintended consequences of their decisions and take all considerations into account.

● **Innovation/creativity/exploiting opportunity/visionary**

The entrepreneur must be creative and develop new ideas or new ways of doing things. Entrepreneurs show imagination, resourcefulness and readiness to undertake new projects. They think outside the box to develop new products or new versions of existing products.

● **Future focused/customer focused/identifying opportunities/proactive**

The entrepreneur is always thinking of the future and looking for possible gaps in the market.

● **Resilient/confident/determined/self-belief**

Entrepreneurs are not put off by failure. Entrepreneurs have a strong sense of self-belief and conviction about their own business ideas. They see failure as an opportunity to learn. Having ambition and having a strong desire for success or achievement is central to being an entrepreneur.

Marking scheme

4 x 5 marks (2 + 3)

Read the information supplied and answer the questions which follow.

The Mayfair Hotel

The Mayfair Hotel is a five-star city centre hotel which is celebrating 10 years in business. To celebrate this centenary, the management of the hotel is planning various events. Discuss how the hotel staff could apply entrepreneurial skills to develop the various centenary events.

(20 marks)

Source: 2016 Higher Level Section 3

Suggested solution

- **Innovative/creative**

The staff could come up with new ideas or new ways of doing things. Develop a unique selling point (USP) to distinguish the hotel from other hotels. Innovative/creative (visionary approach) is required.

- **Customer focus**

Customer satisfaction is the key to any successful business, so a customer focus is required. The Mayfair staff needs to determine and prioritise customer needs.

- **Human relations**

The ability to relate well with people. Staff will be working in teams to generate ideas and plan events, so good human relations are vital. They will also be dealing with customers and potential customers.

- **Adaptable**

The ability to change as circumstances change. The business environment is very dynamic so everything may not go exactly to plan. Staff need to be able to adapt to the changing circumstances/need for flexibility.

- **Reality perception**

The ability to see things as they are, not as you would like them to be. Staff must be realistic with their ideas and plans and be realistic about what they can achieve in a specific timescale/reality perception.

- **Proactive**

The ability to act in advance of a future situation, rather than just reacting. Staff need to take control and make things happen rather than waiting for something to happen. Staff need to adopt a proactive approach.

- **Future focused**

Staff need to anticipate future customer need. They need to have a vision which allows them to anticipate customer needs and look towards the future/future focused. Need to stay ahead of the competition.

- **Decision-making/decisive**

The ability to make quick and effective decisions is essential for enterprising people. Management and staff must be able to assess situations, identify options and weigh up the pros and cons before making decisions that will benefit the hotel.

Marking scheme

Four points @ 5 marks each (State 2 marks, discuss 3 marks)

UNIT 3

Managing I

This unit introduces the concept of management. It examines management as a planning and control process. As management is largely implemented through people, there is an emphasis on the management skills of communication, organisation and motivation.

Objective

To enable pupils to understand the importance of management in business and in the community.

- **Chapter 5:** Introduction and Definition of Management
- **Chapter 6:** Management Skills: Leading, Motivating
- **Chapter 7:** Management Skills: Communication
- **Chapter 8:** Management Activities: Planning, Organising, Controlling

5 Introduction and Definition of Management

aims

Be able to:

- Define management.
- Identify the importance of management skills in areas such as the home, school, local community, government departments and business start-ups.
- List the characteristics of managers.

HL ⦁ Differentiate between enterprise and management.

- Explain the contribution of both managers and entrepreneurs to business.

key point

Definition of Management

Management is the process of combining personnel and physical resources (money) to create an environment in which the planned objectives/goals of the organisation can be achieved through people (that is, by assigning activities to subordinates).

Managers

Managers are the people responsible for achieving the objectives of the business.

Management skills

Leading – Influencing and directing people.

Motivating – The factors that cause people to behave in certain ways.

Communicating – The process of transferring information from one person to another.

key point

Managers need the **skills** of leading, motivating and communicating to enable them to carry out the **activities** of planning, organising and controlling.

Management activities

Planning – Setting goals and objectives and deciding how to achieve them.

Organising – Arranging the resources in an organisation to achieve the objectives.

Controlling – Monitoring progress by comparing performance with set targets and correcting any differences.

Management in action

Management is used in many situations:

- **Home**: Household manager **plans** household budget, **controls** household expenditure, **motivates** students to study for exams, **communicates** with banks, insurance companies, etc.
- **School**: School principal **plans** curriculum and timetables, **organises** supervision rotas, **controls** school budget, **motivates** pupils and teachers.
- **Business**: Manager **plans** goals to be achieved, **organises** resources (finance and staff), **motivates** employees, **communicates** with customers/suppliers, **controls** stock, quality and credit.
- **Government departments**: Taoiseach **plans** government policies, **controls** departmental budgets, **leads** the Dáil Éireann, **motivates** public service.
- **Local Community**: Committee head **plans** fundraising events, **controls** expeditions, **leads** members, **motivates** volunteers.

Characteristics of managers

1. Leadership

Mangers must:

- Lead by example, setting high standards to be achieved by others.
- Be always at hand to impart knowledge to employees.
- Be willing to take responsibility and be accountable for the work of others.

2. Decisive

Mangers must:

- Have the ability to make quick and effective decisions and implement them.
- Take responsibly for the outcome of decisions.

3. Hard-working

- Managers must be self-disciplined and motivated to work hard to achieve objectives.

4. Communicator

- Managers must be good listeners and be able to communicate effectively within and outside the organisation.

5. Organiser

- Managers must have the ability to organise the resources of the organisation or business in order to run it efficiently.

6. Time management

- Managers must ensure tasks are completed on time. This involves:
  - Making best use of the time available
  - Prioritising tasks to ensure that the most important ones are completed first.

7. Charismatic

- Managers must have personal appeal and the ability to charm people to get work done.

8. Interpersonal skills

- Managers must understand people, relate to them and be able to deal with them in ways that gets the best results from them.

Difference between enterprise and management

Enterprise

- Enterprise is the business activity that provides the initiative, generates the idea, identifies the opportunity and underlies the confidence, motivation and determination necessary to take the risk to turn the idea into a reality.
- 'Being enterprising' involves taking risks and, ultimately, being responsible for the success or failure of the business.

Management

- Management is the process of getting objectives achieved effectively and efficiently with and through other people. It is concerned with managing people and resources on a daily basis. Managers must ensure that this is well done so that the aims and objectives of the organisation are achieved.
- Management also involves setting short-term targets and long-term goals, checking to see if they are reached and making changes where necessary.
- The key activities of management are planning, organising and controlling.

In summary

The difference between entrepreneurs and managers is that:

- Entrepreneurs generate ideas, **whereas** managers implement ideas.
- Entrepreneurs risk their own money and reputation in setting up a business, **whereas** managers do not take the same risk.
- Entrepreneurs are concerned with the future of the business or coming up with new ideas for new businesses, **whereas** managers are concerned with the day-to-day operation of the business.

For example, Richard Branson set up Virgin, but Virgin management runs it.

6 Management Skills: Leading and Motivating

Management involves getting the best out of people. Managers must use the management skills of leading, motivating and communication.

Leading

Setting an example

A leader should be clearly visible in the organisation, a role model, setting an example of what is required of subordinates in terms of behaviour.

Direction

Directing staff by guiding them on the right course so that everyone co-operates and works together to achieve the goals of the organisation.

Leadership involves directing and assisting people in order to ensure work is done effectively so that objectives can be met.

Leadership allows an individual to positively influence how others behave so that they contribute voluntarily to achieving group goals.

Delegation

- Delegation involves the passing of authority from a manager to a subordinate, to undertake specific work. The accountability for the particular task/project is also assigned.
- The manager must ensure that the person to whom the task is delegated has the necessary skills, and is provided with the necessary resources to complete the task.
- The ultimate responsibility for the task remains with the manager.
- Example: In a large firm the managing director must delegate tasks to the sales manager, accountant, human resource manager, etc.

Benefits of delegation within a business

- The manager is not required to do all the work and has more time for strategic planning.
- The task/project may be completed to a higher standard due to the level of personal accountability provided by delegation.

- Increased employee motivation from job enrichment/improved staff morale/more challenging work.
- Effective time-managment tool: managers can prioritise tasks that need their attention.
- Higher skilled workforce will allow greater management flexibility.
- May improve the work–life balance for the manager.

Styles of leadership

Authoritarian leadership

- No consultation with subordinates.
- All major decisions are made by the leader, orders are issued and expected to be obeyed without question.
- There is little delegation of tasks to subordinates/leader distrusts staff.
- Objectives are achieved using threats, fear and position of authority to get agreement.
- Communication is only one way – top-down.

The three **styles of leadership** are:

- Authoritarian
- Democratic
- Laissez-faire

Evaluation of Authoritarian Leadership
An authoritarian style will produce dissatisfied and poorly motivated workers who will not co-operate with the leader.

Democratic leadership

- Leader consults subordinates and seeks their opinions, and encourages their participation in decision-making and problem-solving.
- Leader delegates authority and responsibility as he/she trusts staff to do the work.
- Persuades and motivates employees rather than giving orders.
- Communication is two-way.

Evaluation of Democratic Leadership
A democratic style will produce highly motivated and co-operative employees, high morale and greater job satisfaction.

Laissez-faire leadership

- Relaxed leadership style.
- The leader sets the objectives and subordinates must decide how to achieve them.
- All authority/responsibility delegated to staff.

Evaluation of Laissez-Faire Leadership
This style of leadership is effective when:

- Employees are highly skilled, experienced, and educated.
- Employees have pride in their work and have the drive to do it successfully on their own.

It is not suitable for every business situation.

- The manager provides little or no direction and gives employees as much freedom as possible.
- There is considerable trust in staff.
- All authority or power is given to employees and they must determine goals, make decisions and solve problems on their own.
- Little or no involvement from management.
- Communication may be difficult.
- Suitable for creative industries.

Importance of effective leadership in an organisation

- An effective leader delegates tasks to employees – staff are trusted and more involved in the business.
- An effective leader sets an example of what is required by subordinates in an organisation.
- An effective leader gives clear directions to employees. They know exactly what is required of them in the organisation.
- A good leader gets everyone to work together to achieve the goals of the organisation.

Outline two styles of leadership and illustrate how each of these styles may be appropriate in different business situations.

(20 marks)

Source: 2012 Higher Level Section 3

Suggested solution

Leadership Styles

Autocratic

- Leader who likes to be in control of things and does not delegate; little consultation with employees, frequently dictating instructions; opinions of employees are not considered.
- All major decisions are made by the leader and orders are issued and directives are made to be obeyed without question.
- Fear and threats are used as motivators; little trust in employees.
- Manager suffers from overloading and the quality of his/her work suffers.
- Subordinates get little experience of management and promotions are mostly external.
- Morale can be low among staff; staff turnover can be high; staff become frustrated and industrial relations disputes follow.

Ilustration: This style of leadership may be appropriate in a crisis or emergency situation where tough decisions may be needed quickly, e.g. turning around a business facing insolvency.

Democratic

- Power is shared with staff.
- Authority is delegated to staff, but ultimately responsibility rests with the manager.
- Opinions/ideas/feedback are sought before decisions are made and decisions tend to be better as a result.
- Trust is built over time with staff; staff feel more valued and motivated.
- Intrapreneurship may occur.
- Decision-making can be slow and delayed.

Illustration: It may be appropriate in a business that promotes teamwork (e.g. Google). Works well in an environment where staff can handle responsibility.

Laissez-Faire

- Management has a facilitative role guiding and does not get involved in the day-to-day running of the business.
- Almost all authority is delegated to staff.
- Huge trust is placed in staff.
- Highly motivated and trustworthy workers use their initiative, leading to very high levels of intrapreneurship.
- Staff are empowered rather than ordered.
- Greater freedom given to staff in setting own goals.
- Managers are free to deal with more strategic matters.

Illustration: It is likely to be used by high-tech industries which rely on well-educated and highly self-directed employees. Prevalent form of leadership in firms engaged in R&D and advertising where creativity is valued.

Marking scheme

Two leadership styles @ 10 marks each

Two marks – naming leadership styles

Two points of information @ 3 marks each

Two marks for reference to a business situation

Two points of information @ 3 marks each

Two marks for reference to a business situation

Motivating

Theories of motivation

Many theories have been developed over the years to help management identify how best to motivate people.

There are two main theories of motivation on how to motivate employees:

Motivation is the willingness of people to work. It is what drives, influences and encourages people to work towards a particular goal.

It involves putting factors in place that cause people to behave in certain ways for the benefit of the business.

Employees' behaviour can be influenced by motivating them to meet their unsatisfied needs.

Maslow's hierarchy of needs

According to Maslow, most people are motivated by a desire to satisfy a group of five specific needs.

Maslow stated that each individual has a hierarchy of needs and he/she will look to satisfy a higher need only when the lower one has been satisfied.

Maslow's hierarchy of needs

Explanation	Needs	How business can satisfy need
The need to reach one's full potential. Being personally fulfilled having developed one's talents to the highest possible level.	Self-actualisation	Challenging job, promotion and the opportunity to reach full potential.
The need for recognition and respect from others.	Esteem	Job titles, recognition for work and effort. Delegation of tasks and responsibility.
The need for interaction with other people. Being part of a group, friendship.	Social	Team work, social outings, staff interaction at work.
Safety and security needs, house, family.	Safety	Secure employment. Health and safety systems.
Most basic survival needs, food, water, shelter.	Physiological	Salaries, good working conditions, canteen facilities.

Evaluation of Maslow's Hierarchy of Needs

- Maslow's hierarchy of needs is very effective because it tells managers that if they want to motivate employees to work harder, they must identify the level of need which each employee is trying to satisfy.
- Managers must then create a suitable work environment to enable employees to satisfy that need.

McGregor's Theory X and Theory Y

McGregor examined the behaviour of individuals at work and what managers believe about employees and formulated two theories called Theory X and Theory Y.

Theory X	Theory Y
1. Employees are lazy, dislike work and try to avoid it.	1. Employees are interested in work, want challenging jobs.
2. Employees lack ambition, dislike responsibility and prefer to be directed.	2. Employees want to be given responsibility and can be trusted to work on their own.
3. Employees dislike change in the workplace.	3. Employees are motivated to change when they are consulted.
4. Employees are motivated only by money; they need to be controlled to make them function.	4. Employees want to achieve their best and gain respect and recognition.

Characteristics of Theory X manager

- Manager controls employees – possible conflict between management and employees.
- Employees are unlikely to use own initiative.
- No consultation in decision-making.
- Little delegation of work.
- Employees become uncooperative and poorly motivated resulting in poor quality goods and services.

Evaluation of McGregor's Theory X

McGregor suggested that Theory X managers adopt an autocratic approach to management by:

- Supervising workers closely
- Offering incentives or using sanctions/threats to ensure employee co-operation. This results in poor motivation and uncooperative employees

Characteristics of Theory Y manager

- Manager delegates work
- Employees given extra responsibilities
- Employee participation in decision-making
- Employees more co-operative and motivated
- More innovation, improved quality, increased profitability

Importance of motivation in business

- Motivated employees will work hard for the success of the business; productivity is improved.
- Motivated employees are more likely to be more innovative and creative, coming up with new ideas to help the business.
- Motivated employees create a positive atmosphere in the workplace. Morale is higher, with less industrial relations problems.
- Motivated employees are more likely to stay with the business in the long term and are willing to undergo training to improve their skills to help the business be more successful.

exam focus

Evaluation of McGregor's Theory Y

McGregor said that Theory Y managers adopt a democratic approach to management which:

- Takes a much more positive view of employees
- Delegates work and gives employees extra responsibilities
- Employees will be motivated and co-operate and will make a better contribution to the business

exam Q

(i) Explain Maslow's Theory of Motivation.

(ii) Illustrate how a manager could motivate workers by applying Maslow's Theory in the workplace.

(20 marks)

Source: 2011 Higher Level Section 3

Suggested solution

(i) Motivation is the willingness of people to work. It is what drives, influences and encourages people to work towards a particular goal.

Maslow put forward a theory on motivation based on a hierarchy of needs.

As one need is satisfied, then the need immediately above it on the pyramid becomes the dominant motivator/takes precedence.

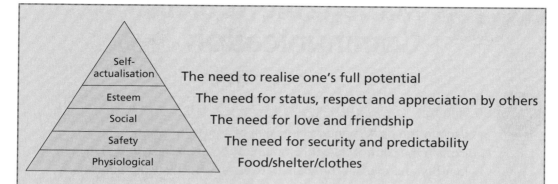

(ii)

- **Physical needs:** A manager can motivate his workers by ensuring they receive a fair wage, bonuses, profit-sharing schemes, in order that the physical needs for food, clothes, shelter, etc. can be met.
- **Safety needs:** Managers can make employees feel safe and secure by:
  - Offering long term contracts of employment.
  - Providing a grievance procedure.
  - Providing free medical check-ups.
  - Sending workers on health and safety courses.
  - Providing a safe working environment, e.g. safety goggles, boots, gloves, hard hats, high-visibility jackets for construction workers.
- **Social needs:** The social needs of employees can be met through offering flexitime, which allows employees to spend more time with their families. Teamwork and social events can help workers form new friendships and relationships.
- **Esteem needs:** Managers can facilitate a worker's esteem needs through offering praise and rewards such as a new job title or an attractive office.
- **Self-actualisation needs:** Management offering workers a career plan, training and development opportunities, empowerment and promotion to positions of responsibility can meet these needs.

Marking scheme

(i) 5 marks (2 + 3)

(ii) Maslow's Hierarchy of Needs in correct order – 5 × 1 mark each

Illustration of how manager could apply Maslow's Theory in the workplace – 5 × 2 marks each

7 Management Skills: Communication

aims Be able to:

- Explain the basic management skill of communication.
- Explain the central role of communication in business and management.
- Identify and explain the main barriers to effective communication.
- Demonstrate business information in the form of memos, reports and business letters and draft a visual presentation from given data.
- Identify the duties of a chairperson and secretary and draft an agenda and minutes of a meeting.
- Distinguish between the methods of communication.
- **HL** Discuss the importance of general communication skills.

Importance of good communication in business

1. Industrial relations

Good communication facilitates problem-solving without the need for industrial action.

key point

Communication is the transferring of information from a sender to a receiver and receiving feedback that the message has been understood.

2. Decision-making

Effective communication is important for successful decision-making as managers need good information. Successful communication of information to and from decision-makers is vital.

3. Downward communication

Communication is necessary when orders or directions are issued from a superior to a subordinate so that the individual understands the task to be performed and avoids mistakes.

4. Goals/Objectives

Communication allows the activities of all the departments to be co-ordinated in order to achieve the goals of the organisation.

5. Introduction of change

Communication forms the basis for the successful introduction of change.

Communication channels

1. Internal communication

Communication between people inside the organisation.

Downward communication

Instructions, orders, directions are transmitted from a superior to a subordinate (e.g. managing director communicating with marketing manager).

Upward communication

Information, messages, complaints are transmitted from subordinate to superior (e.g. employees complaining to management about working conditions).

Horizontal communication

Communication between people at the same level of authority in an organisation to ensure that all sections of the organisation work together (e.g. marketing manager and finance manager meeting to agree a budget for advertising).

2. External communication

Communication between an organisation and outside businesses (e.g. banks, insurance companies, suppliers, customers, etc.).

3. Communication skills

- **Speaking** – The ability to use language appropriate to the listener.
- **Listening** – The ability to listen so that the message is heard and received.
- **Writing** – The ability to write clearly and accurately.
- **Reading** – The ability to read and understand written information.

4. Principles of effective communication

Effective communication can be achieved by considering the following:

- **Accuracy** – All information must be accurate.
- **Brevity** – Communication should be brief and to the point.
- **Clarity** – Language should be clear and easily understood.
- **On time** – Correct timing is essential to allow the recipient time to respond.
- **Feedback** – Communication should allow for feedback from the recipient.

Barriers to effective communication and methods to overcome those barriers

1. Language

If the message is too technical it may be misinterpreted.

How to overcome this barrier: Choose language appropriate to the audience.

2. Not listening

If the recipient is not listening, the information will not be received correctly.

How to overcome this barrier: Repeat the message.

3. Timing

If the message is sent too late, the recipient may not be able to act on the information.

How to overcome this barrier: Plan the message to ensure that enough time is given to the recipient to read, understand and respond to the message.

4. Wrong medium

The medium chosen must be appropriate to the message.

How to overcome this barrier: Use the correct medium (e.g. use a letter to deliver a sensitive personal communication such as the termination of employment).

5. No feedback

The sender may require feedback before taking further action (e.g. the marketing manager may require information from the finance manager before deciding on an advertising campaign).

How to overcome this barrier: Build a feedback mechanism into the process (e.g. schedule a specific time slot for feedback).

Methods of communication

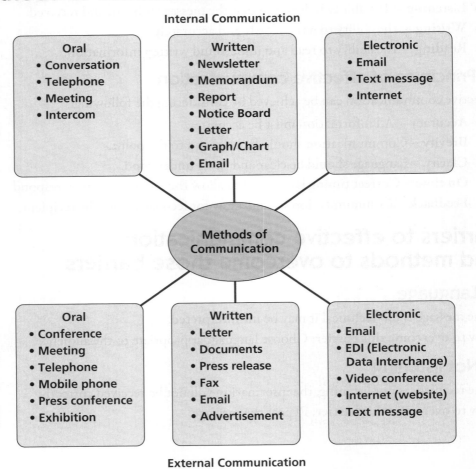

Internal Communication

Oral	Written	Electronic
• Conversation	• Newsletter	• Email
• Telephone	• Memorandum	• Text message
• Meeting	• Report	• Internet
• Intercom	• Notice Board	
	• Letter	
	• Graph/Chart	
	• Email	

Methods of Communication

Oral	Written	Electronic
• Conference	• Letter	• Email
• Meeting	• Documents	• EDI (Electronic Data Interchange)
• Telephone	• Press release	• Video conference
• Mobile phone	• Fax	• Internet (website)
• Press conference	• Email	• Text message
• Exhibition	• Advertisement	

External Communication

Choosing a method of communication

The following factors must be considered when choosing a method of communication:

1. Cost

Businesses must choose a method that will minimise costs. Email is a cheap method of communication.

2. Speed

If the message is urgent, business must choose the quickest method possible. Telephone or electronic communication would be appropriate.

3. Confidentiality

If the information is private, it is important to choose a confidential method of communication. A private meeting would be appropriate.

4. Nature of message

The nature of the message will determine the method to be chosen. If the message is long and detailed and proof of communication is required, written communication would be appropriate.

5. Safety and security

Extra measures should be taken if safety and security is important. Using registered mail or a courier service might be appropriate.

Oral communication

Meetings

A meeting is a gathering of a group of people to share information, exchange ideas and make suggestions to enable collective decision-making.

The **purpose of meetings** is to:

- **Exchange ideas** – Allows people to exchange ideas and information and plan ahead.
- **Make decisions** – Allows decisions to be made by voting on proposals.
- **Co-ordinate departments** – Meetings enable the co-ordinating of activities of various departments.
- **Solve problems** – Problems can be discussed and solutions put forward.
- **Meet legal requirements** – To adhere to legal requirements, all limited companies must hold an AGM.
- **Encourage co-operation and teamwork** – They provide a place for people to work together.
- Enable **face-to-face communication** – They enable people to meet each other in a neutral environment.

Types of meeting

There are different types of meetings, including:

- **Annual General Meeting (AGM)**

  This is a meeting held once a year and attended by the directors and shareholders of the company. The main functions of the AGM are as follows:
  - The shareholders elect a board of directors.
  - The shareholders appoint auditors.
  - The chairperson gives a report on company performance.
  - The auditor's report presents the accounts.
  - Shareholders have an opportunity to question directors in public on company policy.
  - A dividend is declared.

- **Extraordinary General Meeting (EGM)**

  This is a meeting of the shareholders and company directors held to discuss a matter of urgency that cannot wait until the next AGM. There is no other matter discussed at this meeting.

- **Board meetings**

  These are meetings of the board of directors and are usually held on a monthly basis. Progress and performance is discussed and tactical and strategic plans are formulated. Problem-solving is a key function of board meetings.

- **Statutory meetings**

  This is the first meeting of company shareholders about the affairs of the company. A statutory meeting is held once only in the whole life of the company. A statutory meeting is held by every limited company. The meeting should be held within the prescribed period mentioned in the company ordinance.

- **Ad hoc meetings**

  A meeting that takes place at short notice to discuss a matter that requires attention and that has arisen unexpectedly.

Terms

Terms used in meetings include:

- **Agenda** – A list of matters to be discussed at a meeting and the order in which they will be taken.
- **Minutes of meeting** – A written record of the business transacted at a meeting.
- **Quorum** – The minimum number of people that must be present before a meeting can commence.
- **Standing orders** – The agreed rules for running a meeting.

Chairperson

The chairperson is responsible for running the meeting.

Duties of a chairperson:

1. **Planning the meeting** and drawing up an agenda in consultation with the secretary.
2. **Running the meeting**: opening the meeting, ensuring a quorum is present and that the agenda is followed.
3. **Maintaining order at the meeting**, managing discussion, and ensuring compliance with standing orders.
4. **Putting motions to a vote**, having a casting vote in the event of a tie, and announcing the result.
5. **Summarising decisions made** and concluding the meeting.

Secretary

The secretary is responsible for all administration work in the organisation.

Duties of a secretary:

- **Drawing up the agenda** in consultation with the chairperson.
- **Making arrangements for the meeting**, organising the venue, facilities and equipment needed.
- **Sending out notice and agenda** to all entitled to attend in advance of the meeting.
- **Reading minutes** of the previous meeting.
- Giving the **secretary's report**.
- **Taking notes** on discussion and decisions made and writing up minutes of the meeting.
- Arranging the next meeting in consultation with chairperson.

Notice, agenda and minutes of a meeting

Notice

The notice gives the name of the organisation, the type of meeting, the venue, the day, date and time of the meeting and is sent in advance of the meeting.

Agenda

The agenda is the programme for the meeting and contains a list of matters to be discussed and the order in which they will be taken.

Minutes of a meeting

This is a record of the business transacted at a meeting written by the secretary. It includes people present, absences, decisions made, matters discussed, and planning for future meetings.

HL

Agenda and minutes

Draft a typical agenda for, and the minutes of, the AGM of a limited company.

(25 marks)

Suggested solution

Agenda and Minutes of the AGM of a Limited Company

Agenda

Notice is hereby given that the second Annual General Meeting of Redcliffe Ltd will be held in the head office of the company at 8 North Main Street, Wexford, on 10 April 2019, commencing at 1.30 p.m. for the following purposes:

1. Minutes of the 2018 AGM
2. Matters arising from the minutes
3. Chairperson's report
4. Auditor's report and accounts
5. Confirm the interim dividend and declare a final dividend for the year
6. Remuneration and appointment of auditors
7. Election/re-appointment of directors
8. Motions
9. Any other business

By order of the Board of Directors.

John Carey
Company Secretary
Date: 2 April 2019

Minutes of Second Annual General Meeting of Redcliffe Ltd

The second Annual General Meeting of Redcliffe Ltd was held in the head office of the company, 8 North Main Street, Wexford, on 10 April 2019, commencing at 1.30 p.m. The chairperson, Mr Kevin O'Halloran, brought the meeting to order.

The attendance included the directors, sixty shareholders and the auditor.

1. The minutes of the 2018 AGM were read and approved.
2. There were no matters arising from the minutes.
3. The chairperson report was given by Mr Kevin O'Halloran, who reviewed the past year and set out plans for the future.
4. The auditors report was presented and the accounts were adopted.
5. The dividend for the year was agreed at 8c per share.
6. The remuneration of the auditors was agreed and Johnson, Mooney and O'Brien chartered accountants were re-appointed as auditors for the following year.
7. Ms J. Creedon and Mr J. O'Connor were re-appointed directors for a further year.
8. There were no motions before the meeting.
9. As there was no other business, the meeting concluded at 4.15 p.m.

Signed
Kevin O'Halloran
Chairperson
Date: 15 April 2019

Benefits of meetings as a method of communication

1. Meetings allow discussions to take place on different proposals, which in turn allow for good, **effective decision-making/co-ordination of the work of various departments**.
2. Meetings allow **information to be disseminated** to the various stakeholders in the company, e.g. a meeting of management and the employees of the firm regarding industrial relations issues.
3. Meetings are creative forums, e.g. a **brainstorming session** during the idea generation stage of the product development process.
4. Meetings are appropriate when **sensitive or confidential issues** are being discussed e.g. redundancy, dismissal of staff and business contraction/expansion.
5. Meetings allow for **feedback** to be given and received.
6. A **written record** (i.e. minutes) of decisions can be made for future reference.

Notice and agenda

Assume you are the secretary of a local youth club. Draft the notice **and** agenda to be posted to all members of the youth club notifying them of the Annual General Meeting. (The agenda must contain five items.)   (10 marks)

Suggested solution

Notice and Agenda for AGM of Youth Club

Notice is hereby given that the fifth **Annual General Meeting** (1 mark) of the **Wexford Youth Club** (1 mark) will be held in the **Clubhouse, Mary Street, Wexford (1 mark)** on **10 February 2019 (1 mark)** at **8.00 p.m.**   (1 mark)

Agenda for Meeting

1. Minutes of the 2018 AGM   1 mark (compulsory)
2. Matters arising from minutes
3. Chairperson's report   1 mark (compulsory)
4. Secretary's report
5. Treasurer's report   1 mark (compulsory)
6. Subscriptions for 2019
7. Election of officers   plus 2 other items
8. Election of club committee   @ 1 mark each
9. AOB

Signed,
Fiadh O'Rourke
Club Secretary
Date 1st February 2019

Marking scheme
Notice 5 @ 1 mark each
Agenda 5 @ 1 mark each

Written communication

Memorandum (memo)

Memos are an important form of internal communication providing a written record of a message.

Memorandum

Using today's date, draft a memorandum (memo) from Peter Murphy, Marketing Manager, to Mary O'Brien, Managing Director of a retail business, outlining **two** different sales-promotion incentives to encourage sales.

(10 marks)

Suggested solution

Memorandum	(1 mark)
To: Mary O'Brien, Managing Director	(1 mark)
From: Peter Murphy, Marketing Manager	(1 mark)
Date: 9 June 2019	(1 mark)
Subject: Sales promotion incentives	(1 mark)

Please note that the two methods of sales promotion to be used in the business are:

(1) 'Buy one, get one free'	(2 marks)
(2) 'Tokens to be collected for holiday breaks'	(2 marks)

Signature: Peter Murphy
         Marketing Manager   (1 mark)

Business letter

Using a fictitious name and address, draft a letter to the Human Resource Manager of a business setting out four characteristics of managers to be looked for when interviewing candidates for management positions.   **(20 marks)**

Suggested solution

P. C. Henderson
Consultant
2 Bank Buildings
Shardon Street
Waterford
Tel: (061) 6899296
Fax: (061) 6899297
www.pchenderson.com

10 September 2019

Mr Liam Mullins
Human Resource Manager
10 Shanakiel Road
Dungarvan
Co. Waterford

RE: Characteristics of Managers

Dear Mr Mullins

Further to your letter of 5 September, I would recommend that when interviewing candidates for managerial positions in your business you appoint candidates who display the following characteristics:

1. Hard-working

A hard-working manager sticks with the task until the job is done and does not give up when things get difficult.

2. Good human relations

This means being able to work with and understand other people in the organisation.

3. Well-organised

Having a structured and orderly approach to tasks is important.

4. Decisiveness

Good at analysing situations and making choices so that a decision is made and action is taken at the right time.

I hope that this information is to your satisfaction.

Yours sincerely,

P. C. Henderson
Senior Consultant

Report writing

A report is a written document setting out the findings of an investigation into some issue. It also contains conclusions and recommendations.

Reports are used for:

- Giving information about the progress of a project, etc.
- Investigating a problem – findings are presented and solutions are put forward.
- Providing a record of an event and explaining what happened (e.g. an accident).

Structure of a report

1. Title page	Title, writer's name, who report is for, date.
2. Table of contents	Main sections of report, chapters, page numbers.
3. Executive summary	Summary of main findings, conclusions, recommendations.
4. Terms of reference	The purpose of the report; sets out the guidelines to be followed and the problems to be addressed in the report.
5. Findings	Facts discovered are set out in a clear and logical sequence.
6. Conclusions	Evidence is assessed and problems identified.
7. Recommendations	Course of action to be taken.
8. Appendices	Extra information as required.
9. Bibliography	Sources of information used by the writer of the report.

Report writing

Draft a report to the managing director of a limited company explaining the four main barriers to effective communication in business. State relevant assumptions where necessary. (20 marks)

Suggested solution

Title: Report to managing director of Kelly Electronics Ltd on effective communication in business

Report writer: Mr John Hall, Management Consultant

To: Managing Director, Kelly Electronics

Date: 10 May 2019

Table of contents:

Report_____Page 1

Executive summary: The four main barriers to communication are noise, lack of planning, language and not listening.

Terms of reference: To report on the main barriers to communication in business.

Findings: The following are the four main barriers to communication in business:

1. **Noise** – 'Noise' is any interference from outside which leads to messages being misunderstood or, in some cases, the meaning of the message becoming completely changed.

2. **Lack of planning** – The message may not be properly prepared and planned in advance.

3. **Language** – The language must be suited to the audience. If too much technical language is used, the message may not be understood.

4. **Not Listening** – If the recipient is not listening the information will not be received correctly.

Conclusions: The four main barriers that cause communication to fail that were found in the firm are noise, lack of planning, language used and not listening.

Recommendations: Kelly Electronics must develop a plan to overcome these barriers.

Appendices

Bibliography

Signed: John Hall, Management Consultant

Visual communication

Visual communication allows complex information to be understood more easily. It attracts attention, offers variety and helps reinforce the message.

There are many ways in which information can be presented visually, including:

- Graphs
- Pie charts
- Bar charts

1. Graphs

A graph illustrates a trend over time.

2. Pie chart

A pie chart is a circular diagram divided into segments. Each segment shows a figure as a percentage of the total. Pie charts are useful for showing comparisons.

3. Bar chart

A bar chart displays information in a series of separated bars. Each bar is the same width and the height or length of the bars shows the quantities. They are very useful for showing trends and comparisons over a period of time.

Electronic communication

Business today operates in a global market and the ability to communicate is greatly increased by using modern information technology.

1. Internet and the World Wide Web

The internet is a global network of computers facilitating the transmission of data and communication between users.

All computer users who are connected to the internet through an internet service provider can access information via the World Wide Web by using a website address or through a search engine, such as Google (www.google.ie). Broadband is the fastest means of internet access.

key point

Impact of the internet and World Wide Web on Business

- Facilitates e-business – business to business, business to consumer.
- Faster, more cost-effective method of communication – consumers can communicate directly with business.
- A website can be an effective marketing tool – the internet provides access to global markets.
- Increased scope for flexible working conditions and reduced overhead costs where employees avail of teleworking.
- Email provides a record of all communication.

Business can conduct market research through their website.

Users may also communicate with each other via email.

The internet also facilitates e-business, which includes both business-to-business and business-to-consumer activity.

2. Electronic data interchange (EDI)

EDI is an automated method of processing transactions between suppliers and customers; for example, ordering stock, invoicing, making payments, etc. EDI is dependent on suppliers and customers having access to compatible EDI software.

key point

The **impact of EDI on business** is as follows:

- It is a fast method of processing transactions.
- It is a cost-effective method of processing transactions. It reduces labour costs and the cost of stationery/office expenses.
- It is an effective stock control system, leading to reduced stock-holding costs (e.g. insurance, storage, etc.). Automated processing ensures speedier stock re-order.
- The scope for human error is reduced as transactions are automated.

3. Videoconferencing

A meeting between two or more people in different locations that is facilitated by the use of videoconferencing technology. Typically, a telephone line, a monitor and a camera are required in each location.

Videoconferencing substitutes a face-to-face meeting with the same advantages – parties can see and talk to each other. Visuals in the form of charts and diagrams can be used to support the presentation being made.

Videoconferencing can be a time-saving and cost-effective means of communication. It reduces or eliminates the need to travel to a meeting or conference.

The **impact of videoconferencing on business** is as follows:

- Meetings can be conducted from different locations.
- It is cost-effective – people can avoid the necessity to travel, saving both time and money.
- It is quick and easy to set up a videoconference call.
- It may provide the opportunity for more regular meetings as cost is minimised.

4. Email

Email is a way of sending a typed message and computer files directly from one computer to another over the internet.

Each user has an email address and messages are held in a mailbox until read.

The **advantages** of email:

- A fast, efficient, convenient and cheap way of sending messages.
- Copies of a message can be sent to a number of people at the same time.
- Files can be attached to email messages.

However, the use of email in business does present some **problems**:

- **Data security** – Sending information over the internet is not secure. 'Hackers' may gain access to messages or files sent via email.
- **Incorrect address** – Information could easily be sent to the wrong address.
- **Technological availability** – Email can only be used if sender and receiver have computers and email addresses.
- **Computer viruses** – Email can be used to spread computer viruses, which, if opened, may damage a computer system.

5. Teleworking/E-working

This is where an employee works on the move or from home (e.g. using a home computer or laptop).

It is essential to have access to office systems via email, the internet and telephones.

Files can be sent between the home computer and office computer, allowing work to be completed as if the employee were present in the office.

Role of information and communication technology (ICT) and its application in business communications

- **Speed** – Information is transmitted and available worldwide instantly (e.g. email).
- **Location** – Using ICT, decision-makers can be far away from their production activities so that in person communication is no longer necessary (e.g. video-conference meeting).
- **Decision-making** – Decision-making needs up-to-date information (e.g. th marketing department needs up-to-date sales figures). ICT reduces the risk in decision-making.
- **Management structures** – Use of ICT has changed the structure of organisations. Spans of control have been greatly reduced.

Outline how developments in technology have benefited business communications.

(20 marks)
Source: 2014 Higher Level Section 3

Suggested solution

If you need to speak with an employee who is travelling in another country or you need to communicate with your supplier half way around the world, technology such as **email and texting** allows you to do so instantaneously. Urgent messages can be communicated rapidly and effectively using different technologies, including Skype and smartphone technology.

EDI (Electronic Data Interchange) greatly facilitates communication in a global market. Document transfer, automated stock ordering, details of trading figures, etc. can be transmitted globally in a matter of seconds.

Professional networks like LinkedIn have revolutionised the way business people communicate with each other.

The internet, including social networking sites such as Facebook and business networks such as LinkedIn, have facilitated the global marketing of companies.

Network advertising, company **websites** and electronic payment have allowed global e-commerce to flourish.

Intranets or Local Area Networks (LANs) allow employees within the organisation to communicate with each other more effectively. Files can be sent quickly and paperwork is kept to a minimum.

Workers no longer have to be on-site to communicate efficiently. Skype and virtual meetings/videoconferencing allow workers to enjoy flexitime, work from home and communicate efficiently as well as cutting down on the costs associated with live meetings.

CAD (Computer-Aided Design) has revolutionised the design process, making it much easier and faster to develop new products, and allowing companies to react quickly to customer requests and needs. It allows a design to be saved, changed and reworked without starting from scratch. A product designed in one country can be sent electronically to another country to be tweaked by local designers to make it better suited to local tastes.

ISDN (Integrated Services Digital Network) uses telephone lines to communicate, transmit and receive digital information.

File transfer, teleworking, videoconferencing, email, etc. allow vital information to be transferred anywhere in the world. This greatly assists management planning, organising and control and facilitates effective decision-making.

Automated stock control systems/design technology/robotics

Use of technology to handle, analyse and communicate business data.

Marking scheme
Four points @ 5 marks each:

2 marks – stating point

3 marks – developing point

Explain the benefits to a business of having a manager who is an effective communicator.

(20 marks)

Source: 2017 Higher Level Section 3

Suggested solution

Less conflict/fewer industrial relations problems

Effective communication means the receiver gets the message which was sent by the sender. There is **no confusion or ambiguity**. A manager who is an effective communicator will provide an opportunity for feedback to ensure the message is conveyed clearly. This results in less conflict and disagreement among employees.

Less errors

Clear communications are often in written form. This allows the receiver to read them several times to ensure they understand the content of the message. This will result in fewer errors being made.

Less wastage/improved quality

Effective communication from a manager to employees in a timely manner means that tasks can start quicker ensuring there is less wastage and lag times for production.

Quick decision-making/more sales and profits

A manager who is an effective communicator is also an effective listener. He/she can analyse information quickly which means that decisions can be made without delay. This is important in a fast-changing business environment.

Better decision-making

Better decisions are also made based on facts presented, accurate information given in clear language and confusion can be overcome through opportunities for feedback (questions).

Better staff morale/less stress

In a business where managers are effective communicators, employees are empowered by receiving clear instructions, being listened to and having decisions made in an effective manner. This results in a low staff turnover.

Marking scheme

Explain to benefits to a business of having a manager who is an effective communicator.   4 × 5 marks (3 + 2)

Data Protection Act 2018

The Data Protection Act was implemented to create a new legal framework for data protection laws in Ireland.

It was signed into law on 24 May 2018 and changes the previous data protection framework established under the **Data Protection Acts 1988 and 2003**.

Its provisions include:

- Giving further effect to the **General Data Protection Regulation (GDPR)**
- Establishing a new Data Protection Commission as the State's data protection authority.

General Data Protection Regulation (GDPR)

From 25 May 2018 the General Data Protection Regulation (GDPR) replaced existing data protection laws in the European Union.

The new law gives individuals greater control over their data by setting out additional and more clearly defined rights for individuals whose personal data is collected and processed by organisations.

The GDPR also imposes greater obligations on organisations that collect this data. Personal data is any information that can identify an individual person. This includes a name, an ID number, location data (for example, location data collected by a mobile phone) or a postal address, online browsing history, images or anything relating to the physical, physiological, genetic, mental, economic, cultural or social identity of a person.

The GDPR is based on the core principles of data protection which exist under the current law. **These principles require organisations and businesses to:**

- Collect no more data than is necessary from an individual for the purpose for which it will be used
- Obtain personal data fairly from the individuals by giving them notice of the collection and its specific purpose

- Retain the data for no longer than is necessary for that specified purpose
- Keep data safe and secure
- Provide an individual with a copy of his or her personal data if they request it.

Under the GDPR individuals have the right to:

- Obtain details about how their data is processed by an organisation or business
- Obtain copies of personal data that an organisation holds on them
- Have incorrect or incomplete data corrected
- Have their data erased by an organisation, where, for example, the organisation has no legitimate reason for retaining the data
- Obtain their data from an organisation and to have that data transmitted to another organisation (data portability)
- Object to the processing of their data by an organisation in certain circumstances.

Organisations and businesses collecting and processing personal data are required to meet a very high standard in how they collect, use and protect data. Very importantly, organisations must always be fully transparent to individuals about how they are using and safeguarding personal data, including by providing this information in easily accessible, concise, easy to understand and clear language.

The GDPR will also permit individuals to seek compensation through the courts for breaches of their data privacy rights, including in circumstances where no material damage or financial loss has been suffered.

Data Protection Commissioner

The Data Protection Commissioner (DPC) aims to make sure that an individual's rights are being upheld and that data controllers respect data protection rules.

For organisations and businesses who breach the law, the DPC has been given more robust powers to impose sanctions, including the power to impose fines. Under the new law, the DPC will be able to fine organisations up to €20 million (or 4% of total global turnover) for the most serious infringements.

exam focus

Evaluation of the Role of Data Protection Commissioner

- The Data Protection Commissioner is very effective in protecting data subjects by ensuring that individuals have access to their personal data, and getting it corrected or deleted.
- The Data Protection Commissioner also investigates complaints and prosecutes offenders.

8 Management Activities: Planning, Organising and Controlling

 Be able to:

- Explain the basic management activities of planning, organising and controlling.
- Discuss the nature of management activities and their linkages.

Planning

Planning is the process of setting goals or objectives and deciding how to achieve them.

Steps involved in planning

- Carry out SWOT analysis
- Draft mission statement and objectives
- Identify types of planning to be used

SWOT analysis

When planning, an organisation must carry out a SWOT analysis by analysing its internal **Strengths** and **Weaknesses** and identifying external **Opportunities** and **Threats**.

This is an analysis of the present position of a business and is usually done before drawing up plans.

The aim is to maximise the potential strengths and opportunities, while minimising the impact of weaknesses and threats.

| STRENGTHS
Good points of the business which give it an advantage. | → | • High-quality products
• Skilled employees
• Experienced management
• Adequate cash flow
• Unique selling point
• Quality of product |

| WEAKNESSES
Things which make it difficult for the business to achieve its objectives and which must be remedied. | → | • Poor industrial relations
• Weak credit control
• Outdated production technology
• Costs too high
• Lack of expertise
• Lack of capital |

| OPPORTUNITIES
Things businesses can take advantage of in the future. Things which should be exploited where possible. | → | • Expansion opportunity
• Export opportunity
• New markets
• Improvements in the economy |

| THREATS
Things that prevent it from achieving objectives and may pose problems in the future. The business must defend against them. | → | • New competition
• Recession in economy
• New laws being introduced
• Rising wage/insurance costs |

SWOT analysis

HL

(i) What is meant by the term SWOT analysis?

(ii) Conduct a SWOT analysis on a business of your choice.

(Include **two** points under each heading.)

(20 marks)

Source: 2010 Higher Level Section 3

Suggested solution

(i) A management technique/strategic planning method. It is used to assess/ evaluate a business in terms of strengths, weaknesses, opportunities and threats. In a SWOT analysis, strengths and weaknesses are internal factors, while opportunities and threats are external factors. The aim is to maximise the potential of strengths and opportunities, while minimising the impact of weaknesses and threats.

(ii) Ryanair

Strengths

1. Brand name: Ryanair, through its many years in the market place, has developed a very well-recognised brand name.
2. Website: 94% of bookings are through www.ryanair.com. This lowers the cost of bookings.
3. High service performance: Punctual, high rate of flight completion.
4. Small headquarters: Low on overheads.

Weaknesses

1. Distance of some regional airports from advertised destinations: Over time, customers may find this a big inconvenience.
2. Prone to bad press.

Opportunities

1. EU enlargement: A lot of new destinations opened up throughout the EU.
2. Economic slowdown actually helps Ryanair – changes in corporate culture, 'steals' customers from traditional carriers as they seek lower fares in recessionary times.

Threats

1. Dependence on oil markets: Fuel costs huge threat to air travel.
2. Increase of low fare competition: Customers are very price sensitive.
3. Powerless to prevent introduction of duty for fuel or environmental charges/ carbon taxes/travel tax: This would reduce its growth potential as it relies on price stimulation.

Marking scheme

(i) SWOT – 6 marks:
- 4 × 1 mark each
- 2 marks for stating method of planning

(ii) Swot Analysis – 14 marks:
- Name of business – 2 marks
- Four headings @ 3 marks each (2 + 1)
- (Two appropriate points under each heading)

Mission statement and objectives

Mission statement – A mission statement sets out the general purpose and objectives of the organisation, the reason for its existence and what it sees for itself in the future.

Objectives – Objectives of an organisation are aims that it is trying to achieve (e.g. 'to cut costs and become more competitive').

These are the targets to be aimed at – they motivate people to achieve results.
Objectives must be **SMART**:

- **Specific** – They must be clear and precisely expressed (quantifiable).
- **Measurable** – The success of the plan should be easily measured.
- **Agreed** – The plan must be agreed by all the management team.
- **Realistic** – They must be capable of being achieved with the resources available.
- **Timed** – There must be a timescale for achieving the objectives.

Types of planning

Strategic planning (long-term planning)

Strategic plans:

- Are developed over the long term and normally cover five years or more
- Are drawn up by top management and focus on the organisation's mission or purpose
- Provide a guide for where the business is going in the long term, and how it's going to get there.

Strategic planning requires an examination of the organisation's strengths, weaknesses, opportunities and threats so that the objectives can be achieved.

Here are some examples of objectives:

- Achieve entrance into a foreign market or a new market
- Achieve an increase in market share
- Become a market leader

Tactical planning (short-term planning)

The long-term plan is broken down into more manageable short-term plans.

Some short-term plans relate to a particular function of the organisation, e.g. advertising. They cover a period of about one to two years and are developed by a management team which deals with getting the work done to carry out the strategic plan.

Short-term plans have their own objectives. Some examples of short-term objectives are:

- Launch a new advertising campaign aiming to increase sales by 25%
- Improve customer service
- Open a new branch of the business
- Launch a new product
- Reduce employee turnover

Short-term plans are tactical plans. If they are achieved, they help the business to meet its long-term goals.

exam focus

THE IMPORTANCE OF PLANNING FOR THE SUCCESS OF A BUSINESS

It identifies a business's strengths (and builds on them) and weaknesses (which must be overcome).

It identifies a business's opportunities (and exploits them) and threats (which must be eliminated).

It tries to anticipate problems facing the business in the future and identify steps that can be taken to deal with these problems.

It sets targets against which the success of the business can be measured.

Planning helps an organisation cope with change.

Co-ordination

Co-ordination means ensuring that all departments work together with a common purpose of achieving the goals of the organisation.

Example: The production department must contact the purchasing department about types and quantities of raw materials needed.

Read the information supplied and answer the questions which follow.   HL

The Mayfair Hotel

The Mayfair Hotel is a five-star city centre hotel which is celebrating 100 years in business. To celebrate this centenary, the management of the hotel is planning various events. The general manager, Ann Johnson, has suggested organising staff into various project teams, with a project leader to plan for this centenary celebration.

Evaluate how different types of planning contribute to business success. Relate your answer to the Mayfair Hotel, making any appropriate assumptions.

(20 marks)

Source: 2016 Higher Level Section 3

Suggested solution

(Corporate) **Strategic Planning** is long-term planning usually for a period of up to five years. It provides a guide or framework as to where the business/hotel will be in the long run. Strategic plans are usually devised by senior management to ensure the long-term profitability and ultimate existence of the business. A strategic plan may be to grow market share by 20% over the next five years/to increase profitability by 10%/to enter the UK market.

The Mayfair Hotel may have long-term plans such as increasing their market share or becoming a market leader. These plans will allow the business to grow into possible new areas, such as business conferences (providing the latest video and audio conferencing facilities), weddings/banqueting, spa and fitness centre and leisure club, etc. It will help them to increase profits, as developing new facilities will allow them to charge higher prices or have an entirely new source of revenue.

(Functional) **Tactical planning** is short-term planning – usually one to two year plans – which is essential to achieve the business's strategic or long-term plans. The plans are a breakdown of the strategic plans into a set of action items or tactics to help management achieve a number of objectives/goals in the short to medium term.

The staff could conduct market research into the possibility of expanding into the conference/banqueting market. If the research is found to be positive, the hotel may move ahead with its plan to build a conference centre.

OR

Operational planning could involve planning for daily or weekly activities such as timetabling holiday rosters, etc.

The Mayfair Hotel will have operational plans in place for all the various departments in the hotel, such as the kitchen, cleaning department, accommodation, reception, etc. All staff are aware of what needs to be done on a daily and weekly basis, ensuring that guests are well looked after and the hotel runs smoothly.

Manpower planning would involve having the right people with the right skills in the right place throughout the business. It involves doing a human resource audit and estimating future human resource needs.

The Mayfair may require contract/temporary staff at certain busy periods or for specific events, such as conferences and weddings, or specific events relating to the centenary celebrations.

Contingency planning is a plan that is used as a back-up plan for emergency situations. They prevent disruptions in business and thereby may prevent loss of profit and ultimate closure of the business.

The Mayfair may have contingency plans for various emergency situations, which may occur at the hotel, such as closing certain wings of the hotel/shortage of essential supplies/may have a back-up plan for power in the form of a stand-by generator.

Mission statement is a visionary statement outlining the overall purpose of the business and where it is going.

The mission statement would give an insight to the stakeholders into the core values and culture of the Mayfair Hotel.

The Mayfair Hotel may branch out/extend into a new area of business which would be reflected in its mission statement.

Evaluation: Planning helps the hotel by setting goals and devising strategies to achieve them.

Marking scheme
Three points @ 6 marks each:
- 2 marks – naming point
- 3 marks – explaining point
- 1 mark – reference to hotel

Evaluation @ 2 marks

Organising

Organising involves arranging all the resources, people, equipment and finances into the most suitable form to achieve the objectives of the business.

Organising means setting up a formal structure in an organisation so that the activities are co-ordinated and objectives achieved.

An organisation chart shows how an organisation expects to get things done. It will start with the heads of departments and move down to subordinates at lower levels of responsibility.

Good organisation is important for the success of a business because:

- It identifies different levels of authority and sets out who is responsible to whom so that each person can understand his/her role in the achievement of the objectives.
- Work that is shared among the various departments gets completed faster and quality is improved.
- A good organisation structure will improve communication between the various departments. (Good communication is essential for a business that wants to achieve its objectives in the most efficient way possible.)

Types of organisation structure

Functional structure

This is an organisation structure that shows the organisation divided into departments according to their function (such as finance, production, sales and marketing, purchasing, and human resources).

All sales people are grouped together, all production people are grouped together and tasks are carried out more effectively as they are consistent with the training of each individual in his/her department.

A person is in charge of each department who is responsible for achieving its objectives.

The structure is also called 'line organisation' because each person in the line is answerable to the person above. Responsibilities are well-defined and so this type of structure is easy to understand.

Functional structure

Chain of command

The chain of command is the path along which orders/instructions/decisions are passed down from the top to the bottom of the hierarchy and feedback is passed back up. There is a clear structure to the organisation and clear lines of authority exist. Instructions flow downwards along the chain of command and accountability flows upwards.

Span of control

A span of control is the number of subordinates who are delegated authority and report to the supervisor or manager. In the illustration below, the span of control of the managing director is three.

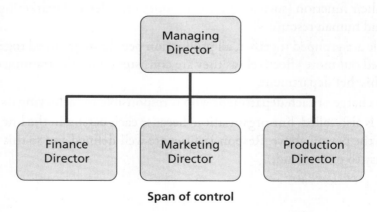

Span of control

A manager's span of control can be wide (many employees) or narrow (few employees). Its size depends on the type/difficulty of work, the quality of the manager and staff, the service being provided and the type of products being made. Products which are easy to make will need less supervision and can have a wider span of control.

Outline the benefits **to a business** of a functional organisational structure.

(15 marks)

Source: 2015 Higher Level Section 3

Suggested solution

Due to specialisation, where each department is concentrating exclusively on one function such as marketing, production, sales or finance, employees and management build up high levels of skill and expertise through repetition and practise.

This leads to efficiency as tasks get done quickly and to a high standard.

The chain of command and line of authority is clear. Clear lines of authority exist and employees know who to report to. There is a person in charge of each department which improves co-ordination and motivation, as employees know what is expected of them and when. There is accountability, as someone is responsible for each section.

There are clear communication channels. The structure helps create a clear communication line between the top and bottom of the business. Instructions flow downward from top management along the chain of command and information is communicated upward. It may result in important information being communicated quickly, leading to quicker decision-making.

Functional organisational structures allow for a wide span of control. There are economics of scale as resources are used efficiently with no duplication of resources. The wide span of control releases top management from micromanaging operations, so that they can focus on the overall strategy of the business.

Promotional paths: Visible hierarchical ladder, providing career paths for employees; provides scope for promotion to the next level so businesses can promote from within, etc.

Marking scheme

3 points @ 5 marks each:

- 2 marks – stating point
- 3 marks – how it benefits the business

(a) Explain the term 'span of control'.

(b) Outline **two** factors that affect the width of the span of control in a business.

(c) Outline a situation where a narrow span of control may be appropriate.

Suggested solution

(a) It refers to the **number of people/subordinates** that **report directly to one manager/supervisor** in a hierarchy.

(b)

1. **Skill of manager/management style:** An experienced, confident and able manager can operate a wide span of control.
2. **Skill of the workforce:** When employees are trusted because of their skill sets and motivation, a wide span of control may operate.
3. **The nature of the work/type of product or service:** When the work involved is repetitive, requiring little responsibility, decision-making or skill, a wide span of control is appropriate. If the work involved requires a high level of expertise, a narrow span of control is appropriate.

(c) A narrow span of control would be more appropriate when the work involved requires a high level of expertise, where nature of work is complex or where workers or management lack experience, etc.

Matrix structure

This type of structure is a combination of two types of organisation structure:

- Functional structure
- Project team structure

It is a team-based approach to problem-solving where the business is involved in complex projects. The emphasis is on combining the skills of many departments to complete the project.

Employees are removed from their normal job to work on the project.

They report to the project leader when working on the project and to their department manager when doing their normal work.

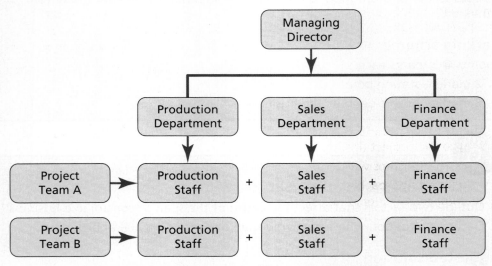

Matrix structure for a manufacturing organisation

Outline two features of a matrix organisation structure.

(10 marks)

Source: 2012 Higher Level Section 1

Suggested solution

- It is a team-based structure with expertise drawn from different departments, e.g. marketing, finance, information technology, production, etc.
- Team members are answerable to the project leader who is responsible for co-ordinating team effort and ensuring task completion.
- It is generally set up to carry out specific projects, such as product development.
- All team members have an input into decision-making/problem-solving.
- Teams can achieve greater output/productivity (synergy).
- Each employee can have two managers – the project manager and the functional manager – which could lead to confusion and conflict.
- Highly specialised employees and equipment are shared by departments.

Marking scheme

Two points @ 6 marks each (3 + 3)

Plus 4 marks (2 + 2)

Discuss the benefits **and** challenges for a business of developing a matrix organisation structure (team structure) to complete specific projects in a business.

(20 marks)

Source: 2016 Higher Level Section 3

Suggested solution

Benefits

Personnel from various different departments bring **new ideas/new ways of thinking** to the project (innovation).

Improves relationships within the team – **improved communication**.

A **co-ordinated approach** to problem-solving can be achieved due to the existence of a team/project leader. Team members have the support of a project leader who is responsible for co-ordinating team effort and ensuring task completion.

Shared skills and expertise – employees can **learn new skills** from each other; professional development and improved motivation for employees.

Responsibility is shared – although a team leader is appointed to take control of the project, the entire team shares responsibility of tasks and all team members have an input into decision-making and problem-solving.

Challenges

Teams can be a **talking shop – 'all talk no action'**. Certain people in the project team may dominate the task so that **only one voice is heard**.

Team development goes through **stages** of forming, storming, norming and performing. Decision-making may be slow as getting agreement at consultation stage could take time. All opinions are considered, which may slow the process down.

It can be **difficult to co-ordinate** employees from different areas; being answerable to two different managers could lead to confusion or a conflict of loyalty.

There can be a **conflicting pull on resources**. Member from the sales production team may unwilling to agree extra funding for the production department, etc.

Marking scheme

4 points @ 5 marks each (2 + 3)

(at least one of each required)

Controlling

Controlling means measuring actual performance to see if it is in line with the target set out in the plan.

Corrective action must be taken if there are deviations from planned performance so that the organisation will reach its target.

Control is concerned with making sure that the objectives are achieved.

Principles of control

1. **Set target** – e.g. increase sales by 25% this year
2. **Measure actual performance** – e.g. after six months, sales had increased by 8%
3. **Compare performance with target** – e.g. result off target
4. **Take corrective action** (to ensure that the business stays on target to achieve its objectives) – e.g. increase advertising

Types of control

The main areas of control in business are:

- Stock control
- Quality control
- Credit control
- Financial control

Stock control

This is the monitoring of stock levels to ensure that there is enough stock to meet demand, while keeping costs to a minimum.

The aim of stock control is to ensure that the business has the correct amount of stock at all times – never too much, never too little.

The following are **benefits of stock control**:
- Cash will not be tied up in too much stock.
- There will be no shortages of raw materials for production.
- Insurance costs will be lower.
- The business will always have the correct amount of stock, ensuring no lost sales and improving sales and profits in the future.
- The firm will be able to identify goods that are on demand, as well as slow-moving goods, which may be subject to deterioration or obsolescence.

Just in Time – This is a method of stock control where materials and products are delivered at the exact time they are needed (e.g. materials delivered just in time for manufacture). The aim is to minimise the cost of holding stock, while, at the same time, never running out of stock.

Quality control

This is checking the efficiency of production to ensure that the product meets the standards expected by customers.

Inspections are carried out during the production process to ensure that high-quality standards are achieved.

A good quality control system can lead to significant cost savings, fewer customer complaints and an improved reputation for the business.

Quality control can be achieved by:

- Obtaining **recognised quality standards** such as the Q Mark and the ISO awards. The Q Mark is a quality standard recognised in Ireland. The ISO (International Standards Organisation) is an internationally-recognised quality standard.
- Having a **quality assurance system** to guarantee customers that the firm's products are of the highest quality.
- Establishing a **Quality Circle** – a group of employees who meet to discuss and solve quality problems.
- **Training** employees in quality control.

Effective quality control is important because it ensures that:
- The goods produced are of the highest standard.
- Costs are reduced as no faulty goods should be sold to customers, which means no repairs and no cash refunds.
- There will be fewer customer complaints and improved reputation for the business.

Credit control

This means controlling the amount of goods sold on credit, monitoring the credit period given to customers and ensuring that payments are made on time.

Credit control involves:

- Confirming the creditworthiness of customers
- Setting credit limits and credit periods
- Establishing penalties for late payments
- Minimising the risk of bad debts

The importance/benefits of a good credit control system:
- Firm controls the amount of goods sold on credit.
- Debtors pay for goods on time.
- Bad debts are kept to a minimum.
- The creditworthiness of customers is checked in advance.
- Firm will not have to rely on bank overdrafts to deal with cash shortages.

HL

Explain the methods a business could consider to minimise the risk of bad debts as part of its credit control system.

(20 marks)

Source: 2015 Higher Level Section 3

Suggested solution

Assess customers' creditworthiness:
The creditworthiness of potential customers is checked in advance, e.g. asking for bank references, trade references, credit bureau.

Set appropriate credit limits and credit periods:
Draw up clear terms and conditions controlling the amount of credit and ensuring that payments are made on time, e.g. a credit limit of €5,000 and a time limit of one month.

Offer incentives such as a cash discount for early or prompt payment.

Policy for late payments/partial payments: agreeing on penalties for late payments and implementing them, e.g. charging interest on overdue accounts.

Have an efficient administration system where invoicing, payment demands and follow-up phone calls and visits occur promptly to ensure payment. Take legal action or threaten legal action to ensure payment. Put credit facility on hold until account is cleared.

Adopt a 'cash sales only' policy with certain customers, etc.

Marking scheme
2 @ 7 marks each (4 + 3) and 1 × 6 marks (3 + 3)
- State Point – 4 marks
- Explain point – 3 marks

Financial control

Financial control is used to monitor the financial position of the business.

A budget is a financial plan that sets out the expected income and expenditure for a future period of time.

A comparison is made between the actual financial performance and the budget figures. The difference (known as a 'variance') should be investigated.

Example: A cash flow forecast shows planned cash inflows and cash outflows for a future period and ensures that the business does not run out of cash.

Read the information supplied and answer the questions that follow.

EducaPrint Ltd is a business publishing schoolbooks in Ireland. John O'Leary, the production manager, suggested introducing some of its original print books in eBook format. He wanted to tap into the improvements in broadband speed and the major developments in mobile devices. The eBooks were launched onto the market in 2013 to great success. EducaPrint Ltd operated a matrix organisation structure for the development of the eBook products.

(i)   Outline the benefits **and** challenges for EducaPrint Ltd of a matrix organisation structure (team structure) for the development of eBook products.   (20 marks)

(ii) Discuss the importance of the management activity of 'planning' for EducaPrint Ltd.   (20 marks)

Source: 2015 Higher Level Section 3

Suggested solution

(i) Benefits

- It is a team-based structure with **expertise drawn from different departments**, e.g. marketing, finance, information technology, production. This enables greater interaction across departments by team members.
- All team members have an **input into decision-making and problem-solving**, which allows for greater output and productivity (synergy). New ideas will evolve and better decisions will be made.
- A matrix structure is generally set up in business to carry out **specific projects**, such as product development within an R and D context. This would be congruent with the development of the eBook products by EducaPrint Ltd.
- Team members have the support of a **project leader** who is responsible for co-ordinating team effort and ensuring task completion; e.g. ensuring the availability of highly specialised employees and equipment for the team.
- Employees should experience **greater job satisfaction** as all members' efforts are taken into account. They are better motivated as participation in teams satisfies the social needs of employees (Maslow's theory on motivation). Staff morale improves.

Challenges

- Each employee can have **two managers**, the project manager and functional manager, which could lead to confusion and conflict.
- Employee's communication skills and interpersonal skills will need to improve as they are working in a group and dealing with different personalities.
- Successful teams progress through the team development stages of forming, storming, norming and performing. During the storming stage, conflict and personality clashes may occur which could lead to industrial relations problems.
- **Decision-making may be slow** because getting the agreement of the team during consultation stage may take some time. This matrix organisational structure may not be appropriate in a crisis or emergency situation where tough decisions have to be made quickly, e.g. turning around a business, which is facing insolvency.

(ii)

- Planning is the setting out of **specific goals and objectives** for the business; it involves the putting in place of **strategies** that allow the business to achieve the stated goals and objectives. Planning ensures that EducaPrint Ltd considers its future and how it will achieve continued success.

- Planning gives EducaPrint Ltd purpose and direction and **reduces risk** and uncertainty.

- **SWOT analysis** is an initial step in the planning process. The aim of EducaPrint Ltd is to play to its strengths and opportunities, while seeking to minimise the impact of weaknesses and threats.

- **Mission Statement:** This is a visionary statement outlining who the business is, what the business does and where the business is going: e.g. EducaPrint Ltd is a business publishing schoolbooks and eBooks in Ireland. The mission statement would give an insight to the stakeholders into the core values and culture of EducaPrint Ltd.

- **Strategic Planning:** This is long-term planning covering a period of five years or more. It is usually drawn up by senior management and it outlines how the long-term goals of the firm are to be achieved; e.g. EducaPrint Ltd may decide to expand its successful business model into the UK publishing market.

- **Tactical Planning:** This is short-term planning, which breaks the strategic plan into shorter, more manageable periods. It deals with the 'now' part of the plan. It is usually drawn up by middle management; e.g. EducaPrint Ltd might attempt to target a new group of customers next year.

- **Contingency Planning:** This is back-up planning to cope with emergencies, unforeseen events or unexpected circumstances. Contingency plans benefit EducaPrint Ltd by preventing disruptions to business and thereby preventing loss of profits and possible business collapse; e.g. EducaPrint Ltd may have alternative suppliers of paper available for its traditional print books.

Marking scheme

(i) Two benefits @ 5 marks each (2 + 3)

Two challenges @ 5 marks each (2 + 3)

(Must have two references to EducaPrint Ltd)

(ii) Three points: 2 @ 7 marks each (4 + 3) and 1 × 6 marks (3 + 3)

Applied Business Question (ABQ) (Higher Level)

Based on Units 1, 2 and 3

This is a compulsory question for Leaving Certificate 2019/2024

Atlantic Surf

Shay Doherty, a native of Summerstown, is the owner of Atlantic Surf, a surfing school located on the seafront at Summerstown Beach in County Donegal. In 2008 Shay was enjoying life in Australia and perfecting his big-wave surfing skills when he read an article in *National Geographic* describing the quality of the giant waves surfers were experiencing along the west coast of Ireland. Inspired by the article, and having always wanted to have his own business, he decided to return home from Australia to set up Atlantic Surf. Having tried and failed in business in the past, Shay realised that he needed to carry out some market research and get assistance with this venture. Shay contacted the Irish Surfing Association (ISA) and received valuable advice on health and safety legislation, on how to network and on the importance of having a web presence. He prepared a business plan and received a business start-up grant of €10,000 from Donegal Local Enterprise Office. He used the grant, together with €30,000 he had saved while working in Australia, to establish Atlantic Surf, an ISA-approved surfing school.

From the outset, Shay understood that location would be a key factor driving business success. While researching property sites, he spotted a suitable retail premises located on the seafront at Summerstown. The property was advertised as being available for immediate use for an annual rent of €10,000. Given the economic climate at the time and the collapse in property prices in Summerstown, Shay believed that a better deal could be agreed. He telephoned the landlord and suggested a more realistic price of €7,500. This price was rejected and both parties entered into negotiations with the objective of concluding a legal contract. In April 2009, just before celebrating his twenty-eighth birthday, Shay was delighted when the landlord said yes to an annual rent of €8,000. Shay secured the premises and paid €8,000 to the landlord. The necessary documentation for the rental was signed in the solicitor's office in time for the busy summer surfing season.

Shay decided to open a 'one-stop surf shop' in the rented premises and appointed Karen, a champion surfer, as its manager. The shop sells high-quality stock, including wetsuits, surfboards, kitesurfing equipment and Atlantic Surf branded beach clothing. In addition, it rents out wetsuits and surfboards. From the beginning, Karen adopted a 'cash sales only' policy with customers and negotiated a 30-day credit period with suppliers. While very pleased with the high stock turnover of the Atlantic Surf branded beach clothing, she had some concerns because the annual stocktake revealed a high level of kitesurfing equipment still unsold. To assist with cash flow, Karen decided to use the website to highlight offers, such as six surfing lessons for the price of five if payment is made in advance. Karen believes quality development is key to business success and she is hoping to apply for quality standard certification in the near future.

(A) Illustrate what it means to be an entrepreneur with reference to Atlantic Surf. (20 marks)

(B) 'For a contract to be legally enforceable, certain essential elements must exist.' Discuss this statement with reference to the rental of the premises by Shay Doherty for Atlantic Surf. (30 marks)

(C) Evaluate the effectiveness of the systems of management control in operation at Atlantic Surf. (30 marks)

(80 marks)

Suggested solution

(A) Being an entrepreneur in Atlantic Surf involves:

Innovation/Creativity

Entrepreneurs are good at coming up with new ideas. They are constantly looking for ways of improving what they do. Entrepreneurs show imagination, initiative, resourcefulness and readiness to undertake new projects. They think outside the box to develop new products or new versions of existing products.

Link:

'He read an article in National Geographic *describing the quality of the giant waves surfers were experiencing...'*

Risk-Taker

Being an entrepreneur involves taking both personal and financial risk in pursuit of a business idea. Successful entrepreneurs are not afraid of taking risks. They are realistic risk-takers.

Link:

'He (Shay) used ... €30,000 he had saved while working in Australia to establish Atlantic Surf'.

Initiative/Exploiting opportunity

Shay showed initiative by bringing his surfing experience/skill to Ireland and taking advantage of Ireland's growing reputation for quality waves. Shay saw an opportunity presenting itself in the growing interest in surfing along the west coast of Ireland.

Link:

'Inspired by the article ... he decided to return home from Australia in 2008 to set up Atlantic Surf.'

Resilient/Confident

Entrepreneurs are not put off by failure. Entrepreneurs have a strong sense of self-belief and conviction about their own business ideas. Shay showed confidence and belief in Atlantic Surf. He sees failure as an opportunity to learn. Having ambition and having a strong desire for success or achievement is central to being an entrepreneur.

Link:

'Having tried and failed in business in the past ... he decided to return home from Australia to set up Atlantic Surf.'

Future focused

Reference to the importance of a business plan ...

Link:

'He prepared a business plan and received a business start-up grant of €10,000 from Donegal Local Enterprise Office.'

Reality Perception

Sees things for what they are.

Link:

'Shay realised that he needed to carry out some market research and get assistance with this venture.'

Networking/Persuasive abilities

Entrepreneurs recognise the importance of a wide range of contacts to provide guidance and support.

Entrepreneurs need to be able to persuade others.

Link:

'Shay contacted the Irish Surfing Association (ISA) and received valuable advice on health and safety legislation, on how to network and on the importance of having a web presence.'

Marking scheme

(A)	Illustrate what it means to be an entrepreneur with reference to Atlantic Surf. Point, theory, link. (Separate relevant link for each point)	3 explanations: 2 × 7 marks (3 + 1 + 3) 1 × 6 marks (3 + 1 + 2)	20 marks

(B) 'For a contract to be legally enforceable, **certain essential elements** must exist.' Discuss this statement with reference to the rented premises at Atlantic Surf.

Offer

A promise by the person making the offer to be bound by the offer provided the terms of the offer are accepted. The offer can be made orally, in writing or by conduct, and is a clear indication of the offeror's willingness to enter into an agreement under specified terms.

Link:

'He telephoned the landlord and suggested a more realistic price of €7,500.'

Acceptance

It must be identical to the offer without any changes or conditions and communicated to the offeree in the time specified.

Link:

'Shay was delighted when the landlord said yes to an annual rent of €8,000.'

Agreement

For agreement to exist, there must be a clear, complete and unconditional offer and an acceptance of that offer.

Legality of form

Certain contracts, to be considered legal, must be drawn up in a particular manner. Some contracts must be in writing if they are to be legally valid. These include: insurance policies, hire purchase agreements, the sale of property or land, share transactions, consumer credit and bank loans.

Link:

'The necessary documentation for the rental was signed in the solicitor's office.'

Consideration

Each party in a contract must give something of value to the other party. Something of value must be exchanged. So long as consideration exists, a court of law will not question its adequacy, provided it is of some value.

Consideration is usually some monetary payment, but it could also be something valuable exchanged as part of the contract.

Link:

'Shay secured the premises and paid €8,000 to the landlord.'

Capacity to contract

All natural persons (human beings) and legal/corporate persons, such as companies, have the legal right to enter freely into a contract.

The following generally do not have the capacity to contract:

- Infants (those under 18 years of age), except in certain cases, e.g. necessities
- Persons under the influence of drink or drugs
- Insane persons
- Bankrupt persons
- Diplomats
- Companies operating outside their powers/ultra vires.

Link:

'In April 2009, just before celebrating his twenty-eighth birthday ...'

Intention to Contract

Both parties to the contract must be aware that they are entering into a legally binding agreement that could see them in court if they fail to keep their side of the agreement. With domestic and social arrangements there is no intention to create a legally binding contract.

Link:

'... both parties entered into negotiations with the objective of concluding a legal contract.'

Legality of purpose

Contracts must be compliant with the laws of the land. Contracts may not be for an illegal activity such as smuggling or defrauding the state of taxes.

Link:

'While researching property sites he spotted a suitable retail premises.'

Marking scheme

(B)	Elements of Contract Law Name, theory, link. (Separate relevant link for each element)	4 elements 2 × 8 marks (3 + 3 + 2) 2 × 7 marks (3 + 2 + 2)	30 marks

(C) Evaluate the effectiveness of the systems of management control in operation at Atlantic Surf.

Stock Control

Stock control is concerned with keeping optimum stock levels so that Atlantic Surf doesn't have too much stock or too little stock. Effective stock control means that you have the optimum level of stock/adequate stocks in your business to meet the needs of your consumers, while at the same time keeping them to a minimum.

Optimum stock levels leads to efficiencies because you have the right stock in the right place at the right time to meet production requirements and satisfy consumer demand. Stock control can achieve efficiencies by eliminating the costs associated with carrying too much or too little stock, i.e. high storage and administration costs resulting from too much stock, production stoppages due to a lack of raw materials and components for production, and lost sales orders because of a lack of finished goods for sale.

Link:

'While very pleased with the high stock turnover of the Atlantic Surf branded beach clothing ...'

OR

'She had some concerns because the annual stocktake revealed a high level of kitesurfing equipment still unsold.'

Evaluation

In my opinion, Atlantic Surf is not effective in controlling stock levels. The high levels of unsold stock could go out of fashion and then it would have to be sold at a loss.

Quality Control

Quality control is concerned with checking/reviewing/inspecting work done to ensure it meets the required quality standards of the business. It could involve physical inspections, quality circles, etc.

As part of a quality control system Atlantic Surf may achieve a quality control symbol, such as an ISO 9001 award. This symbol would be recognised worldwide and would be of major benefit to Atlantic Surf in marketing its products internationally.

Effective quality control leads to efficiencies in business because consistently high quality products are being sold, resulting in repeat purchasing, consumer loyalty and the ability to charge higher prices.

Link:

'The shop sells high-quality stock including wetsuits, surfboards, kitesurfing equipment and Atlantic Surf branded beach clothing.'

OR

'Karen believes quality development is key to business success, and she is hoping to apply for quality standard certification in the near future.'

Evaluation

In my opinion, Atlantic Surf is effective in controlling quality as it states that 'the shop sells high-quality stock'. Also the achievement of the quality standard certification would reassure customers that their product is of high quality.

Credit Control

Credit control means controlling the amount of credit given to customers and the payment period given to customers. Good credit control ensures that payments are made in full and on time. It involves checking creditworthiness of customers, setting credit limits, credit periods and deciding on penalties for late payments. It seeks to minimise bad debts.

Link:

'From the beginning, Karen adopted a "cash sales only" policy with customers.'

Evaluation

In my opinion, Karen's approach of a 'cash sales only' policy will improve liquidity as cash is paid immediately making it easier for the business to pay short-term debts.

Financial Control/Budgetary Control

The aim of financial control is to ensure overall business profitability and liquidity (ability to pay bills due). Financial control involves preparing cash flow budgets, ratio analysis and employing cost control measures (e.g. utilities, wages, etc). These can provide an early warning of possible financial problems.

Link:

'To assist with cash flow, Karen decided to use the website to highlight offers such as "six surfing lessons for the price of five" if payment is made in advance.'

OR

'She negotiated a 30-day credit period ...'

Evaluation

In my opinion, Atlantic Surf is not effective in financial control. They should use budgets to forecast their future financial needs.

Marking Scheme

(C)	The effectiveness of the systems of management control Name, theory, link, evaluation (Quality, credit, stock, financial) (Separate relevant link for each type of control)	Three management control techniques/systems 3 @ 10 marks each (3 + 4 + 2 + 1)	30 marks

UNIT 4

Managing II

The theme of this unit is the applications of management. It looks at those functions that are common to managing a household and a business. It examines organisational applications, including human resource management and the changing role of management.

9 Household and Business Manager 1: Finance

Cash flow forecast – household and business

The purpose of a cash flow forecast for a business

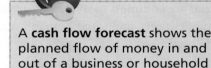

- It identifies when a business might find itself facing a **cash flow problem**.
- It identifies times of high expenditure and **shortages** so that finance can be arranged to deal with the deficit.
- It identifies future cash **surpluses** so that the business can make plans to invest this extra money.

> **key point**
>
> A **cash flow forecast** shows the planned flow of money in and out of a business or household over a period of time.

- Comparing figures in the cash flow forecast with the actual receipts and payments figures allows the business to see if it is on target with its cash flow projections, aiding **financial control**.
- It shows future cash inflows and outflows, their sources and timing, which assists in the **decision-making process**.
- A cash flow forecast is vital for a **business starting up** and is essential if making an **application for a loan** to show that repayments can be made.

Household Cash Inflows and Outflows

Inflows	Outflows
Wages/salaries	Fixed expenditure (mortgage/rent)
Interest	Irregular expenditure (telephone/electricity)
Child benefit	Discretionary expenditure (holidays/entertainment)
Social welfare payments	
Tax rebate	
Loans	

Business Cash Inflows and Outflows

Inflows	Outflows
Cash sales	Purchase of assets
Receipts from debtors	Purchases of goods
Interest	Payments to creditors
Grants	Payment of taxes
Share capital	Payment of expenses
Sale of assets	Paying dividends to shareholders
Tax refund	

exam Q

The cash flow forecast for Amrod Ltd for the final quarter of 2015 is set out below: HL

2015	October	November	December	Total
	€	€	€	€
Total Receipts	70,000	180,000	90,000	340,000
Total Payments	100,000	165,000	120,000	385,000
Net Cash	(30,000)	15,000	B	(45,000)
Opening Cash	20,000	A	5,000	C
Closing Cash	(10,000)	5,000	(25,000)	(25,000)

(i) Explain the reasons Amrod Ltd would prepare a cash flow forecast.

(ii) Calculate the figures represented by the letters **A, B** and **C** on the cash flow forecast. (**Show your workings in your answer book.**)

(iii) Explain how Amrod Ltd might deal with the financial problem identified in this cash flow forecast.

(25 marks)

Source: 2015 Higher Level Section 3

Suggested solution

(i) • It will help Amrod Ltd manage its cash flow and live within its means. It acts as a financial control mechanism that can be used to measure actual cash flow against planned cash flow, encouraging Amrod Ltd to plan its finances sensibly and live within its means and not to overtrade. Avoids cash flow problems as costs are considered in advance to ensure the company has sufficient funds.

• It will help Amrod Ltd identify periods of time in the future when the business will have an excess of expenditure over income, i.e. a deficit, and then take corrective action/assess the best methods to deal with the cash shortfall/enable Amrod Ltd to use its **scarce resources** more effectively.

- It will help Amrod Ltd identify problems of time in the future when the business will have a surplus of income over expenditure. Amrod Ltd can then make plans to place these **surplus funds** on deposit with a financial institution or make expansion decisions.
- It will help Amrod Ltd **gain access to finance** from financial institutions as the cash flow forecast is an integral part of the business plan given to banks and other potential investors. Supports applications for loans and grants, etc.

(ii) **A** = (€10,000) = 2 marks
   B = (€30,000) = 2 marks   (€90,000 – €120,000) = 1 mark
   C = (€20,000) = 2 marks

(iii) **Financial Problem**

The deficit months are October and December.

How to address:

Avail of a short-term source of finance:

- Amrod Ltd could arrange a bank overdraft facility with its bank to finance problem months where the business is running a deficit. The overdraft facility provides extra flexibility for Amrod Ltd when it needs it most. However, care should be taken because the rate of interest charged on a bank overdraft is high. Other short-term sources could be considered, such as trade credit (delaying payment to creditors/seeking an extension period of credit from creditors).
- Adjust receipts: Its receipts in October and December could be increased by changing its marketing mix, e.g. lowering price to sell more, increasing the price depending on elasticities, designing new products or more effective promotion campaigns/reducing period of credit given to debtors/cash sales only.
- Adjust payments: The business could decrease its cash payments by sourcing cheaper suppliers, restructuring loan repayments or asking employees to take a wage decrease. By moving €10,000 of payments from October to November, the company would break even at the end of October, etc.

Marking scheme

(i) Two points @ 5 marks each (2 + 3)

(ii) Three figures (2 × 2 marks and 1 × 3 marks (2 + 1))

(iii) 8 marks (2 × 4 marks (2 + 2))

Sources of finance

Most households and businesses need finance to pay bills or purchase assets.

Sources of finance can be **short-term**, **medium-term** or **long-term**. Businesses must match the source of finance with its use.

Short-term sources of finance (less than one year)

Short-term finance

Sources and Uses of Short-term Finance	
Household	**Business**
Sources:	**Sources:**
Bank overdraft	Bank overdraft
Creditors	Creditors – trade credit
Accrued Expenses	Accrued expenses
Credit card	Taxation
Uses:	**Uses:**
Pay day-to-day expenses	Purchase stock
Purchase clothes	Pay wages/expenses
Purchase services	Pay creditors

This is finance for less than one year and is used to finance short-term assets, such as stock and pay expenses.

The main sources of short-term finance include:

- Bank overdraft
- Creditors
- Accrued expenses
- Taxation
- Credit cards

Bank overdraft

A bank overdraft is a short-term loan given to current account holders designed to meet short-term expenditure needs.

The current account holder is given permission by the bank to withdraw more than the amount in the account up to a specified limit.

Security is not usually required.

Interest is calculated on a daily basis on the overdrawn balance.

Creditors

Suppliers give an agreed period of credit to their customers, who then sell the goods and have the use of the money until the invoice has to be paid.

No interest is charged and no security is required. However, if the invoice is not paid by the due date, discounts may be lost.

Accrued expenses

These are expenses that do not have to be paid until after the service has been provided (e.g. telephone, electricity).

By delaying the payment of these bills, the business can use the money as a short-term source of finance for other purposes.

Taxation

The business collects taxes on behalf on the Revenue Commissioners (e.g. PAYE, PRSI and VAT).

These taxes are held by the business for a period of time before being forwarded to Revenue.

Credit card

A credit card allows a cardholder to purchase goods and services up to a specified limit.

At the end of the month, the credit card company sends a statement.

No interest is charged if the balance is paid by the due date.

Medium-term sources of finance (one to five years)

Sources and Uses of Medium-term Finance	
Household	**Business**
Sources:	**Sources:**
Hire purchase	Hire purchase
Leasing	Leasing
Personal loan	Medium-term loan
Uses:	**Uses:**
Cars	Computers
Televisions	Office equipment
Electrical appliances	Vehicles
Furniture	Machinery

Medium-term finance

This is finance for one to five years and is used to finance office equipment, vehicles and machinery. The main sources of medium-term finance include:

- Hire purchase
- Leasing
- Term loan.

Hire purchase

Purchasing assets and paying by instalments over an agreed period of time.

Buyer obtains immediate possession and use of the asset but does not become the legal owner until the last instalment is paid.

The rate of interest is high and interest is charged on the initial sum borrowed.

No security is required to obtain the finance.

Leasing

Leasing is a medium-term source of finance for households and businesses and involves the renting of an asset from a finance company.

The lessee has the possession and use of the asset during the period of the lease but does not own it.

The lessee does not have to use a cash lump sum to buy the asset.

No security is required.

Lease repayments can be set against profits to reduce tax.

Medium-term loan

A term loan from the bank is repaid in fixed instalments over an agreed period.

It is negotiated with the bank after completing a loan application form and is granted for a stated reason.

Banks may demand security (collateral) in the event of non-repayment.

Interest on a business term loan can be offset against tax in the profit and loss account.

Long-term sources of finance (over five years)

exam focus

Sources and Uses of Long-term Finance	
Household	**Business**
Sources: Long-term loan Mortgage Savings	**Sources:** Long-term loan/debenture loan Owner's capital/share capital Retained earnings
Uses: Buy a house Pay for house improvements	**Uses:** Purchase of land and buildings Pay for business expansion Buy another business

Long-term finance

This is finance for more than five years and is used to purchase property, build an extension or expand a business.

The main sources of long-term finance include:

- Long-term loans
- Share capital
- Retained earnings

Long-term loans

Long-term loans for a household are available from banks and building societies to purchase a residence. These are called mortgages and are secured on the asset purchased. A debenture loan is a long-term loan to a company, usually for expansion.

Security for the loan will usually be the title deeds to the property.

Interest payments on loans are an allowable expense against tax in the profit and loss account.

They are used for large capital expenditure.

Share capital (equity)

Share capital is provided by the shareholders (owners) who buy shares in a company.

Shareholders receive a share of the profit in the form of a dividend if the company makes profit.

Ordinary shareholders have votes at the AGM giving them a say in the running of the business – one share = one vote.

There are no interest payments and no security has to be provided to raise this finance.

Equity capital is used to purchase expensive assets that will last more than five years.

Retained earnings

This is profit not paid out in dividends but re-invested back into the business as extra capital for expansion or for purchasing assets.

It is a free source of finance and no security is required.

If this source of finance is continuously used, shareholders may become dissatisfied with the lack of dividends.

Read the information supplied and answer the questions that follow.

Sarah Fleming is a wedding dress designer and has worked for over 20 years in the bridal and clothing industry. She specialises in creating unique wedding dresses with an emphasis on personal service. Business is good and Sarah has applied for a bank loan of €10,000 to finance expansion.

(a) Outline **three** factors that Sarah's bank may consider when assessing her bank loan application. (15 marks)

(b) (i) Explain the term 'short-term finance'.

(ii) Outline **two** sources of short-term finance Sarah may consider to meet her working capital needs. (20 marks)

Source: 2014 Higher Level Section 3

Suggested solution

(a) Creditworthiness

The bank will look at Sarah's credit history and her record in terms of repayment of previous loans. Any bad debt history will affect her loan application.

Ability/capacity to repay the loan/business plan:

Sarah will be expected to provide a business plan outlining her trading history and predicted profit trends for the short and medium term. Profitability/liquidity/gearing.

Amount/purpose of the loan/time period for the loan:

The larger the loan amount required, the riskier it is for the bank in terms of default. As a consequence, the loan application may be affected. Furthermore, it will be expected that the loan application is for a productive purpose, e.g. business expansion.

Availability of security:

A valuable asset, such as premises, will be required as collateral for the loan. In the event of a default, the bank will be able to sell the asset to recover its loan.

Level of own investment/grants, etc.

(b) (i) Short-term finance is finance available for a period of up to one year. It should be repaid within 12 months and should be used for short-term needs.

(ii) Bank overdraft

This is a facility offered by a bank that allows current account holders to withdraw more money from their account than they actually have in it.

Interest is charged on the outstanding balance on a daily basis. It can be recalled by the bank at any time. Sarah could use an overdraft facility to purchase stock or pay the wages of part-time staff.

Accrued expenses

This source of finance frees up money by delaying the payment of regular bills such as utilities, rent or insurance. This would free up cash for Sarah to pay for supplies which, in turn, could be sold allowing these bills to be paid later.

Trade credit

Sarah may buy stock for resale on a 'buy now and pay later' basis. The amount of credit available may be dependent on her reputation and creditworthiness. There is no direct charge, but cash discounts can be sacrificed if Sarah chooses to buy raw materials and stock on credit.

Factoring debts/short-term loan from a Credit Union

Marking scheme

(a) 3 × 5 marks (2 + 3)

(b) (i) 4 marks

(ii) 2 points @ 8 marks each (4 + 3 + 1) (name, explain, reference to Sarah's usage)

Be able to:

- Outline the difference between managing a household and managing a business in relation to insurance.
- Explain the importance of insurance to a business.

Insurance

Insurance is a contract whereby a person (the insured) pays a fee (premium) to an insurance company (the insurer), which in return promises to compensate the person for any financial loss suffered.

Risk management

Risk management is having a planned approach to the handling of the risk to which an individual or business is exposed. It involves:

- Identifying all possible risks facing a business (e.g. risk of fire)
- Identifying the cause of the loss (e.g. personal injury)
- Measuring the likelihood of the event occurring
- Calculating the costs of the methods of protecting the business from loss (e.g. reduce risks by insurance, training of staff in health and safety).

Methods of risk reduction

1. Take out insurance in order to transfer the risk to an insurance company for a premium where the company will compensate for any loss suffered.
2. Train personnel in health and safety, and provision of safety equipment and/or protective clothing.
3. Appoint a health and safety representative in the workplace who would report safety issues, provide a health and safety statement, identify hazards and carry out regular safety inspections.
4. Install security systems, alarms, security guards, CCTV.
5. Introduce safer production processes to improve employee health and safety.

Principles of insurance

1. Insurable interest

- The insured person must have a personal financial interest in the item being insured.
- The policyholder must benefit by the continued existence of the item and suffer by its loss.
- The owner of property has an insurable interest in the property.

The **principles of insurance** are:
1. Insurable interest
2. Utmost good faith
3. Indemnity
4. Subrogation
5. Contribution

Example: Everyone has an insurable interest in their personal possessions, such as their house, but your next door neighbour would not have an insurable interest in your house.

2. Utmost good faith

- All material facts must be disclosed to the insurer.
- A material fact is one that would influence the insurer into accepting or rejecting the risk or in setting the premium.
- This means that all the information that might have a bearing on the decision to enter the contract must be supplied on the proposal form, even if the information is not requested.
- The insurer can declare the contract void and claims made by the insurer can be refused if all the facts are not disclosed.

Example: A person with a heart condition looking for life assurance would have to disclose this to the insurance company as this is a relevant fact related to life assurance.

3. Indemnity

- There must be no profit from insurance – only recovery of actual loss.
- The contract is for the reinstatement of the actual property insured. That is, putting the claimant in the same position as was the case prior to the accident or loss.

Example: A two-year-old car insured for €20,000, but with a market value of €15,000, is written off in an accident. The maximum compensation for the loss suffered is therefore €15,000.

4. Subrogation

- Having paid compensation to the insured, the insurer takes over the rights of the insured to sue a third party who was responsible for causing the loss.

Example: If A injures B, and B is paid compensation by the insurance company, then the insurance company can sue A to recover the money.

- When an insured property is written off, the insurer also has the right to take over what is left of the property after compensation is paid.

5. Contribution

- If the loss suffered is insured by more than one insurer, then the amount claimed is divided proportionally between them.
- The loss is shared by the insurers. Contribution usually occurs where two or more companies insure the same risk (e.g. insuring the same property with two different insurance companies).

Underinsurance

Average clause

- The average clause states that if a partial loss is suffered and the property is underinsured, then only a proportion of the amount insured will be paid.
- The full value of the loss is not paid – all claims are reduced to a proportion of the insured value.

John O'Neill owned a house worth €350,000 and had insured it for €300,000 when a fire caused a partial loss of €63,000.

(i) Calculate the amount the insurance company will pay. (Show your workings.)

(ii) Explain your answer. (10 marks)

Source: 2008 Higher Level Section A

Solution

(i) Answer €54,000

(ii) The average clause applies for partial loss. As the house is underinsured, only a proportion of the amount insured will be paid.

> *Workings*
>
> $$\frac{\text{Value Insured} \times \text{Loss}}{\text{Value of House}} = \text{Compensation}$$
>
> $$\frac{€300,000 \times €63,000}{€350,000} = €54,000 \text{ Compensation}$$

Relationship between risk and cost

The relationship between risk and cost is:

- The higher the risk, the higher the cost.

  Example: Car Insurance – a male, aged 20 and holding a first learner permit, will be a higher risk and thus pay a higher premium than a female aged 40 who has been insured for a number of years and holds a full licence.

Insurance and assurance

Insurance is a protection against a risk that **may** happen – for example, a fire or accident. **Assurance** provides for a risk that **will** happen – such as death.

Types of Insurance a **household** should have:
1. Motor insurance
2. House and contents
3. Health insurance
4. Life assurance
5. Mortgage protection
6. Permanent health insurance

1. Motor insurance

- **Third-party fire and theft insurance**

  Compensation is provided to third parties for damage to them and their property by the insured while driving a car.

  It does not cover the insured person or his/her car for damage caused by the insured. Compensation is paid to the insured only when damage results from a fire or theft of the car.

- **Comprehensive insurance**

  Comprehensive insurance provides compensation to third parties for damage to them or their property by the insured while driving a car. It also covers the insured person's car against all risks.

2. House and contents

Covers buildings and contents against fire, flooding, burglary or accidental damage. It would provide compensation to the owner in the event of loss or damage to the specified items covered by the policy.

3. Health insurance

Covers the cost of hospital care in the event of accident or illness. Private healthcare insurance is provided by VHI Healthcare, Laya Healthcare and Aviva Health.

4. Life assurance

Life assurance provides compensation on the death of the insured. Types of life assurance include:

- **Whole life assurance** – The insured pays a premium for the rest of his/her life and compensation is paid to dependents on the death of the insured.

- **Endowment life assurance** – The insurance pays the premium, and compensation is paid either on the insured reaching a certain age or on their death, whichever comes first.

5. Mortgage protection

If the borrower dies before the mortgage is fully paid, the policy will cover the balance due on the mortgage.

6. Permanent health insurance

This covers a person's income if they are unable to work because of an accident, serious accident or disability.

Taking out insurance/insurance documents

1. Insurance proposal form

An application form that must be filled out if a person or firm is taking out insurance. All material facts must be disclosed and the proposal form is governed by the principal of utmost good faith.

2. Premium

Fee paid annually to the insurance company by the person seeking insurance. In return, the insurance company will compensate the insured for the loss or damage covered by the agreement.

3. Policy

Contains details and terms of the insurance agreement. Policy excess means the insured has agreed to forgo, say, the first €250 of any compensation.

4. Claim form

This form is used by the insured when seeking compensation for a loss that has occurred. It describes what happened and the amount being claimed.

Insurance Terms

Claim

When a risk which is covered by an insurance policy actually occurs, the insured can apply to the insurance company to get money to cover the loss.

Assessor

An assessor investigates the insurance claim on behalf of the insurance company – inspects the damage to the property/item and decides how much compensation should be paid.

Compensation

This is the amount of money paid by the insurer to the insured after a claim has been made for a loss which has occurred and the insurer has established that the claim is genuine.

Read the information supplied and answer the questions that follow.

Private Motor Insurance Proposal Form *Declaration*

I/We declare to the best of my/our knowledge and belief that the information given on this form is true and complete in every respect.

(i) Outline the function of an *insurance proposal form*.

(ii) Explain the principle of insurance, referred to in the extract from the above private motor insurance proposal form.

(iii) Outline *two* other principles of insurance that apply to insurance contracts.

(20 marks)

Source: 2015 Higher Level Section 3

Solution

(i) Insurance proposal forms are used to apply for insurance cover and the company is given full particulars of the risk against which the insurance protection is desired. Insurance proposal forms help the insurance company to calculate the premium based on all the potential risks in relation to the insurance policy.

(ii) **Utmost good faith:** All **material facts** must be revealed. The person taking out the insurance must answer all the questions truthfully. Failure to do so can make the insurance cover worthless. If the insurance contract is obtained by way of fraud or misrepresentation, it is void, e.g a driver should declare truthfully the number of penalty points on his/her licence.

(iii) **Indemnity:** An insured person cannot make a profit from an insurance claim, i.e. insurance can at best put an insured person in the same financial position as they were prior to a loss occurring. If a car is written off in an accident, the insured receives its replacement value and not the original sum paid for it.

Insurable interest: The insured must gain from the existence of the exposure unit and suffer from its loss. You can insure your own car but not your neighbour's. In essence, you can't insure something unless you have a vested interest in it.

Subrogation: If a third party is responsible for damaging your car in an accident and you are compensated by your own insurer, your insurer can then sue the other driver. Subrogation says that when you accept an insurance settlement the insurer gets your right to sue the third party. This prevents you collecting twice for the same damage and gives your insurer a way to recoup their losses. Fundamentally, the principle is linked to indemnity, ensuring that a person doesn't profit from insurance.

Contribution: This principle states that if you hold more than one insurer liable for your losses, they have to share the loss. If you take out two policies on your car, you can't collect from both insurers. One company would pay you and then collect from the second, or both companies would share the compensation payment between them. Fundamentally, the principle is linked to indemnity, ensuring that a person doesn't profit from insurance.

Marking scheme

(i) 5 marks (2 + 3)

(ii) 5 marks (2 + 3)

(iii) 2 × 5 marks (2 + 3) (Name – 2 marks, explain – 3 marks)

Business insurance

1. Motor vehicle insurance

All cars, vehicles and delivery trucks owned by a business must be insured. The same types of policies and rules apply as for households.

2. Property insurance – buildings and contents

This policy covers buildings, equipment and stock against loss or damage as a result of fire or accident.

3. Public liability insurance

This protects the business against claims by members of the public from injury or loss resulting from an accident on the business premises.

Types of Insurance a **business** should have:

1. Motor vehicle insurance
2. Property insurance – buildings and contents
3. Public liability insurance
4. Employer's liability insurance
5. Fidelity guarantee insurance
6. Product liability insurance
7. Burglary insurance

4. Employer's liability insurance

This policy protects employers against claims made by employees as a result of an accident at work.

5. Fidelity guarantee insurance

This protects the business against financial losses as a result of theft or fraud by an employee.

6. Product liability insurance

This protects the business against claims by members of the public for loss or damage suffered as a result of a defective product.

7. Burglary insurance

This protects the business against loss/damage caused by theft/break-ins.

The importance of insurance for business

1. Protection against risks

The business will be protected against risks. A large claim against the business or loss of property could put the business in severe financial difficulty.

2. Business survival

The business can continue and survive despite unforeseen events (e.g. fire or flood).

3. Improved safety standards

Insurance companies will insist on improved safety and security standards before granting insurance cover. This should reduce the number of accidents in the workplace.

Explain what it means to be 'underinsured' **and** outline **one** possible effect of being underinsured on a business.

(15 marks)

Source: 2014 Higher Level Section 3

Suggested solution

Underinsured means the business has inadequate insurance cover. The insured fails to insure for the full value of the policy. In the event of a claim for total loss or partial loss, underinsurance may result in economic losses to the policy holder, since the claim would exceed the maximum amount that can be paid out by the insurance policy.

The motivation for being underinsured is the lower premiums paid by the policy holder; however, the losses arising from a claim will far outweigh savings experienced in reduced insurance premiums as a consequence of the inadequate insurance.

Possible effects on business:

Underinsurance could result in a serious financial crisis in a business depending on the asset that is insured. For example, if a building is insured for €300,000 and is subsequently destroyed in a fire and the cost to replace the building is €500,000, the business will have to make up the difference of €200,000 from its own resources.

The lower premiums will reduce the business costs and thereby increase profits. This could be intentional with the full knowledge of the risk. However, the losses arising from a claim may far exceed any marginal savings in insurance premiums.

It may not be intentional. Businesses should review and update cover annually (e.g. stock may have increased in value due to inflation).

Marking scheme

Three points of information @ 4 marks each

One possible effect @ 3 marks

HL

Read the information supplied and answer the questions that follow.

Bianua Ltd, a medium-size company operating in the agrifood sector, supplies quality prepared food products in Ireland and in the UK market.

Draft a business letter from EXON Insurance plc to Bianua Ltd, using today's date, identifying the possible risks and the appropriate types of insurance for Bianua Ltd. Use fictitious names and addresses.

(20 marks)

Source: 2014 Higher Level Section 3

Suggested solution

EXON Insurance plc
(Address, Telephone No., Email, Directors, etc.)

Your ref:
Our ref:

Date 14/06/18

Bianua Ltd
(Address)

Re: Business risks and the appropriate types of insurance policy for the company

Dear Mr/Ms

The following is a list of possible business risks and the appropriate types of insurance for the company.

The risk of structural damage to the factory, warehouse or office building.

Buildings insurance – provides protection against loss or damage to the structure of the building caused by fire, flood or storm.

The risk of damage to stock, raw materials, components, etc.

Contents insurance – provides protection against loss or damage to contents caused by burglary, fire or flood.

The risk of being involved in a road traffic accident.

Motor insurance – it is compulsory by law to have third party insurance. Other policies include 'third party, fire and theft' and comprehensive.

The risk of losing an important member of staff.

Key person insurance – protects the business against the loss of a valuable staff member.

The risk of a customer injuring themselves while on the premises.

Public Liability Insurance – protects the business against claims made by the public as a result of accidents while on site.

The risk of a worker injuring himself while carrying out his or her job.

Employer Liability Insurance – Covers the business against claims made by employees as a result of accidents in the workplace.

The risk of having cash or stock stolen by an employee.

Fidelity Guarantee Insurance – Protects the business against dishonesty or fraud committed by an employee.

The risk of the company's products being harmful to the public.

Product Liability Insurance – Protects the business in the event of a customer making a claim as a result of defective products that may have caused harm.

Other: Goods in transit/consequential loss.

I look forward to hearing from you.

Yours faithfully

Signature
Position held

Enc.

Marking scheme

Layout 8 marks:

- Letterhead 1 mark; date 2 marks
- Inside name and address 1 mark
- Salutation 1 mark; Re: 1 mark
- Complimentary close 1 mark
- Author's signature 1 mark

Identifying Risks

8 marks: Four risks @ 2 marks

Appropriate types of insurance

4 marks: Four types of insurance @ 1 mark

11 Household and Business Manager 3: Taxation

aims

Be able to:

- Outline the difference between managing a household and managing a business in relation to taxation.
- Explain the implications of taxation to a business.
- Identify activities common to managing a business and a household in relation to finance, insurance and taxation, including the completion of relevant forms.
- Identify activities that are different in managing a business and a household in relation to finance, insurance and taxation.

Taxes paid by households and individuals

Tax is charged by the government on the income of individuals and businesses and on goods and services. This money is used by the government to finance its spending and to provide services.

1. Income tax (PAYE)

This is charged on people's wages/salaries. Income tax is deducted by the employer from wages/salaries and sent to the Revenue Commissioners. This is called the PAYE system (Pay As You Earn). PRSI (Pay Related Social Insurance) is also collected through the PAYE system, as well as the Universal Social Charge.*

The PAYE system

The PAYE system applies to anyone who earns income from employment.

Form 12A

Form 12A must be completed by all employees before commencing employment.

It is used to apply for a certificate of tax credits and a standard cut-off point.

Tax credit

A tax credit reduces the amount of tax payable by the taxpayer and is determined by personal circumstances.

*The Universal Social Charge is a tax payable on income from all sources.

exam focus

Taxes paid by **households and individuals**:

1. Income tax (PAYE)
2. Value added tax (VAT)
3. Capital Gains Tax
4. Capital Acquisitions Tax
5. Deposit Interest Retention Tax (DIRT)
6. Motor Tax
7. Employee PRSI
8. Universal Social Charge

exam focus

The PAYE system requires the completion of a number of tax forms, including:

- 12A
- P60
- P45
- P21

Tax credits that a person may be entitled to include:

- Personal tax credit (single, married, etc.)
- PAYE tax credit
- Dependent Relative tax credit
- Home Carer tax credit

> Gross tax less tax credits = tax payable

Standard cut-off point

This is the amount of a taxpayer's income on which they pay tax at the standard rate. Any income earned over the standard cut-off point will be subject to the higher rate of tax. In the absence of a certificate of tax credits, emergency tax must be deducted by the employer.

Form P60

Issued by an employer to an employee after the end of the tax year.

It shows gross pay, income tax and PRSI paid by the employee for the tax year.

Form P60 will be required by the employee when claiming a refund on overpaid tax or overpaid PRSI contributions.

Form P60 can also be used as proof of income for various purposes (e.g. education grants, medical services, etc.).

Form P45

Issued by an employer to an employee on leaving employment.

Form P45 provides details of the amount of gross pay, tax and PRSI paid by the employee up to the date of leaving employment.

Form P45 will be required by an employee when:

- Entering new employment – the new employer will require the P45 to calculate the correct amount of tax payable
- Claiming social welfare benefits
- Claiming a tax refund

Form P21

This is known as a balancing statement and all PAYE taxpayers are entitled to receive a P21 annually. It compares tax paid with the amount of tax that should have been paid. If tax was overpaid by a taxpayer, they are entitled to a refund. If tax was underpaid by a taxpayer, a demand for further tax will be made.

Income tax calculation

From the following information, calculate the net annual take-home pay of Ms Joan McCormack for 2018.

Joan McCormack is an employee of Lynch Printers and earns a gross salary of €84,000. She is allowed the following tax credits:

Single person tax credit of €1,650 and PAYE tax credit of €1,650. The income tax rates are 20% on the first €34,550 (standard cut-off point) and 40% on the balance. Employee PRSI is €3,360. The universal social charge (USC) is €5,880.

Suggested solution

Joan McCormack – Net Annual Take-Home Pay

Gross Salary				€84,000
Tax				
€34,550 @ 20%	€6,910			
€49,450 @ 40%	€19,780			
Gross Tax		€26,690		
Less Tax Credits				
Single person	€1,650			
PAYE	€1,650	(€3,300)		
Tax to be paid			€23,390	
PRSI			€3,360	
USC			€5,880	
Tax, PRSI and USC				€32,630
Net annual take-home pay				€51,370

2. Value added tax (VAT)

Value added tax is paid by households when they buy goods and services.
VAT is added to the price of the goods or services. Here's an example:

Price of computer (excluding VAT)   €800
Add value added tax 23%   €184
Price of computer (including VAT)   €984

Householder will pay €984, and of this amount €184 is VAT.

3. Capital gains tax

This is tax paid by the household on profit from the sale of assets, such property or shares.
Capital gains tax does not apply to the profit on the sale of a principal private residence.

4. Capital acquisitions tax

This tax is paid by the recipient of:

- A gift taken, other than on death
- An inheritance taken on death

The amount of tax payable depends on the amount of the gift or inheritance and the relationship between the giver and receiver.
A certain amount of the gift or inheritance is tax-free.

5. Deposit interest retention tax (DIRT)

The interest a person receives on a savings account in a bank, building society or post office is subject to a tax called Deposit Interest Retention Tax (DIRT). The tax is deducted by the bank before the interest is paid to the person and is sent to Revenue.

6. Motor tax

Motor tax is paid to the local authority on all motor vehicles owned by the household. The amount payable depends on the car's emissions levels.

7. Employee pay-related social insurance (PRSI)

Every person in employment must pay PRSI. It is a compulsory payment and is calculated as a percentage of the employee's gross wages. There is a wide range of benefits available to people who have paid PRSI, including jobseeker's benefit, illness benefit, maternity benefit, and dental and optical benefits.

Income tax question

(a) Explain PAYE.

(b) Outline **two** main features of the PAYE tax systems.

(c) Explain the difference between the terms *tax rates* and *tax credits*.

(d) The following forms are used in PAYE taxation: P60, P45, P21. Outline the purpose of these.

Suggested solution

(a) Pay As You Earn – this is a direct tax paid by employees on their income/wages/salaries. It is deducted at source by the employer at a specified rate and forwarded to the Revenue Commissioners. It is a statutory deduction from wages/salaries.

(b) Progressive: Falls heaviest on high-income earners

Efficient: Business collects the tax for the exchequer

Direct: It is a direct tax on income earned from employment

Form-based: 12A, P60, P45, P12, P21, etc.

(c) Tax rates: Income is taxed at two different rates. The rate at which tax is paid depends on the level of taxable income. The current tax rates are the standard rate of 20% up to a certain income and the higher rate of 40%.

The standard or lower rate of 20% applies to the tax band of €34,550 and the higher rate 40% applies to the balance of taxable income.

Tax credits:

Gross Tax – Tax Credits = Tax Payable

Under the tax credit system, a taxpayer is entitled to tax credits/range of allowances depending on each person's personal circumstances, which can change from year to year, e.g. married person's tax credit or civil partner's tax credit, employee (PAYE) tax credit, etc.

These tax credits are used to reduce tax liability calculated on gross pay. Tax credits are non-refundable. However, any unused tax credits in a pay week or month are carried forward to subsequent pay period(s) within the tax year.

Examples of tax credits include: Blind Person's Credit, Dependent Relative Credit, Guide Dog Allowance, Home Carer Credit, Incapacitated Child Credit, One Parent Family Credit, PAYE Credit, Widowed Parent Credit.

(d) P60

- This must be given by the employer to the employee at the end of the tax year.
- It shows the employee gross pay for the year.
- It also shows tax and PRSI deductions made during the year.
- It can also be used as proof of earnings.
- It can be used as proof of income if applying for a loan or a mortgage.

P45

- This must be given by the employer to the employee if an employee leaves a job or is made redundant during the tax year.
- It shows the gross pay for the year to date and the tax and PRSI deductions made.
- It shows the date of leaving.
- It can be given to a new employer or to the Department of Social Protection if claiming Jobseeker's Benefit.

P21

- This is a statement of total income, tax credit and tax paid for a particular tax year.
- It is issued on request by the Inspector of Taxes to PAYE taxpayers.
- It compares the amount of tax paid with the amount that should have been paid.
- It can be used to claim a tax refund if tax was overpaid.
- It can be used to demand further tax payment if tax was underpaid.
- It differs from a P60 because a taxpayer may have more than one source of income or may be jointly assessed, which means that a P60 from one employer would not give the full information.

Audrey Stapleton is an employee at BAT Resources Ltd and earns a gross annual salary of €78,000. Her employer provides her with a holiday voucher worth €2,000. This is treated as a benefit-in-kind for tax purposes and is taxed accordingly.

The standard rate band for a single taxpayer is €34,550. (This means that the first €34,550 is taxed at the 20% standard tax rate, and the remainder is taxed at the higher tax rate of 40%.)

Audrey has the following tax credits: Single Person Tax Credit €1,650, PAYE Tax Credit €1,650 and Dependent Relative Tax Credit €70.

The Universal Social Charge (USC) rates on Audrey's gross income are 0.5% on the first €12,012, 2% on the next €7,360, 4.75% on the next €50,672, and 8% on the balance of her gross income. Audrey pays employee PRSI at the rate of 4% on her gross income.

(a) Calculate Audrey Stapleton's net monthly take-home pay. (20 marks)

Source: 2013 Higher Level Section 3

Suggested solution

Tax Computation for Audrey Stapleton

	€	€	€
Gross Salary			78,000
Add Benefit in kind			2,000
Gross Income			80,000 **(2m)**
PAYE Tax payable calculation			
€34,550 @ 20%		6,910 **(1m)**	
€45,450 @ 40% **(1m)**		18,180 **(1m)** OF	
Gross PAYE Tax		25,090 **(1m)** OF	
Less Tax credits			
Single Person	1,650 **(1m)**		
PAYE	1,650 **(1m)**		
Dependent Relative	70 **(1m)**		
	3,370	(3,370)	
(A) Net Tax Payable		21,720 **(1m)** OF	
(B) Employee's PRSI			
€80,000 @ 4%		3,200 **(2m)**	
(C) Universal Social Charge (USC)			
€12,012 @ 0.5%	60.06 **(1m)**		
€7,360 @ 2%	147.20 **(1m)**		
€50,672 @ 4.75% **(1m)**	2,406.92 **(1m)** OF		
Balance of €9,956 @ 8%	796.48	3,410.66 **(1m)** OF	
Total Statutory Deductions			
(A+B+C)			28,330.66
Net Income (Take-home Pay) p.a.			
(€78,000 − €28,330.66)			49,669.34
Net Income (Take-home)			
(49,669.34 ÷ 12) **(2m)**			4,139.11
			OF = Own Figure

Marking scheme

14 figures @ 1 mark each

Three figures/actions @ 2 marks each

Taxes paid by business

1. Income tax – self-assessment

Self-assessment income tax applies to all self-employed people.

Self-employed people calculate their own tax liability for the year and pay it by 31 October of that year.

They must also send in a full tax return for the year by 31 October of the following year.

Self-assessment tax returns are subject to random audits by Revenue inspectors to ensure that the returns made are accurate.

Taxes paid by **businesses** include:
1. Income tax – self-assessment
2. Value added tax (VAT)
3. Corporation tax
4. Commercial rates
5. Employer's PRSI

2. Value added tax (VAT)

VAT is a tax on consumer spending. It is chargeable when a business sells goods or services to a consumer.

A business charges VAT on sales and is entitled to deduct from this amount VAT paid on purchases.

VAT owed by a business must be sent to the Revenue Commissioners every two months. There are various rates of VAT depending on the product or service sold.

3. Corporation tax

Corporation tax is charged on profits of companies resident in the state.

The rate of corporation tax is 12.5% on trading income.

4. Commercial rates

Rates are a charge payable by all commercial businesses to fund services provided by local authorities, including housing, water supply and sewerage, roads, etc. Rates amounts are based on property valuations.

5. Employer's pay-related social insurance

Employers must also pay PRSI. It is calculated as a percentage of an employee's gross wages. This is the employer's contribution to the national social insurance fund, which pays for social insurance benefits and pensions.

Effects of taxation on business

1. Collecting and recording tax is a huge cost for business. They do not get paid anything for collecting tax for the state.
2. Tax reduces profit, which reduces the dividends paid to shareholders and the amount of retained profit in the business.
3. Customs duties increase the price of raw materials imported, thus increasing the cost of production.
4. High rates of personal taxation reduce the incentive to work and seek promotion.

Similarities and differences in managing a household and managing a business

Similarities

1. Taxation
Both households and businesses must pay taxes, so income tax/PRSI is common to both. Businesses must also pay VAT on purchases and corporation tax on profits.

2. Insurance
Both must assess risk and insure people and property.

3. Finance
Both must raise suitable sources of finance. Households need finance for the purchase of a house, car and other expenses (such as the education of children and family holidays). Businesses need working capital to finance operating expenses and long-term finance to fund the purchase of fixed assets.

4. Official Forms
Both household and business must complete forms such as tax forms, loan applications and insurance proposal and claim forms.

5. Records
Both must keep financial records and keep documents such as tax forms and insurance policies safe.

6. Management Activities
Both must plan, organise and control to achieve goals and objectives.

Differences

1. Taxation
Different taxes apply to households (PAYE, capital acquisitions tax) and to businesses (VAT, corporation tax).

2. Insurance
Businesses need to cover a wider range of risks than households (e.g. public liability, employee's liability and fidelity guarantee).

3. Finance
Businesses have a wider range of sources of finance (e.g. share capital).

4. Scale of Operation
Business is on a much bigger scale then a household (e.g. finance and personnel).

5. Motivation
Motivation in business is mainly profit, whereas in a household the main motivating factor is family love.

6. Legislation
A business is subject to much more legislation than a household. Areas such as company law and competition law do not directly affect households.

7. Management Expertise

Specific kinds of management expertise are regularly used in running a business. Bookkeeping and budgeting skills are relevant to the running of a household, but not to the extent required in business.

Pay as You Earn (PAYE), Value Added Tax (VAT), and Corporation Tax are examples of taxes relevant to a business.

(i)   Explain each tax underlined above.

(ii) Evaluate the implications of each tax for a business.

(25 marks)

Source: 2011 Higher Level Section 3

Suggested solution

Pay as You Earn

- PAYE is a direct tax on income earned from employment.
- PAYE is remitted by the business every month to the Revenue Commissioners.
- It is deducted at source by the employer and passed on to the Revenue Commissioners.
- Taxpayers receive a certificate of tax credits which is forwarded to employers and which will reduce the amount of tax they have to pay.

Implications for business (evaluation)

- The collection of PAYE is an administrative cost for business. It is a bureaucratic system requiring the completion of many different taxation forms, e.g. 12A, P60, P45, P12 and P21.
- It is a progressive tax because the more income you earn, the more tax you pay. High rates of PAYE are a disincentive for people to do overtime, which affects a business's ability to meet sales orders.

Value Added Tax

- VAT is an indirect tax charged on the sale of goods and services.
- Businesses register for VAT and receive a VAT number.
- VAT is remitted for the business every two months to the Revenue Commissioners.
- The VAT paid is the difference between the VAT paid on purchases and collected from sales.
- VAT is charged at different rates, depending on the type of goods or services involved.

Implications for business (evaluation)

- The collection of VAT is a significant administrative cost for business.
- High rates of VAT on raw materials and components increase the cost of production for business affecting margins and cash flows.

- High rates of VAT increase the purchase price for consumers. This reduces the demand for goods and services of business.
- The government's reduction in VAT rates in the tourism sector from 13.5% to 9% encouraged growth in the tourism sector.

Corporation Tax

- Corporation tax is a tax on the profits made by companies.
- The current rate of corporation tax is 12.5% for manufacturing businesses.
- Expenses of the business are allowable when calculating the taxable profits of the business.
- Companies must prepare annual final accounts to show their taxable profit.

Implications for business (evaluation)

- Corporation tax in Ireland is relatively low by international standards. This encourages Irish entrepreneurs and foreign investors to set up here. If corporation tax was to increase, it could act as a disincentive to FDI.
- Corporation tax reduces the size of profits and consequently the amount available as retained earnings. This could put pressure on the business to borrow money, leading to high gearing.

(No repeat points in either explanations or implications for each tax.)

Marking scheme

(i) 3 × 6 marks (3 + 3)

(ii) 7 marks (3 + 2 + 2)

12 Human Resource Management

Human resource management

Human resource management is the function of management that recruits, trains and rewards the workforce so that the objectives of the firm are achieved.

1. Manpower planning

Manpower planning involves:

- Identifying the human resource needs of the organisation and ensuring that they are met
- Conducting an audit of existing staff skills and expertise
- Identifying additional staff needed
- Preparing a plan to recruit or reduce human resources.

2. Recruitment and selection

Recruitment – The process of attracting suitable candidates to apply for vacancies in a firm.

Selection – Selecting the most suitable candidates for the job.

Stages in recruitment and selection

Prepare a job description

This describes the duties and responsibilities of the job. It includes details of the job, conditions of employment place of work, etc.

exam focus

The **functions of human resource management** are:

1. Manpower planning
2. Recruitment and selection
3. Training and development
4. Employer–employee relationships
5. Performance appraisal
6. Rewarding employees
7. Teamwork

Prepare a person specification

This describes the ideal person to do the job. It includes the skills, qualities, experience and qualifications that the person should possess to do the job effectively.

Advertising the job – The human resource manager uses the information from the job description and person specification to draw up an advertisement for the job. Candidates may be asked to submit a CV or complete an application form.

Attract a group of suitable candidates

The next job of the human resource manager is to encourage suitable candidates to apply for the job.

A. Methods of recruiting employees:

- Advertising in newspapers or local radio is a popular way of recruiting staff. Newspapers carry recruitment supplements and reach a wide audience
- Posting an advertisement online (such as on Irishjobs.ie)
- Using the local job centre
- Using Solas, which keeps a register of jobseekers
- Headhunting (targeting a good employee in another firm and encouraging him/her to change jobs)
- Using recruitment/employment agencies
- Recruiting at colleges and training centres

B. Internal and external recruitment

Internal – Finding someone from those already employed in the business.

External – Finding someone from outside the business.

The advantages of **internal recruitment** are:

- **Motivation** – Employees will see that hard work and commitment can be rewarded through promotion
- Less expensive to promote internally
- **Knowledge** – Existing employees know the business better than external recruits
- The business knows the employee's achievements, strengths, weaknesses, etc.

The advantages of **external recruitment** are:

- An external candidate may have new ideas or new ways of doing things
- The person with the most suitable skills can be employed
- An outsider will bring a range of experiences gained in other organisations.

C. Decide on the application process

The most common methods are:

- Application form
- Curriculum vitae (CV)

Application form

Many firms develop their own application forms, asking a series of questions regarding education, work experience, interests and hobbies, etc. The application form is completed by the applicant and returned to the firm.

Curriculum vitae (CV)

The CV sets out:

- Personal details
- Skills and qualities
- Education and qualifications

- Achievements
- Employment history
- Referees

The applicant applies for the job by sending his/her curriculum vitae along with a covering letter to the company.

Screening of applicants

Once the application forms or CVs are received, the selection process begins. Screening is carried out to compile a short list of candidates for the job.

Selection tests

A number of selection tests may be carried out to assist in the selection process:

- Intelligence tests – measures general intelligence
- Aptitude tests – tests a candidate's skills
- Personality tests – measures personality type.

Interview

The interview allows the employer to acquire information about the candidate and assess their suitability for the job. It also enables the candidate to obtain information about the job and the organisation. Interviews can be one-on-one, in a panel interview, or in a group interview.

Checking references
The checking of references is undertaken to confirm the information already obtained and to establish past performance.

Offer job to successful candidate
A written offer of the job is made to the most suitable candidate. A contract of employment is drawn up and is signed by both parties and given to the employee.

3. Training and development
Training involves supplying the skills and knowledge needed by employees to do their jobs better.

Types of training

Induction training
The training received by new employees to help them in the workplace. It includes:

- Health and safety training
- Presentation of the organisation's rules and codes of ethics
- An introduction to co-workers and management.

On-the-job training
Involves experienced staff teaching the employee the skills and knowledge required for the job in the workplace.

Off-the-job training
Involves doing courses outside the workplace (e.g. in a training centre or college).

Staff development
Development involves preparing the employee to take on more responsibility and new challenges in the workplace. This includes certificate/diploma/degree/post-graduate courses, management courses, etc.

Importance/benefits of training and development:

- Better quality service to customers, resulting in fewer complaints.
- Improved quality of production.
- Flexible and adaptable workforce allowing for changes to take place; new work methods and technologies are facilitated.
- Less industrial relations problems; staff are better cared for and more motivated.
- Lower labour turnover due to high staff morale.
- Adds to the reputation of the firm, thereby attracting quality staff.

4. Employer–employee relationships

The human resource manager is responsible for ensuring good industrial relations in business. The term 'industrial relations' refers to the quality of the relationship that exists between employer and employees in business.

If relations between employer and employees are good, workers will be motivated to work hard and morale will be high.

A **good industrial relations climate and high morale in the organisation** can be achieved by:

- **Open communication** – Regular meetings between management and staff
- Providing for the **health, safety** and **welfare** of staff
- **Valuing employees** – Recognising the contribution of employees to the organisation
- **Grievance procedures** – Ensuring that employees have a formal means of making a complaint
- **Teamwork** – Developing teams within the organisation
- **Reward** – Rewarding employees fairly for effort.

The **importance/benefits of a good employer–employee relationship in business** include:

- **Motivation** – Employees are motivated to work to the best of their ability.
- **Co-operation** – Employers and employees are working towards the same goal/objectives.
- **Less risk of industrial action** – Fewer labour problems if good relations exist.
- **High productivity** – Employees have a positive attitude towards work.
- **Problem-solving** – Problems are resolved quickly as there are agreed procedures for solving disputes.

5. Performance appraisal

This is the process of reviewing the performance of an employee in business.

Performance appraisals involve a meeting/interview between the human resource manager and employee to:

- Examine their performance and discuss their progress
- Set targets/objectives/expectations
- Discuss any problems the employee may be having
- Identify training and development needs/resources needed by the employee to achieve targets
- Discuss the employee's pay and rewards.

Many organisations now relate reward (i.e. salary scales) to how the employee performs in the organisation.

The importance/benefits of conducting performance appraisals in business:

- **Review rewards** (benefits structures) – It may be used in determining pay increases or promotion.
- **Decide about selection and training** – It helps a business decide if too much or too little training is being delivered in various departments of the business. (For example, they may need to reduce training in some departments that have a high staff turnover and thereby reduce business costs.)
- **Retain the right staff/identify poorly performing staff** – It helps a business identify top talent and ensure that these employees are retained and guided towards reaching the business plans and objectives. A business can also identify employees who are not reaching their potential and take steps to address the issue.
- **Improve industrial relations** – Conflicts in the workplace may be highlighted through performance appraisals. This enables the business to help solve problems between management and employees and helps improve industrial relations in the workplace.
- **Increase productivity** – Performance appraisals are important for staff motivation, communicating and fostering a positive relationship between management and staff. This leads to greater productivity from employees.
- **Identify hidden strengths** – Performance appraisals help to identify hidden strengths in staff members, which can then be brought out for the good of the business. This can be achieved by developing individual skills and thus improving the overall performance of the business. It can be used to assess employees' potential for promotion.
- **Delegate tasks** – Managers can decide to delegate tasks to certain employees who are performing well in business. This will relieve pressure on managers.
- **Form judgements** – It requires the human resource manager to form a judgement on a person's work by reviewing the quality of the work and the progress that the person has made or the capability of the person.

6. Rewarding employees

It is the function of the human resource manager to negotiate the remuneration package employees are to receive. This package can include both financial and non-financial rewards.

Financial rewards

- **Time Rate**

With time rate, payments of a fixed amount per hour for a fixed number of hours per week are made to the employees.

If the employee works more than the fixed number of hours, overtime is paid at different rates above the minimum, e.g. time and a half or double time.

- **Piece rate**

This relates to payment given to employees for each unit produced or job completed. The more units produced, the more the employee earns.

- **Bonus**

This relates to the payment given to employees for reaching a certain target, e.g. for producing units above an agreed limit.

- **Commission**

This is a type of financial reward where payment is made according to the value of the amount sold, e.g. payments to a sales person (say, 10%) in proportion to the level of sales achieved. It has the advantage of directly encouraging sales.

- **Profit-sharing schemes**

This is a scheme where some of the organisation's profits are paid to employees on an agreed basis. This scheme is administered and profits are paid to employees to motivate them to become more productive.

- **Employee Shared Ownership Scheme**

Shares in the organisation may be given to employees instead of cash bonuses, maintaining employee interest in the job.

Share options in the organisation may be given to employees interested in the job. Share option schemes give employees an option to buy shares in a company at a specified price some time in the future.

Non-financial rewards

- **Benefit-in-kind**

This is also known as a perk or a fringe benefit. It takes the form of goods or service given to employees rather than money. Benefits-in-kind are often used to raise the status of a position in a firm and to boost morale.

Examples include meal vouchers, company cars and health insurance.

(Note: Benefit-in-kind can be considered financial or non-financial depending on whether it is taxable or not.)

- **Promotion**

Movement to a more responsible senior level in the organisation. While this will also carry a higher wage, it is often a job title, bigger office or the availability of a personal assistant that is the real reward, as per Maslow's self-esteem needs.

- **Job Satisfaction/Job enrichment/Job enlargement**

Employees are rewarded because the job satisfies their social needs (teamwork) and self-actualisation needs (opportunity to do further study). The nature of the work and the opportunities it presents (travel) reward the employee, e.g. a volunteer with a Third World relief agency or charity.

- **Flexitime**

This allows employees the freedom to choose their own work hours within an agreed time frame; e.g. workers may have to be in the workplace between 10 a.m. and 1 p.m.

only. This allows employees to work from home and organise, for example, their childcare arrangements more efficiently.

- **Job sharing**

This involves employees sharing a position, e.g. two employees have a job split between them. This is a flexible approach to employment and recognises that employees may wish to prioritise leisure time over work time.

7. Teamwork

A team is a group of people working together towards a common objective.

Stages in team formation

Objectives are set for the team and then people with the right skills are selected. The process of team development takes place as follows:

- **Forming** – The team is formed and begins to meet and discuss the project.
- **Storming** – Team members argue with each other until their various roles are clarified. (This is called 'storming'.)
- **Norming** – The team then begins to work as an effective unit. They set 'norms' or rules and standards for working together.
- **Performing** – The team begins to perform and achieve its goals.

exam focus

IMPORTANCE/BENEFITS OF TEAMS IN ORGANISATIONS

- **Motivation** – Teamwork encourages greater effort and recognition is given to everyone's achievements.
- **Better decisions** – People working in teams are likely to reach better decisions.
- **More ideas** – Members of a team are more forthcoming with ideas and solutions.
- **Support** – Team members share responsibility and help each other out.
- **Same objectives** – All team members are working towards the same objectives.

Explain the following functions of a Human Resource Manager.

(i)   Training and development

(ii) Recruitment and selection

(iii) Employer/employee relations

Suggested solution

(i) Training and development

- **Training** involves supplying the skills, knowledge and attitudes needed by employees to do their jobs better.
- Training improves skill levels and increases staff morale.
- Types:

  On-the-job training: This means acquiring the skills and knowledge required for the job in the actual workplace by observing experienced employees performing their duties, e.g. staff being shown how to use company software by the manager/work shadowing a colleague.

  Off-the-job training: This means training that takes place outside the work place, usually with specialist trainers. It could be lectures, demonstrations or university courses, all at venues away from the workplace, e.g. staff being sent on a training course at an outside venue.

- Development involves preparing the employees to take on new/extra responsibility and new/greater challenges in the workplace.
- **Includes:** Employees taking certificate/diploma/degree/post-graduate courses, management courses, which would enable them to take on other tasks in future.
- It prepares employees for promotion, increases their self-esteem and gives them a broader understanding of the business.
- However, it can be costly for the firm; other employees may resent not being offered courses; trained employees might transfer to another firm.

(ii) Recruitment

Recruitment means the process of attracting suitable candidates to apply for vacancies in a firm. It involves job description, person specification, advertising and receiving applications.

Internal recruitment

Internal recruitment means finding someone from among those who already work in the business. It involves offering a position to an existing employee. It can involve promoting an employee or asking an employee to move to a different department or office.

External recruitment

External recruitment means finding someone who does not already work in the business. It involves offering a position in the business to someone from outside the business. An individual from outside the business can bring a fresh perspective, new ideas or greater expertise.

Job description

This document shows details of the position/vacancy to be filled, including the job title, work details, duties and responsibilities of the job, conditions of employment and place of work.

Person specification

This describes the qualities that the successful candidate for the job should have. These would include academic qualifications, previous work experience and relevant personal characteristics and skills.

Selection

Deciding on the most suitable candidate for the position. This involves screening, short-listing, interviews/aptitude tests, reference checks, making an offer to a successful candidate, drawing up an employment contract, and notifying unsuccessful candidates.

(iii) Employer/employee relations

It is essential to maintain good industrial relations in an organisation. This results in positive attitudes from staff, higher productivity, co-operation and a good atmosphere in the workplace.

Poor relations would lead to lack of motivation, stress, disputes, absenteeism and low productivity.

HR manager must:

- Establish agreed procedures for dealing with issues/disputes
- Create a pleasant work environment
- Communicate openly, honestly and fairly with employees
- Meet regularly with shop steward and listen to employees' grievances
- Organise social activities for employees
- Facilitate training/management courses for employees
- Ensure health/safety/welfare of employees is prioritised.

Outline the financial rewards used for motivating employees.

(15 marks)

Source: 2017 Higher Level Section 3

Suggested solution

Time rate

The employee is rewarded with a fixed amount per hour for a fixed number of hours. Hours worked over and above the fixed number of hours are paid at a higher rate called overtime, e.g. time and a half or double time.

Piece rate

The employee is rewarded per item produced/job completed. This method may lead to quality control problems as employees may try to get as many items produced as possible to increase his/her earnings.

Commission

The employees are paid a **percentage of the total sales** they have achieved. This is normally paid in addition to a flat payment. It has the advantage of directly encouraging sales.

Salary

A salary is paid to the employees in equal amounts, either weekly, biweekly or monthly.

Benefit-in-kind (if taxable)

The use of an asset as a form of reward, e.g. company car available for private use. It could include preferential loans, free or subsidised accommodation, etc.

Bonus

A sum of money raised for reaching a certain target, e.g. producing units above an agreed limit.

Profit-sharing scheme

This is a scheme where some of the business profits are paid to employees on an agreed basis. The scheme is administered and profits are paid to employees to motivate them and to become more productive.

Employee shared ownership scheme

Shares may be given to staff instead of cash bonuses, maintaining employee interest in the job. Share option schemes give employees an option to buy shares in a company at a specified price some time in the future.

Marking scheme

3 × 5 marks (2 + 3 Name, explain)

Read the information below and answer the questions which follow.

SuperSave

SuperSave, a supermarket chain located in the south-west, is considering updating its IT system to link all its stores and to modernise all its operations. It intends to implement a new Quality Assurance programme throughout all its stores. It is also considering a major recruitment campaign.

Discuss the benefits of both internal and external recruitment for management positions for a business such as SuperSave.

(20 marks)

Source: 2016 Higher Level Section 3

Suggested solution

Benefits of internal recruitment

Morale improves in business as staff have greater variety and promotion opportunities/career progression. It can act as a motivator and strengthen employee commitment to the business.

Employees skills, capabilities and attitude to work will be well known by management.

Employee has a working knowledge of how the firm operates – reduces need for cost of induction training.

Reduces labour turnover as the opportunity for promotion exists.

Less disruption within the business; vacancy can be filled quicker and cheaper; reduced cost of advertising, etc.

Benefits of external recruitment

Best candidate for the job can be recruited; wider range of candidates.

New employee brings fresh ideas; more open to change.

Wide ranging experience from previous employment/better skill set/higher calibre.

No existing relationships in the business – may reduce chance of conflict; less tension among existing staff.

Marking scheme

Four points @ 5 marks each (2 + 3)

(Two internal, two external required)

Outline the benefits of *performance appraisal* for **employees** in a business.

(15 marks)

Source: 2016 Higher Level Section 3

Suggested solution

Rewards/Monetary and non-monetary: It may be used in determining pay increases for employees and other awards such as share option schemes, benefits in kind, etc.

Motivation/Job satisfaction: Performance appraisal is important for staff motivation, communicating and fostering a positive relationship between management and staff; it ensures a high performance standard, where staff work to their full potential and are happy in the job.

Industrial relations: Potential conflicts in the workplace may be highlighted through performance appraisals. This enables the business to help address and solve problems or resolve issues between management and employees and helps improve industrial relations in the workplace and provide clarifications.

Training and development: The performance appraisal interview can identify training and career development needs for employees and provide appropriate training. Can evaluate the effectiveness of training programmes already provided.

Feedback: It provides an opportunity for employees to give and receive feedback, which may improve the employee's job satisfaction/motivation.

Evaluate the performance of management and employees: The goals set the previous year and the employee's achievements during the year are discussed and reviewed. Problem areas are identified. Priorities and goals are set by mutual consent for the following year. There is two-way communication and the employees are appraised on their own performance.

Promotion path/Recognition: This identifies hidden strengths in employees, which can be used and recognised. Achievements are recognised through promotion; helps promotion decisions.

Marking scheme
Four points × 5 marks (2 + 2 + 1)

Name – 2 marks

Explain – 2 marks

How it benefits employees – 1 mark

Outline the benefits of *teamwork* for the employees in a business.

(15 marks)

Source: 2011 Higher Level Section 3

Suggested solution
Employees experience **greater job satisfaction** as all members' efforts are taken into account. They are better motivated as participation in teams satisfies the social needs of employees (Maslow).

Employees' **communications skills and interpersonal skills** improve as they are working in a group and dealing with different personalities. This is a good experience for employees, as effective communication skills will help prepare employees for leadership roles within the business.

When working in isolation, employees might find it difficult to make **tough decisions**. However, with the mutual support and protection of a team, these tough decisions are easier for employees to make, e.g. a decision on making workers redundant.

Successful teams progress through the team development stages of forming, storming, norming and performing. A successful team will mean **less industrial relations problems and less conflict**, saving the employee the stress associated with industrial action.

Marking scheme
3 × 5 marks (2 + 3)

13 Changing Role of Management

The changing role of management

People working in management today have to cope with rapid change.

The following are among the factors that force managers to change.

1. Changing consumers

Management must respond to changes in consumer tastes and focus on high-quality goods and services to achieve customer satisfaction.

2. Changing technology

There have been rapid developments in ICT in recent years. The advent of video-conferencing, e-business and the internet has led to significant changes in the conduct of business. As a result, most organisations are in a state of change.

3. Changing employees

Employees are better educated and want a say in decision-making. Companies must respond to this change and provide opportunities for employees.

4. Competition

Organisations face competition on a global scale, so in order to compete, smaller firms have to change their structures and operations.

5. Changing legislation

Management must respond to new Irish and EU laws that affect business (e.g. employment laws, consumer rights, etc.).

Change from controller to facilitator

In a changing business world, businesses must change their management style from 'controller' to 'facilitator'.

Controller manager

The manager was:

- The Boss – Gave orders to employees which are to be carried out without question.
- The Controller – Constant supervision and direction from manager – employees had no say in decision-making.
- The Critic – Told employees where they went wrong.
- The Expert – Knew all the answers – employees did it his/her way.

Facilitator manager

The manager is:

- **The Leader** – Gives direction.
- **The Coach/Trainer** – Trains employees to develop their skills and fully utilises their talents.
- **The Resource Provider** – Provides all the necessary resources to carry out the job (finance, training, technology).
- **The Facilitator** – Does the following:
  - Provides advice and support
  - Delegates responsibility to employees
  - Encourages new ideas
  - Consults staff on issues concerning their job
  - Promotes new relationships through involvement and empowerment of employees.

Employee participation

Achieving employee participation

Employee participation can be achieved by:

- Involving employees in the affairs of the firm
- Offering share ownership
- Job enlargement, rotation, enrichment.

Involving employees in the affairs of the firm

This can be achieved through:

- **Work councils** – Allows representatives of the workers to have a say in the plans and strategies of the firm.
- **Worker directors** – Employees are elected to the board of directors. This gives employees a say in decision-making.

Offering share ownership

Employees are given an opportunity to purchase shares in the company. They become owners and have a vote at the AGM.

Job enlargement, rotation, enrichment

Employees can also participate in the organisation through:

- Job Enlargement
- Job Rotation
- Job Enrichment.

Job Enlargement

- Increasing the number of tasks in the job.
- Provides more varied work and reduces boredom.

Job Rotation

- Switching workers between a number of jobs.
- Greater variety will lead to greater job satisfaction.

Job Enrichment

- Employees are given a variety of more difficult tasks with more authority and more responsibility.

Empowerment

Empowerment is placing real power, responsibility and decision-making in the hands of the workers who work close to the customer.

Empowerment is more than delegation in that real power is given to employees, including the freedom to decide what to do and how to do it. Employees are then responsible for the achievement of the goals set.

Workers who deal with customers every day are given great influence over the operation of the enterprise. Decision-making and control is in the hands of the workers, who use their skill and knowledge in the interests of the organisation.

BENEFITS OF EMPOWERMENT IN ORGANISATIONS

- Improved service to customers.
- Improved morale – Workers have control over how they work.
- Improved skills – Gives the workers the opportunity to improve existing skills and develop new skills.
- Improved motivation – Empowerment allows staff to influence business decisions.
- Improved productivity – Empowerment makes the working of the organisation more effective and because employees are using their own initiative, productivity is improved.

Total quality management (TQM)

Total quality management is a process which tries to ensure quality in all aspects of a firm's operation so that it can produce the best products or services for its customers.

Total quality management puts the focus of the firm into meeting and satisfying the needs of its customers. Employees are given responsibility to ensure that the products meet the requirements of customers.

There are basically **five principles** to a TQM approach:
1. Focus on customers
2. Continuous improvement
3. Empowerment
4. Teamwork
5. Quality assurance

1. Focus on customers

Business must find out what customers want and then make that product to meet their requirements.

2. Continuous improvement

To achieve continuous improvement, management must concentrate on improving processes and products, improving quality and reducing costs.

Continuous improvement is a step-by-step bettering of business processes.

3. Empowerment

TQM will not happen without the empowerment of workers. They must be given real power, including the responsibly and authority to decide what to do. They must be allowed make decisions and changes where necessary to improve the quality of the product.

4. Teamwork

For TQM to succeed, there must be teamwork – people working in groups to achieve improvement in specific areas. The sharing of ideas and solving of problems together in groups makes work more rewarding and satisfying.

5. Quality assurance

Quality assurance means management ensuring that the product or service is of the highest quality and that quality standards are agreed and met throughout the organisation to insure customer satisfaction. Quality must be the responsibility of all employees.

BENEFITS OF TOTAL QUALITY MANAGEMENT IN ORGANISATIONS

- Improved quality – There should be an improvement in the quality of products produced.
- Reduction in cost – There will be less waste.
- Workers are better motivated – Because they see management are committed to quality.
- Increased sales – The firm will develop a reputation for providing quality goods, which will increase sales.
- Increased customer satisfaction – Products and services are of the highest standard.

Strategies for managing change

1. Management Commitment

There must be total senior management commitment for the proposed changes. If this is not present, the change process will not progress.

2. Consultation

Consultation must take place with trade unions and employee representatives regarding the proposed changes and the effects of the change on them. Employees must understand fully the implications of change on them.

3. Communication

Effective communication between all parties throughout the change process is essential. This will reduce uncertainty and insecurity.

4. Negotiation

Negotiations between management and employees on options for implementing change, remuneration packages, productivity agreements, changes in work practices and a general improvement in working conditions may all be part of the change process.

5. Funding

Finance is required for training and retraining of employees in the new skills needed to do the work as a result of the change.

6. Reward

Employees must be rewarded for implementing the change process. This means remuneration packages for staff.

Managing technology

How technology has changed the way management operates

Technology has changed the way management operates in the following ways:

1. Information and Communication Technology (ICT)

Management use technology to communicate developments. The use of the internet, email, EDI, fax and videoconferencing have greatly facilitated information exchange.

Electronic Data Interchange (EDI) – used to exchange business documents in a highly **efficient way**.

Videoconferencing – This enables people in businesses worldwide to communicate person-to-person.

2. Decision-making

Management use computers for financial forecasting and planning. Data can be downloaded, enabling them to make critical decisions more quickly.

3. Production

Advances in production technologies have resulted in higher levels of automation. For example,

- **Computer-Aided Design (CAD)** allows a business to design new products or **redesign existing products**.
- **Computer-Aided Manufacture (CAM)** is computer software that controls the manufacturing process.

4. Motivation

Many organisations are using computers, the internet and fax to enable employees and managers to work from home – Teleworking. Productivity and motivation may increase because employees are free to work at home at their own pace.

5. Marketing

Most companies use a website to advertise and sell their goods and services. Market research can also be carried out on the internet.

Impact of technology on personnel

- **Teleworking**

ICT enables managers and employees to work on a computer from home or from other remote locations and be linked to the office computer. The time and cost of travelling to and from work is reduced.

- **Reduced workforce**

Technology has replaced many jobs leading to redundancies. Fewer workers are required in offices and on production lines.

- **Training**

In many occupations, the training of workers can be done by or with the help of computers and the many different software packages available.

- **Job satisfaction**

Technology makes routine or boring tasks easy to carry out, increasing job satisfaction.

Impact of technology on business costs

The introduction of technology may **increase business costs** in the following ways:

- **Investment in technology**

There is a high capital cost associated with new communication and production technology, including installation and maintenance costs.

- **Training costs**

Training costs can be high and must be ongoing to keep up-to-date with technological developments.

New technology can also reduce business costs

The introduction of technology may **reduce business costs** in the following ways:

- **Better quality goods** – Better quality products, less waste and fewer complaints can lead to significant cost savings.
- **Reduced administration costs** – Teleworking reduces the amount of office space required and reduces administration costs.
- **Less Travel** – Videoconferencing reduces the amount of travel to meetings.

Impact of technology on business opportunities

- **New products** – Some new products owe their existence and success to technology (e.g. reserving airline seats and hotel reservations from any part of the world at any time).
- **Marketing** – Many businesses now use the internet to market their goods and services. By creating a website, a large number of potential customers can be reached at minimal cost.
- **New methods of conducting business for individuals** – Using a home computer or laptop allows people to engage in many business-related activities from home (using online banking, seeking insurance quotes, working from a home office, etc.).
- **E-business** – Many business functions can be carried out using the internet (e.g. EDI [Electronic Data Interchange], where goods can be ordered automatically from a supplier when stocks fall below a certain level).

HL

Discuss the benefits **and** risks of empowering employees within a business.

(20 marks)

Source: 2012 Higher Level Section 3

Suggested solution

Benefits

- Decision-making and control is in the hands of employees who use their greater skills and knowledge for the benefit of the business; decisions are made quicker.
- Employees become more responsive to the needs of customers and come up with ideas to solve issues leading to more satisfied customers.
- Employees are more motivated, have greater job satisfaction. They feel valued, which improves morale and increases loyalty.
- Employees are better trained and better prepared for promotion.
- Management can focus on strategic planning.

Risks

- If empowerment is introduced without adequate training for employees, then mistakes can be made.
- Employees may be unhappy with the extra responsibility and/or lack of training and their stress levels may increase. This can cause demotivation among employees.
- The lack of control and day-to-day supervision may encourage some empowered employees to take unnecessary risks, leading to bad decision-making.
- Empowerment means management are handing over control, responsibility and power to subordinates. Some managers may be cautious of this reallocation of power and loss of control. This can lead to conflict between themselves and employees.

Marking scheme

4 × 5 marks (2 + 3)

(At least one benefit and one risk required)

Outline **two** strategies that management could use to help employees adapt to change.

(10 marks)

Source: 2011 Higher Level Section 1

Suggested solution

Benefits

1. Management need to **communicate** clearly why change is necessary and the consequences of not taking any action. For example, management could point out that increased competition may lead to a loss of market share and redundancies, and that a change in work practices involving greater productivity is a strategy that could prevent this. It will reduce uncertainty and tension among employees.

2. Management needs to **consult** with the employees before introducing change so that employees will be more willing to accept the changes introduced (inputting into the decisions made).

3. Management needs to **reward** employees for embracing change, e.g. bonus payments and wage increases for accepting and using new technology.

Other strategies could include empowerment, total quality management (TQM), training, industrial democracy, teamwork and adequate funding.

Marking scheme

Two strategies @ 5 marks each (3 + 2)

Monitoring the Business

aims Be able to:

- Understand the importance of accounts and business data in the monitoring of the business enterprise.
- Calculate and interpret the main profitability, liquidity ratios and debt–equity ratio.

Accounts and business information

Financial information tells the owners or shareholders and the management how the business is performing and allows them to make decisions. It also provides useful information to other interested parties.

Trading account

This shows the gross profit or gross loss made by a business in the trading period.

Gross profit is the profit made by buying and selling goods before deducting expenses.

key point

Final Accounts

The financial statements used by a business are:

- Trading account
- Profit and loss account
- Balance sheet

> Sales − Cost of Sales = Gross Profit/Loss

> Cost of Sales = Opening Stock + Purchases − Closing Stock

Profit and loss account

This shows the net profit or net loss made by a business in the trading period that is profit after deducting expenses.

> Gross Profit − Expenses = Net Profit

Balance sheet

A balance sheet is a statement of assets, liabilities and share capital of a business on a particular day.

A balance sheet shows:

- **Assets:** Profit a business owns.
- **Fixed assets:** Permanent assets in the business.
- **Current assets:** Assets that can be easily turned into cash (e.g. stock, debtors, bank, cash).
- **Liabilities:** Debts that a business owes.
- **Current liabilities:** Debts that have to be repaid within one year (e.g. creditors, bank overdraft, expenses due).
- **Long-term liabilities:** Debts that will be repaid in the long term (e.g. mortgage, long-term loans).
- **Share capital:** Money invested in the company by its owners or shareholders.
- **Reserves:** Retained earnings built up over a number of years and used to finance expansion.
- **Working capital:** Money available to pay short-term debts as they arise. It is calculated by deducting current liabilities from current assets.

Current Assets − Current Liabilities = Working Capital

If current assets are greater than current liabilities, working capital is positive and the firm is said to be liquid.

If current liabilities are greater than current assets, working capital is negative and the firm is said to have a liquidity problem and to be overtrading, i.e. cannot pay its debts as they arise.

Interpretation of accounts using ratios

A company can be assessed in the following areas:
- **Profitability:** Profitability ratios measure the efficiency of a firm in generating profit.
- **Liquidity:** Liquidity ratios measure the ability of a business to pay its short-term debts.
- **Debt–Equity:** Ratio that identifies how the business is structured financially.

1. Profitability ratios

Profitability ratios shows how successful the management was in making profit in the business.

The profitability ratios are:

- Return on Capital Employed/Return on Investment
- Gross Profit Percentage/Margin
- Net Profit Percentage/Margin.

	Ratio	Formula	Information Given by Ratio
1.	Return on Capital Employed/Return on Investment	$\dfrac{\text{Net Profit} \times 100}{\text{Capital Employed}}$ Ans = %	Shows the return on the total amount of money invested in the business. Should be compared with the return from risk-free investments in financial institutions.
2.	Gross Profit Percentage/Margin	$\dfrac{\text{Gross Profit} \times 100}{\text{Sales}}$ Ans = %	This is gross profit as a percentage of sales. This is profit made from buying and selling before paying expenses.
3.	Net Profit Percentage/Margin	$\dfrac{\text{Net Profit} \times 100}{\text{Sales}}$ Ans = %	This is net profit as a percentage of sales. This is profit made after payment of expenses.

Question and Solution – Profitability Ratios

Financial information published in financial statements such as profit and loss accounts and balance sheets are useful for decision-making. Consider the following figures and answer the questions that follow:

	2017	2018
	€	€
Sales	400,000	500,000
Expenses	40,000	50,000
Net Profit	60,000	70,000
Capital Employed	600,000	650,000

(i) For 2017 and 2018 calculate the gross profit margin, the net profit margin and the return on investment.

(ii) Analyse these profitability trends and discuss how shareholders might use them in making decisions.

(40 marks)

Suggested solution

(i)

Profitability Ratios	Formula	2017	2018
1. Gross Profit Margin	$\dfrac{\text{Gross Profit} \times 100}{\text{Sales}}$ ❷	* $\dfrac{100,000 \times 100}{400,000}$ ❸ ❶ 25% ❶	* $\dfrac{120,000 \times 100}{500,000}$ ❸ ❶ 24% ❶
2. Net Profit Margin	$\dfrac{\text{Net Profit} \times 100}{\text{Sales}}$ ❷	$\dfrac{60,000 \times 100}{400,000}$ ❶ ❶ 15% ❶	$\dfrac{70,000 \times 100}{500,000}$ ❶ ❶ 14% ❶
3. Return on Investment	$\dfrac{\text{Net Profit} \times 100}{\text{Capital Employed}}$ ❷	$\dfrac{60,000 \times 100}{600,000}$ ❶ ❶ 10% ❶	$\dfrac{70,000 \times 100}{650,000}$ ❶ ❶ 10.76% ❶

Net Profit + Expenses
* 2017 Gross Profit = 40,000 + 60,000 = 100,000
Net Profit + Expenses
* 2018 Gross Profit = 70,000 + 50,000 = 120,000

(ii)

The gross profit margin has decreased from 25% in 2017 to 24% in 2018. This indicates that the firm's profitability has decreased, and it is less efficient in buying and selling, even though sales and gross profit both increased.   (2 marks)

The net profit margin has decreased from 15% in 2017 to 14% in 2018. The firm's profitability has disimproved over the year, even though the net profit has increased from €60,000 to €70,000. The expenses increased from €40,000 to €50,000, and as the net profit is calculated after deducting expenses, this indicates that the firm is less efficient at controlling expenses in 2018.

Expenses must be examined closely for possible savings and unusual unnecessary increases, and controlled.   (2 marks)

Return on investment has improved from 10% in 2017 to 10.76% in 2018. A return of 10.76% is very good when compared with the return from risk-free investment of 2% to 3% at present.   (2 marks)

How Shareholders Might Use Profitability Ratios When Making Decisions

Profitability ratios are very useful to shareholders when making decisions about their investment in a business:

- return on investment shows the return on the total funds invested in the business. It indicates how successful management was in making profit in the business. (2 marks)
- shareholders are to invest in business the return on investment should be higher than the return to be earned elsewhere in banks, building societies or other risk-free investments because of the element of risk involved. (2 marks)
- In this business, the return in 2018 of 10.76% would be attractive to shareholders as it is much better than alternative investments. (2 marks)

2. Liquidity ratios

Liquidity is the ability of a business to pay its short-term debts as they arise. It is measured by subtracting current liabilities from current assets.

Current Assets – Current Liabilities = Working Capital

Working capital is the day-to-day finance available for running a business. If working capital is positive, the firm is said to be **liquid**. If working capital is negative, the firm is said to be **overtrading**, i.e. it cannot pay its debts as they arise.

The liquidity ratios are:

1. Current Ratio/Working Capital Ratio
2. Acid Test Ratio/Quick Acid Ratio

	Ratio	Formula	Information Given by Ratio
1.	Current Ratio	$\dfrac{\text{Current Assets}}{\text{Current Liabilities}}$	Tells us whether the company has enough current assets to pay its current liabilities. The recommended ratio is 2:1 – that is, current assets should be double current liabilities.
2.	Acid Test Ratio	$\dfrac{\text{Current Assets} - \text{Closing Stock}}{\text{Current Liabilities}}$	This ratio measures a firm's ability to meet its short-term debts out of liquid assets. Stock is omitted from current assets as it may not be quickly turned into cash. Thus it is a better measure of liquidity. The recommended ratio is 1:1, so that a healthy firm should have €1 in liquid assets for every €1 owed in short-term debts.

Question and Solution – Liquidity Ratios

Examine the following figures from Savin Ltd.

HL

	2017	2016
Current Assets	€91,500	€80,450
Current Liabilities	€62,400	€43,200
Closing Stock	€49,000	€40,100

(i) Calculate for 2017 and 2016:
- Current Ratio
- Acid Test Ratio

(ii) Applying your knowledge, comment on two trends that you notice developing in the business. Suggest what you would do about them.

(30 marks)

Suggested solution
(i)

Ratio	Formula	2017	2016
Current Ratio	$\dfrac{\text{Current Assets}}{\text{Current Liabilities}}$ ❷	❶ $\dfrac{91,500}{62,400}$ ❶ 1.46:1 ❶	❶ $\dfrac{80,450}{43,200}$ ❶ 1.86:1 ❶ *want* 2:1
Acid Test Ratio	$\dfrac{\text{Current Assets} - \text{Closing Stock}}{\text{Current Liabilities}}$ ❷	❶ $\dfrac{91,500 - 49,000}{62,400}$ ❶ ❶ $\dfrac{42,500}{62,400}$ ❶ 0.68:1 ❶	❶ $\dfrac{80,450 - 40,100}{43,200}$ ❶ ❶ $\dfrac{40,340}{43,200}$ ❶ 0.93:1 ❶ *want* 1:1

(18 marks)

(ii) **Trends and Suggestions**

Current Ratio

Trends Developing

The ratio has decreased from 1.86:1 in 2016 to 1.46:1 in 2017. This is well below the ideal ratio of 2:1. The trend shows a worsening of the liquidity in the business. This has been **caused** by a large increase in current liabilities. (3 marks)

Suggestions for Action
Some action is necessary to improve the situation. Current liabilities have to be reduced by raising cash from some source, perhaps by selling stock at reduced prices to increase cash flow and so pay creditors and a bank overdraft. Reducing the length of credit to debtors would also improve the liquidity position. (3 marks)

Acid Test Ratio
Trends Developing
The acid test ratio has disimproved from 0.93:1 to 0.68:1. Both of these ratios are well below the ideal ratio of 1:1 and indicate that the firm will have difficulty in paying its debts as they fall due. The business has only got 68 cent available to pay each €1 of short-term debts. (3 marks)

Suggestions for Action
Cash must be obtained from some source. Maybe giving discounts to debtors to pay quickly would allow the firm to reduce its current liabilities. (3 marks)

3. Debt–equity ratio

This shows the relationship between debt capital and equity capital in a company.

Debt Capital = Long-term debt
Equity Capital = Ordinary Share Capital + Reserves

Debt Capital : Equity Capital

The ratio shows how much the business has borrowed relative to amount invested by owners:

- **Low Gearing**: Debt capital is less than equity capital. This means business has borrowed less money than the amount invested by shareholders.
- **High Gearing**: Debt capital is greater than equity capital. This means business has borrowed more money than the amount invested by shareholders.
- **Neutral Gearing**: Debt capital = equity capital. The business has borrowed the same amount of money as that invested by shareholders.

Advantages of low debt–equity ratio (low gearing)

1. **Owner's Capital**
   A greater amount of the capital of the company is provided by the owners.
2. **More Profit Available for Dividends**
   As there are no major interest commitments, a large proportion of the profits is available to pay dividends or to reinvest in the company.

3. **Easier to Borrow in the Future**

The business can borrow more easily in the future.

4. **Easy to Sell Shares in the Future**

It should be easier to sell additional shares in the future because of good dividends to shareholders.

Consequences of high debt–equity ratio (high gearing)

1. **High Interest**

High interest payments on borrowings must be met before the company can pay dividends to shareholders.

2. **Difficult to Sell Shares in the Future**

It may be difficult to sell shares in the future because of the poor outlook on dividends.

3. **Difficult to Borrow in Future**

Additional borrowings may be almost impossible to get since assets will have been used as security for loans already issued.

4. **Low Dividends–Low Share Price**

If profits fall, interest on loans must still be paid. There may be little profit left to pay dividends to shareholders. Shareholders may become dissatisfied with their investment and may sell their shares, resulting in a fall in the share price.

Question and Solution – Debt–Equity Ratios

(i) Using the figures given below, calculate the debt–equity ratio of SES Ltd for the years 2016 and 2017. (Show your workings.)

	2016	2017
Long-term Loans	300,000	364,000
Ordinary Share Capital	450,000	450,000
Retained Earnings	50,000	70,000

(ii) Comment on the significance of the trend in the debt–equity ratio over the two years for the existing shareholders.

(20 marks)

Suggested solution

(i) The debt–equity ratio provides an indication of the financial structure/gearing of the business.

> The debt–equity ratio is calculated as follows:
> Debt Capital : Equity Capital

	2016	2017
Debt–Equity Ratio	❶ ❷ 300,000:500,000 0.6:1 ❷	❶ ❷ 364,000:520,000 0.7:1 ❷

(2 Calculations @ 5 marks (1 + 2 + 2))

(ii) Significance of the trend in the debt–equity ratio over the two years for the existing shareholders.

The debt–equity ratio in 2016 was 0.6:1, while the debt–equity ratio for 2017 has **increased** to 0.7:1. This is a worrying trend for the existing shareholders.

Significance

- Higher interest payments may reduce profits.
- If profits fall, the payment of dividends to ordinary shareholders will be affected.
- Reduction in dividends may lead ordinary shareholders to sell their shares. The increased supply of shares on the market will reduce the market price of the shares.

(2 Comments @ 4 marks each (2 + 2))

The importance of the profit and loss account and balance sheet for the good financial management of a business

Profit and loss account

The profit and loss account has two sections:

- Trading account
- Profit and loss account.

Trading Account

The trading account shows:

- **Sales** – cash sales and credit sales
- **Cost of sales** – all costs incurred producing the goods

> Cost of sales = opening stock + purchases – closing stock

- **Gross profit** – profits after all the costs have been taken away

$$\text{Sales} - \text{Cost of Sales} = \text{Gross Profit}$$

Profit and Loss Account

All expenses of the business are deducted from gross profit to arrive at net profit.

$$\text{Gross Profit} - \text{Expenses} = \text{Net Profit}$$

THE IMPORTANCE OF THE PROFIT AND LOSS ACCOUNT

The profit and loss account shows:

- The figure for **net profit** for the year. By comparing the figure with the previous year the performance of the business can be assessed.
- The level of **expenses**. If expenses have increased from the previous year, they must be investigated and controlled to increase profits.
- How much of the net profit **is retained** in the business and how much is distributed to the shareholders in **dividends**. Prudent financial management ensures that the level of profit retained is adequate for future expansion or investment.

Balance sheet

A balance sheet is a statement of assets, liabilities and capital of a business on a particular day.

Assets

- **Fixed assets**: Permanent assets in the business (e.g. land, buildings and machinery).
- **Current assets**: Assets held in the business for less than one year (e.g. stock, debtor's cash and bank).

Liabilities

- **Current liabilities**: Amounts the business owes and are due to be paid within one year (e.g. creditors, bank overdraft, accrued expenses).
- **Long-term liabilities**: Debts that will be repaid in the long term, i.e. over five to 25 years (e.g. long-term loans).
- **Share capital**: Money invested by the owners, which made up of issued share capital and profit and loss account.

THE IMPORTANCE OF THE BALANCE SHEET

The balance sheet shows:

- The **value** of the fixed assets in a business and whether there is adequate **security** available for future borrowings.
- The company's **liquidity position** – the ability of the firm to pay its debts as they arise. Working capital is calculated by deducting current liabilities from current assets. The current ratio should be 2:1, otherwise the firm may be in danger of overtrading.
- How the business is **financed**. The debt–equity ratio compares the amount of equity in the business with the amount of debt capital. The lower the ratio, the less is being paid out in interest payments.

Users of accounts and business information

The following parties are interested in the performance of a business.

1. **Owners/shareholders**

   Owners/shareholders will be interested in:
   - How much profit the business made.
   - How much they can expect in dividends.
   - The value and security of their investment.

2. **Management**

   Accounting information is important to management in assessing the performance of a business. It is also useful in decision-making.

3. **Financial institutions**

   Financial institutions will be interested in:
   - The liquidity position of the firm and its ability to pay interest and repay loans and overdrafts when due.
   - Whether to give finance to the firm in the future.

4. **Creditors and suppliers**

   Creditors and suppliers will be interested in the liquidity position of the business and in particular:
   - Whether it can pay for goods supplied on credit.
   - Whether it is advisable to give credit in the future.

5. **Potential investors**

   Investors will be interested in:
   - The return on their investment in dividends.
   - The long-term share values and security of investment.

6. **Employees**

Employees will want to assess:
- Security of employment and prospects of promotion.
- The future prospects of the company.
- The company's ability to meet wage demands in the future.

7. **Revenue Commissioners**

The Revenue Commissioners require accounts and information to accurately calculate the tax liability of the organisation.

(i) Using two ratios in each case, analyse the profitability and liquidity trends in Calty Construction Co. Ltd, from the following figures for 2017 and 2018.

(ii) Suggest how the trends might be improved.

	2017	2018
Current Assets	15,900	16,800
Net Profit	15,100	12,285
Equity Share Capital	100,000	105,000
Current Liabilities	8,100	7,400
Closing Stock	9,100	12,400
Gross Profit	45,150	40,950
Retained Earnings	20,000	21,000
Sales	169,500	157,500

(40 marks)

Suggested solution

(i)

(a) Gross Profit Margin

	2017	2018
$\dfrac{\text{Gross Profit} \times 100}{\text{Sales}}$ ❶	❶ $\dfrac{45,150 \times 100}{169,500}$ ❶	❶ $\dfrac{40,950 \times 100}{157,500}$ ❶
	= 26.64% ❶	= 26% ❶

The gross profit margins decreased from 26.64% in 2017 to 26% in 2018. The margin is steady, even though sales and gross profit have both decreased. ❷

(b) Net profit margin

	2017	2018
$\frac{\text{Net Profit} \times 100}{\text{Sales}}$ ❶	❶ $\frac{15{,}100 \times 100}{169{,}500}$ ❶	❶ $\frac{12{,}285 \times 100}{157{,}500}$ ❶
	= 8.9% ❶	= 7.8% ❶

The net profit margin decreased from 8.9% in 2017 to 7.8% in 2018. This reflects the reducing sales and gross profit figures. ❷

(c) Return on Investment

	2017	2018
$\frac{\text{Net Profit} \times 100}{\text{Capital Employed}}$ ❶	❶ $\frac{15{,}100 \times 100}{120{,}000}$ ❶	❶ $\frac{12{,}285 \times 100}{126{,}000}$ ❶
	= 12.58% ❶	= 9.75% ❶

The return on investment decreased from 12.58% in 2017 to 9.75 % in 2018.

It is still better than the return on risk-free investments of 2% to 3% at present. ❷

(d) Liquidity

Current Ratio	2017	2018
$\frac{\text{Current Assets}}{\text{Current Liabilities}}$ ❶	❶ $\frac{15{,}900}{8{,}100}$ ❶	❶ $\frac{16{,}800}{7{,}400}$ ❶
	= 1.96 : 1 ❶	= 2.27 : 1 ❶

The current ratio has increased from 1.96:1 in 2017 to 2.27:1 in 2018. It is slightly above the recommended ratio of 2:1. While current assets have increased and current liabilities decreased, the level of stock held has increased. There is a danger of obsolescence and increased costs for storage and insurance. ❷

(e) Acid Test Ratio

	2017	2018
$\frac{\text{Current Assets} - \text{Closing Stock}}{\text{Current Liabilities}}$ ❶	❶ $\frac{15{,}900 - 9{,}100}{8{,}100}$ ❶	❶ $\frac{16{,}800 - 12{,}400}{7{,}400}$ ❶
	$\frac{6{,}800}{8{,}100}$	$\frac{4{,}400}{7{,}400}$
	= 0.83 : 1 ❶	= 0.59 : 1 ❶

The acid test ratio has deteriorated from 0.83:1 in 2017 to 0.59:1 in 2018. The ratio in both years is well below the ideal ratio of 1:1 and indicates that the business will have difficulty in paying its debts as they fall due. The business has only 59 cent available to pay each €1 of short-term debts in 2018. (2 marks)

(ii)

1. A decline in the gross profit margin can be improved by:

   - Increasing selling price, if there has been an increase in cost of sales.
   - Changing the sales mix towards more products with a higher profit margin. (2 marks)

2. A decline in the net profit margin can be improved by:

   - Controlling expenses – all expenses areas should be examined and tightened for possible savings, and investigate unusual and unnecessary increases. (1 mark)

3. **Acid Test Ratio**

   The firm's liquidity position is deteriorating so cash must be obtained from some source by:

   - Giving discount to debtors to pay, thereby quickly improving the cash position, which would allow the firm to pay its current liabilities.
   - Selling stock at reduced prices to increase cash flow and pay current liabilities. (2 marks)

Marking scheme

Any two trends @ 2 marks each.

(A) Equinox Design Ltd is a graphic design business.

From the figures given for 2016, calculate the following for Equinox Design Ltd. (Show your workings.)

(i) Net profit margin

(ii) Current ratio

(iii) Return on investment

(iv) Debt–equity ratio

Equinox Design Limited: Information for 2016	
Sales	€200,000
Net Profit	€30,400
Current Assets	€20,000
Current Liabilities	€16,000
Issued Ordinary Share Capital	€300,000
Long-Term Loan	€400,000
Retained Earnings	€60,000

Equinox Design Limited: Results for 2015	
Net Profit Margin	20.5%
Current Ratio	2:1
Return on Investment	8%
Debt/Equity Ratio	0.7:1

(B) (i) Analyse the profitability **and** liquidity of Equinox Design Ltd for 2016, with reference to the results for 2015 shown in the box above.

(ii) Should Equinox Design Ltd expand its business? Outline one reason for your answer.

(iii) Outline **two** limitations of using ratios to analyse the final accounts of a business.

(25 marks)

Source: 2017 Higher Level Section 3

Suggested solution

(A) From the figures given below for 2016, calculate the following for Equinox Design Ltd. (Show your workings)

(i) Net profit margin 15.2%

(ii) Current ratio 1.25:1

(iii) Return on investment 4%

(iv) Debt–equity ratio: 1.1:1

Net Profit Margin	$\dfrac{\text{Net profit} \times 100}{\text{Sales (1m)}}$	$\dfrac{30,400 \times 100}{200,000 \text{ (1m)}}$	15.2% (1m)
Current ratio	Current Assets Current Liabilities (1m)	20,000:16,000 (1m) (1m)	1.25:1 (1m)
Debt–Equity ratio	Debt Capital : Equity Capital	$\dfrac{30,400 \text{ (1m)} \times 100}{300,000 + 400,000 + 60,000}$ (1m) + (1m) + (1m)	4% (1m)
Return on investment	$\dfrac{\text{Net Profit} \times 100}{\text{Capital Employed (1m)}}$	400,000:(300,000+60,000) (1m) + (1m) + (1m)	1.1:1 (2m)

Each formula and figure merits 1 mark, except the answer to Debt Equity, which merits 2 marks. Answers must be in the correct format to be awarded marks.

(B) (i) Profitability

The Net Profit Margin (NPM) has decreased from 20.5% to 15.2%

The Return on Investment (ROI) has decreased from 8% to 4%.

Analysis of trends: (Two trends)

NPM: A major review of its costs will be required as well as a review of its sales strategy; cheaper raw materials/increase selling prices.

This decrease in ROI (profitability) will concern the shareholders of the business, as they may get a better return for their investment elsewhere.

Liquidity

The Current Ratio has decreased from 2:1 to 1.25:1

Analysis of trend:

This is unsatisfactory for the business, as while still having enough to pay their short-term debts, liquidity has declined. This will be of concern to supplier. Could sell off slow-moving lines to improve liquidity, etc.

(ii) No.

The business should not expand as all key financial indicators are in decline.

OR

It may find it difficult to acquire long-term finance for expansion as the debt–equity ratio has increased. Interest must be paid irrespective of profits. Debt finance is already at €400,000.

(iii) Financial ratios do not consider the following:

1. Staff relations with management not taken into account and the climate in business is difficult to assess.

2. **Assets** may not be shown at their true value.

3. Ratios are based on **past** figures and not on projected future figures.

4. Final Accounts only hold for a **certain** year. Balance Sheets are only true for the **day they are written**.

5. Does not consider business environment, i.e. **competition/recession/outside influences, etc.**

6. **Inflation/deflation** may impede the comparison of ratios from one period to another.

7. **Different accounting policies may be** used from one year to the next.

Marking scheme

(i) Profitability: 8 marks
- NPM trend, 2 marks
- ROI Trend, 2 marks
- Analysis of both trends, 2 marks + 2 marks

Liquidity: 6 marks
- Trend, 2 marks
- Analysis of trend 2 + 2 marks

(ii) Should Equinox Design Ltd expand its business? (2 marks)
Outline one reason for your answer. (3 marks)

(iii) Outline **two** limitations of using ratios to analyse Final
Accounts of a business. 6 marks (2 + 4)

The following figures are taken from the final accounts of Flame Ltd for 2013.

Flame Ltd	2013
	€
Authorised Share Capital	900,000
Issued Share Capital	450,000
Long-Term Loan	200,000
Retained Earnings	150,000

(i) Explain the term 'debt–equity ratio'.
(ii) Calculate the debt–equity ratio for 2013. (Show your workings.)
(iii) Discuss the importance of the debt–equity ratio when deciding on new
sources of finance for Flame Ltd.

(20 marks)

Source: 2014 Higher Level Section 3

Suggested solution

(i) The debt–equity ratio is an analysis of the capital structure of the business.
It indicates what proportion of capital is made up of long-term loans and what
proportion of capital is made up of reserves and issued ordinary share capital.

(ii)

Debt	: Equity
200,000	: 450,000 + 150,000
200,000	: 600,000
.33	:1

(iii)

- Flame Ltd is a lowly geared company, which means the majority of the capital has been provided by the owners in the form of share capital and retained earnings.
- Flame Ltd can raise further capital by selling shares up to a limit of €450,000 (Authorised – Issued).
- Raising finance through additional loans is an option for Flame Ltd because it does not have too many existing loans, as it is lowly geared.

Marking scheme

(i) 4 marks (2 + 2)

(ii) 10 marks:
- Formula 2 marks each
- Three figures @ 2 marks each
- Answer 2 marks

(iii) 6 marks (3 + 2 any two points)

Applied Business Question (ABQ) (Higher Level)

Based on Units 2, 3 and 4

This is a compulsory question for Leaving Certificate 2020/2025

Harte Shoes Ltd

Harte Shoes Ltd is a small family-run manufacturing business located in Monaghan, which has operated in the highly competitive footwear industry since the 1970s. At its peak, the company employed highly skilled shoemakers and a very effective sales team. Martin Harte, the owner, began to realise that the centuries-old footwear industry was in decline, largely as a result of cheaper imports from manufacturers in Eastern Europe. He decided to review the company's corporate strategy in order to make his company viable in the future.

His solution was based on the ever-increasing popularity of Irish dance worldwide. The outstanding success of productions such as *Riverdance*, *Lord of the Dance* and the popularity of competitions such as the Irish dance World Championships have seen a global increase in the numbers of girls and boys learning Irish dancing. Martin's goal was to create a range of soft and hard dance shoes, using the finest and most durable leather, and so well engineered that they would provide protection and comfort for Irish dancers worldwide.

He sought the assistance of Enterprise Ireland's 'Get Export Ready' scheme. Enterprise Ireland appointed Christine Landers, a Development Adviser, to Harte Shoes Ltd and she carried out a SWOT analysis. From this, it was clear that Harte Shoes Ltd had manufacturing expertise and that growing markets existed in the UK, America and Australia, due to the global popularity of Irish dancing. However, she noted the lack of a computer-aided design system (CAD) to assist with the production of shoes, especially in light of the fact that competitors from Eastern Europe had invested heavily in Information and Communications Technology (ICT). She also noted the absence of a quality website to facilitate online selling.

Martin discussed the SWOT analysis with existing employees and, at that meeting, a way forward was agreed. Martin invested a further €50,000 into the business to be used for modernising plant and equipment. Grant aid received from Enterprise Ireland was used for a new CAD system and a website was established to showcase the new brand and to get orders from clients. Employees were given the required training and development through upskilling courses organised by the company. Significant productivity improvements were achieved by introducing bonus shares for employees and offering a fair redundancy scheme. Martin was delighted with the innovative approach adopted by the design team in creating a range of quality hard and soft dance shoes. He welcomed their suggestions on the technical aspects of manufacturing hard dance shoes, which included fibreglass heels and toes to increase the clicking sound so important to Irish dance. His team developed a newly patented production technique enabling them to produce a dance shoe that is the lightest and loudest in the marketplace.

(A) Do you think that Martin Harte displayed enterprising skills/characteristics? Explain your answer with reference to the text of the ABQ. (20 marks)

(B) (i) Define the management activity of planning.

(ii) Explain the elements of a SWOT analysis and conduct the SWOT prepared by Christine Landers. (30 marks)

(C) Evaluate the effectiveness of the approach taken by Martin to help Harte Shoes Ltd adapt to change. (30 marks)

(80 marks)

Suggested solution

(A) Yes.

Innovative/Creative

Entrepreneurs are good at coming up with new ideas and better ways of doing things. They are constantly looking for new ideas and ways of improving what they do. They think outside the box to develop new products or new versions of existing products.

Link:

'His solution was based on the ever-increasing popularity of Irish dance worldwide'.

Initiative/Exploiting opportunity

Martin showed initiative by bringing his footwear manufacturing expertise into the growing Irish dance market. He saw an opportunity present itself (a niche market) for Irish dancing shoes and he exploited it.

Link:

'Martin's goal was to create a range of soft and hard dance shoes, using the finest and most durable leather and so well engineered that they would provide protection and comfort for Irish dancers worldwide.'

Risk-Taker

Being an entrepreneur involves taking both personal and financial risk in pursuit of a business idea. Successful entrepreneurs are not afraid of taking risks. They are realistic risk-takers.

Link:

'Martin invested a further €50,000 into the business to be used for modernising plant and equipment.'

Customer focus/Future focus

Entrepreneurs are very aware of customer needs and are willing to change their business model to meet those needs.

Link:

'He began to realise that the centuries-old footwear industry was in decline ...'

Reality Perception/Realistic

An entrepreneur sees things/situations for what they are and not as he/she would like them to be.

Link:

'Martin Harte, the owner, began to realise that the centuries-old footwear industry was in decline ...'

Networking/Persuasive abilities/Human relations

Entrepreneurs recognise the importance of a wide range of contacts to provide guidance and support. Entrepreneurs need to be able to persuade others.

Link:

'He sought the assistance of Enterprise Ireland's "Get Export Ready" scheme.'

Marking scheme

(A)	The Enterprising skills/characteristics		yes = 2 marks
	Name skill/characteristic	2 marks	
	Explain theory	2 marks	3 × 6 marks (2 + 2 + 2)
	Separate relevant link	2 marks	

(B) (i) Planning is the setting down of **specific goals and objectives** and the putting in place of **strategies** that allow you to achieve the stated goals and objectives of the business.

(ii) Harte Shoes Ltd

Strengths: Internal attributes and resources that support a successful outcome; aspects of a business which it is good at can be developed into a competitive advantage.

Examples: Strong brand/good market share/skilled workforce/manufacturing efficiency/strong financing.

Link:

'... highly skilled shoemakers and a very effective sales team'.

OR

'... Harte Shoes Ltd had manufacturing expertise ...'

Weaknesses: Internal aspects of a business which are underdeveloped and could damage the success of the business/work against a successful outcome of the business.

Examples: Poor credit control/obsolete technologies/weak management/outdated facilities/inadequate R&D.

Link:

'... the lack of a computer-aided design system (CAD) to assist with the production of shoes ...'

OR

'... absence of a quality website to facilitate online selling.'

Opportunity

External factors which a business could use to its advantage; factors outside the business which have the ability to benefit the business.

Examples: Falling exchange rate/consumer demand/strong economy.

Link:

'... growing markets exist in the UK, America and Australia due to the global popularity of Irish dancing.'

Threat

External factors that could jeopardise the business or could have negative impact on a business.

Examples: EU regulations/shortage of raw materials/changing market tastes.

Link:

'... that competitors from Eastern Europe had invested heavily in Information and Communications Technology (ICT).'

Marking Scheme

(B)	(i) Define planning (ii) Explain SWOT/Conduct SWOT • Name – 2 marks • Explain – 2 marks • Link – 2 marks (Link must be related to correct element)	6 marks (3 + 3) 24 marks 4 × 6 marks (2 + 2 + 2)

(C) Communication/Consultation: Communication should be honest and open. Management should explain the need for the changes and the consequences of not taking any action to ensure the survival of the firm. The benefits of change should be explained to staff. This will reduce uncertainty and tensions among employees.

Link:

'Martin discussed the SWOT analysis with existing employees ...'

OR

Change is implemented by having a consultative process with employees, e.g. calling a meeting and discussing and seeking opinions and views of staff with a view to reaching a compromise. Forced change may be resisted.

Link:

'He welcomed their suggestions on the technical aspects of manufacturing hard dance shoes ...'

Evaluation

Negotiation: Management may discuss with employees and their representatives the changes in work practices required with a view to coming to some agreement in relation to pay and conditions of employment without damaging industrial relations.

Link:

'Significant productivity improvements were achieved by introducing bonus shares for employees and offering a fair redundancy scheme.'

Evaluation

Rewards: Staff should be rewarded for taking part in/embracing change. Rewards will encourage the workforce to engage with change and see change as positive. Rewards should take account of the demands of the change.

Link:

'Significant productivity improvements were achieved by introducing bonus shares for employees and offering a fair redundancy scheme.'

Evaluation

Facilitator: Management could change from a controller to facilitator (helping employees perform the tasks rather than controlling them), etc.

Link:

'He welcomed their suggestions on the technical aspects of manufacturing hard dance shoes which included fibreglass heels and toes to increase the clicking sound so important to Irish dance.'

Evaluation

Empowerment: Staff should be involved in the decision-making process, giving them a sense of ownership in the process of change. Employees are encouraged and empowered to come up with ideas and these opinions and ideas are taken into account. This allows employees to feel they have a voice and encourages them to take on extra responsibility. With the increased responsibility comes increased enthusiasm for the job and doing it right.

Link:

'Martin was delighted with the innovative approach adopted by the design team in creating a range of quality hard and soft dance shoes.'

OR

'He welcomed their suggestions on the technical aspects of manufacturing ...'

Evaluation

Adequate Funding/Resource provider: Finance and funding of human and physical resources provided with an emphasis on new technology.

Link:

'Grant aid received from Enterprise Ireland was used for a new CAD system and a website was established ...'

OR

'Martin invested a further €50,000 into the business to be used for modernising plant and equipment.'

Evaluation

Training and Development: Staff must be trained in the management and use of new technologies so as to achieve efficiencies and provide a better service to customers.

Link:

'Employees were given the required training and development through upskilling courses organised by the company.'

Evaluation

Emphasis on quality/TQM/Quality Circles:

The focus of change has to be on the quality of output and quality management which is firmly based on teamwork.

Link:

'His team developed a newly patented production technique enabling them to produce a dance shoe that is the lightest and loudest in the marketplace.'

OR

'... a range of soft and hard dance shoes, using the finest and most durable leather, and so well engineered that they would provide protection and comfort for Irish dancers worldwide.'

Evaluation

Total commitment by management/Lead by example

Management is totally committed to creating a business that welcomes change/develops a culture of change.

Link:

'He decided to review the company's corporate strategy in order to make his company viable in the future.'

Marking scheme

(C)	The change strategies (Identify, explain, link, evaluate) (Separate Relevant Link for each approach)	30 marks 3 × 10 marks (3 + 3 + 3 + 1)

UNIT 5

Business in Action

This unit views business as a living, dynamic activity. It examines a business start-up from the generation of the original idea to the development of the business plan. There is an emphasis on the relationship between the business and its customers and on how the business must develop in response to changes in the market.

Objective

To enable pupils to understand the stages involved in setting up a business enterprise.

- **Chapter 15:** Identifying Opportunities
- **Chapter 16:** Marketing
- **Chapter 17:** Getting Started
- **Chapter 18:** Business Expansion

15 Identifying Opportunities

 aims Be able to:
- Explain the importance of researching business ideas.
- Identify techniques for developing business ideas and researching them.
- Contrast the main sources of new product ideas.

Sources of new product or service ideas

Business ideas and opportunities come from a wide variety of sources. These include:

- **Internal sources** – by examining their own strengths and weaknesses
- **External sources** – by looking at the opportunities and threats in the marketplace

Internal sources

1. The research and development department

The R&D department in a business is typically staffed with technical experts such as scientists and engineers seeking to devise new applications and products.

Example: Pfizer – the world's largest research-based pharmaceutical company – invests more than $7 billion annually in research and development to create new products to treat diseases.

2. Employees

Idea generation and development techniques (such as brainstorming) can be encouraged by rewarding employees who come up with ideas with cash bonuses and fringe benefits or any incentive that encourages the idea-generation process (entrepreneurship).

3. Existing products of business

Employees may improve or develop new products or services based on existing products of the business.

4. Community needs

Recognising community needs and wants that are not being met at present may provide an opportunity to fill a gap in the market.

Example: A late-night takeaway or a shop in a housing estate.

5. Hobbies or occupations

These can be a source of new product ideas.

External sources

1. Changes in society

Changes in society (such as new legislation) can give rise to a need for new products and services.

Example: Legislation banning the use of mobile phones while driving led to the development of hands-free mobile phones.

2. Customers

Customers can often suggest ideas for improvements in a product and innovative ideas may come from customer feedback, customer complaints or the changing needs of customers.

3. Competitors

Ideas can be found by monitoring competitors to see what products they are developing and what customers they are neglecting.

4. Market research

A business may carry out market research or surveys to find out what product or service is not provided. The firm can identify customer needs and wants by using a variety of research approaches, including customer surveys and interviews.

5. Organisations/state agencies

Organisations such as Enterprise Ireland, the Central Statistics Office, and country and city enterprise boards can provide statistical information which may be used to produce a successful product or service idea.

6. Products in other countries

Products or services that are available in other countries but not yet in Ireland could be adapted for the Irish market. If a product has not been patented, it may be freely copied.

Market research

- Market research is the systematic gathering of important and relevant information about markets and trends.
- Market research provides a business with a method of collecting important information on customers and their likes and dislikes in an organised and systematic way so that the information is accurate and reliable.

Read the information supplied and answer the question that follows.

Google's '20% Time' strategy gives engineers time and space to work on their own projects.

Outline the internal **and** external sources of new product ideas for technology companies like Google.

(20 marks)

Source: 2013 Higher Level Section 3

Suggested solution

Internal

- **Brainstorming sessions.** This involves people from different areas of the business coming together and creatively thinking up new ideas. Some of these ideas are rejected, while some are given further consideration. The diversity of the team assists in the creativity process.
- **Sales personnel.** Market research or feedback from sales representatives is a major source of product innovation and new product ideas.
- **Ideas from employees** through suggestion schemes or suggestion boxes. A good idea may be rewarded by a bonus. A good intrapreneurial culture exists within Google, fostering innovation, e.g. Google's '20% Time' strategy gives engineers time and space to work on their own projects.
- **The R&D department** may discover a new product or improve an existing product through research and development; for example, Google spent in the region of 13% of its revenue ($3.7 billion in 2011) on research and development.

External

- **Monitoring competitors** and copying some of their product ideas, while being mindful of patent and copyright law, e.g. Samsung and Apple.
- **Import substitution** where a product that is currently being imported is substituted by a home-produced product of a similar quality or price.
- **Use a market research company** to identify gaps in the market and market trends. Companies can then exploit these gaps or niche markets.
- **Customer complaints/feedback** could result in changes in or further developments of existing products.
- **Foreign travel or trade shows** such as the Web Summit could inspire companies to make a new product for the domestic market.

Marking scheme

Two internal sources @ 5 marks each (2 + 3)

Two external sources @ 5 marks each (2 + 3)

Total 20 marks

Reasons why businesses carry out market research

- **Market:** It provides information about the size of the market and whether it is growing. It also provides information about the characteristics of the market (age of people in it, their income, their location).
- **Competitors:** It reveals information about competition in the market, their products, the market share and their strengths and weaknesses.
- **Marketing mix:** It helps a business decide on the marketing mix it will use to sell its products in terms of the Four Ps – product, price, promotion and place (the product, its price, the method of promotion and the place where it will be sold).
- **Consumer reaction:** Businesses can find out the reasons why consumers buy a particular product and what influences their buying behaviour.
- **Reduces risk:** Market research makes it more likely that a product will succeed. It reduces the risk of the business using resources to produce products that the consumer does not want.
- **Sales:** It assists a business in working out the likely sales for its products.

Market research techniques

There are many different types of market research, including:

- Desk research
- Field research

Desk research

Desk research is based on secondary sources of information (i.e. on research that has already been conducted by others). Internal and external sources of information may be used in desk research.

Example: The total number of cars sold in 2018 can be found through research conducted by the CSO or the Society of the Irish Motor Industry (SIMI).

Internal sources of information are available in the firm's files and will include:

- Company reports
- Customer feedback
- Sales figures, marketing records, and salespersons' reports on file

External sources of information include:

- Reports from state agencies (CSO, Enterprise Ireland, SOLAS)
- Trade Associations (such as SIMI)
- Websites
- Trade statistics for the country (imports and exports)
- Household budget surveys

Field research

This is research based on primary sources of information. Field research seeks to discover new information about a target market.

Field research methods include:

- Surveys
- Questionnaires
- Observation

Example: A car dealership that wishes to check the satisfaction ratings of customers who purchase new cars may gather this information by using a questionnaire.

Surveys

The main purpose of a survey is to determine from the responses how consumers will react to new products or services.
Survey methods include:

- Personal interviews
- Telephone interviews
- Postal surveys
- Online surveys

Potential customers are interviewed by researchers and responses recorded.
A representative sample of people from the entire market is selected for the survey.

Questionnaires

The data-collection method is usually carried out with questionnaires. Questionnaires must be prepared in such a way that the information is useful and relevant. A questionnaire contains a series of structured questions designed to generate information required to meet the objectives of the research.

Observation

This is a technique that requires a researcher to observe and watch the reactions and behaviour of individuals.
Example: A researcher in a bank observing the average queue length for each hour of the day.

Read the information supplied and answer the question that follows.

An Irish company, All-Weather Wellies Ltd, identified a niche market for colourful wellington boots of all sizes. The wellington boots are sold mainly online to people who enjoy 'the great outdoors' and festivalgoers. The company wishes to expand and add accessories, such as umbrellas, scarves and hats, to the product range.

Outline the market research techniques available to All-Weather Wellies Ltd for developing its product range.

(20 marks)

Source: 2013 Higher Level Section 3

Suggested solution

Desk Research

- Desk research involves accessing information that has already been gathered.
- It is secondary research and can be both internal and external.
- Desk research is relatively cheap, which keeps business costs down, thereby ensuring a competitive business.
- Different types of desk research include the internet, internal sales reports, trade reports, Central Statistics Office publications, newspapers, etc.
- Desk research can provide information on competitors and consumer spending patterns.
- The daily sales records of All-Weather Wellies Ltd would indicate if consumer spending patterns have changed and if they are ready for different accessories in the range.
- The CSO would provide information on the population details of towns (i.e. age, sex, family structure, etc.) and its household budget survey would give information on households' spending patterns on different types of goods.

Field Research

- Field research involves going into the marketplace to gather first-hand or new business information. It is primary research, which is carried out by making direct contact with customers or potential customers.
- Field research tends to be expensive and time-consuming but it does provide specific information on the behaviour of the target market.
- Field research methods or techniques include: surveys, observation, questionnaires and customer panels. Surveys involving personal interviews and questionnaires with a sample of the population can be very effective tools in accessing and collecting detailed information about consumers' tastes, behaviours and attitudes in the marketplace. Surveys could be carried out on site at concerts by field researchers employed by All-Weather Wellies Ltd.
- Observation involves viewing consumers in action, e.g. the number of customers selecting a particular product during a particular period in the store. Field research for All Weather-Wellies Ltd ascertains attitudes and opinions of its customers, and they can make specific changes to their products and product portfolio based on the feedback received.
- Field research allows the company to satisfy its customer needs more effectively, encouraging customer loyalty and increasing the profits of the business.

Marking scheme

Two techniques @ 10 marks each

Name: 2 marks

Two points of information @ 3 marks each

Relevant reference to All-Weather Wellies Ltd: 2 marks

Read the information supplied and answer the questions that follow.

Stitch Express

Stitch Express is a business set up by Alex Dunne, originally offering clothing alterations, dress restyling and repairs. The business has grown and Alex believes it is time to update his marketing strategy. Following market research, Alex introduced a dry-cleaning service. There are a few competitors in the market, so Alex decided to review his pricing and promotion policies. Alex believes he will need to rebrand the business as a result of introducing the dry-cleaning service.

(i) Outline the advantages **and** disadvantages of using secondary (desk) research techniques for collecting information on a market.

(ii) Illustrate **one** source of desk research and **one** source of field research that Stitch Express might use, giving a reason for your answer in **each** case.

(25 marks)

Source: 2016 Higher Level Section 3

Suggested solution

(i) Advantages

Usually faster to complete than primary research as it may be carried out online – research reports/press reports/CSO publications, etc.

Relatively inexpensive compared to primary research, thereby keeping business costs down.

More and more sources are available online, so results can be checked for accuracy. Desk research can provide information on competitors and consumer spending patterns.

It can be a starting point to allow business to focus primary research on a particular area identified through secondary research.

Disadvantages

Information is also available to your competitors.

Accuracy of information cannot be completely verified or it can be difficult to find the original source.

Information collected may be out of date. Information may be biased, depending on who developed it.

(ii) Desk: (quantitative data)

CSO statistics – to determine population trends (age, sex, family structure) and forecasts/rate of pedestrian and traffic flow past business compared to that of rivals/footfall in a location.

Household budget survey (CSO) would give information on household spending patterns for different types of goods.

Internet – could view the pricing and promotion strategies of competitors from their websites to help develop its own pricing or promotion policies.

Daily sales records would indicate if consumer patterns have changed and if consumers would be interested in the new service.

Government publications – Enterprise Ireland, etc.

Previous market research reports, such as trade association reports.

Own previously published reports.

Press – newspaper and magazine articles – useful general information.

Reason for your choice must be given.

Field: (opinions and attitudes – qualitative data)

Questionnaires/Surveys – where individuals are asked specific questions and detailed information is received about consumers' tastes, behaviours in the marketplace.

Focus groups – selected individuals are involved in discussions about the product or service, using a scripted series of questions or topics.

Personal interviews – provide more subjective data.

Observation – viewing customers in action and purchasing patterns are observed by trained staff.

Reason for your choice must be given.

Marking scheme

(i) 3 × 5 marks (2 + 3)

(at least one of each required)

(ii) 2 × 5m (2+ 2 + 1)

(Name, explain, reference to Stitch Express)

New product and service development process

The development of a new product or service goes through a number of stages:

1. Idea generation

Initial ideas for the new product are identified. This can take the form of brainstorming, where many ideas are discussed, or market research.

2. Product screening

The ideas are analysed and the impractical and unworkable ideas are eliminated, leaving the one which has the best potential to succeed in the market place.

A SWOT analysis may help identify ideas with potential.

3. Concept development

This involves turning an idea into an actual product or service that will appeal to customers. A **unique selling point** (USP) is identified, which will distinguish it from other products.

4. Feasibility study

This is carried out to assess whether the product is viable and can be successfully developed and brought to the market. Break-even analysis is done to check if the product can be profitable.

5. Prototype development

An original working model of the product is developed and tested. It is produced to see if the product can be made and what materials are required to make it. The prototype is used to test the product to see what improvements can be made.

6. Test marketing

The product is tested on a sample of consumers. Consumer feedback is gathered at this stage.

7. Production and launch

The product is put into production and introduced to the market. The firm will select a suitable marketing strategy to persuade consumers to buy the product.

Read the information supplied and answer the questions that follow.

In 2015 a Slovakian company, AeroMobil, revealed its prototype of the AeroMobil 3.0 – a flying car. It is a road-ready vehicle with foldable wings. It can navigate both city traffic and airspace.
Source: Forbes Magazine, **March 2015**

Describe the stages in the new product development process up to and including prototype development. Refer to the AeroMobil 3.0 vehicle in your answer.

(25 marks)
Source: 2017 Higher Level Section 3

Suggested solution

Idea generation

- Initial ideas for the new product are thought up systematically. They can be internal or external.
- Ideas may be generated by brainstorming sessions, market research, staff suggestions, customer suggestions/feedback on existing products or services, competitors, R&D, etc.
  The company created the idea for a 'flying car'.

Product screening

- All **ideas are vetted** and the impractical and unworkable ideas are dropped, leaving the most viable ones for further examination and development.

- Careful screening helps businesses avoid huge expenses in developing ideas that are subsequently not marketable and ensures that good opportunities are not lost.
The car would have to have foldable wings to travel on both road and in air.

Concept development

- This involves **turning the idea into an actual product** or service that will appeal to/meet the needs of customers.
- A unique selling point (USP) is identified, which will differentiate it from other products on the market.
The unique selling point is that the car is capable of flying and being driven. A flexible model.

Feasibility study

- This is carried out to assess if a product has potential. It looks at whether it can be produced technically (**production feasibility**) and if it will be profitable (**financial feasibility**). Will it meet government regulation regarding safety standards and will it be marketable, etc.? Safety considerations would be a big concern for AeroMobil.
- It seeks answers to questions such as: what demand will there be for the product? What will it cost to produce and can the business afford it?
The flying car would be a very expensive/luxury product.

Prototype development

- This stage involves **developing a sample or model of a product**. It is produced to see if it can be made, what materials are required to make it and if it appeals to customers.
- It can be used to test the product to see if it conforms to certain standards and to determine what adjustments/improvements can be made before deciding to go into full production.
In 2015 a Slovakian company AeroMobil revealed its prototype of the AeroMobil 3.0 – a flying car.

Marking scheme

5 × 5 marks (2 + 2 + 1)

Stages must be in the correct order for full marks to be awarded.

Some reference to AeroMobil 3.0 required in each point for 1 mark.

Feasibility study, test marketing, product screening and **prototype development** are stages in the new Product Development Process.

(i) List the four stages above in the **correct** order.

(ii) Outline your understanding of any **three** of these stages.

(20 marks)

Source: 2015 Higher Level Section 3

Suggested solution

(i)

1. Product Screening
2. Feasibility Study
3. Prototype Development
4. Test Marketing

(ii)

Product screening (screening ideas): All ideas are vetted and the impractical and unworkable ideas are dropped, leaving the most viable ones for further examination and development. Careful screening helps businesses avoid huge expenses in developing ideas that are subsequently not marketable and ensures that good opportunities are not lost.

Feasibility Study: This is carried out to assess if a product has potential. It looks at whether it can be produced technically (production feasibility) and if it will be profitable (financial feasibility). It seeks answers to questions such as 'what will it cost to produce?' and 'can the business afford it?'

Prototype Development: This stage involves developing a sample or model of a product. It is produced to see what materials are required to make it. It can be used to test the product to see if it conforms to certain standards and to determine what adjustments/ improvements can be made before deciding to go into full production.

Test Marketing/Product Testing: Involves doing a small-scale trial to identify possible faults and to assess customer reaction. The product is tested on a sample of potential consumers before going into full production.

Marking scheme

(i) 5 marks

(ii) 3 × 5 marks (2 + 3)

Medron plc

Medron plc manufactures medical devices and its R&D department is currently working on a prototype for a tube to be used in vascular surgery.

Outline the reasons why businesses engage in prototype development.

(15 marks)

Source: 2016 Higher Level Section 3

Suggested solution

It is an opportunity to refine the original design to create a fully functioning product (eliminate bugs). The product can be tested in use to identify problems with the product and improvements that could be made.

It identifies the effectiveness of machinery and equipment used to make the product. It is an opportunity to address engineering/production issues during the production process.

It determines if you can source the materials when required (required amount and appropriate quality).

To determine the financial cost of producing the prototype.

Prototype can be used for test marketing.

Marking scheme

3 × 5 marks (2 + 3)

16 Marketing

Marketing

Marketing is defined by the Institute of Marketing as 'The process responsible for identifying, anticipating and satisfying customer requirements profitably.'
It is the process of:

- **Identifying customer requirements** through market research. It is only by finding out the needs of customers that the business can respond to those needs.
- **Anticipating customers' future needs**.
- **Satisfying the identified need** by producing products and services in the quality and quantity required by customers.

Marketing concept

The marketing concept has been defined as:

- Understanding the needs and wants of customers
- Developing products to satisfy consumers' needs
- Supplying the desired product more efficiently than competitors
- Making every effort to satisfy customer wants profitably

Advantage to a business of adopting the marketing concept

A business will be able to compete in the most competitive of markets, because it will produce what its customers need rather than attempt to get customers to purchase what the firm has produced.

Marketing strategy

The marketing strategy (or marketing plan) will be made up of a plan on how the policies relating to the Four Ps (product, price, place and promotion) will be used to achieve the marketing objectives.
Particular emphasis is placed on 'market segmentation policy' and the needs of customers in different markets.
A SWOT analysis should be carried out in advance of drawing up a marketing plan.

Advantages of marketing plan

It sets out the steps needed by a firm to achieve its objectives. Management must choose the best way forward to achieve the objectives.

The business can measure its performance against the goals set in the marketing plan, thus helping to control the business. Changes can be made if required.

The marketing plan helps to present the case for finance to financial institutions. It can be used to show where the enterprise is going.

Market segmentation

Market segmentation involves dividing up the market into clearly identifiable sections which have common characteristics.

It allows a firm to identify its target market.

The main ways to segment a market include:

- **Demographic** – This involves dividing a market according to factors such as age, income, gender.
- **Physiological** – This involves dividing the market according to attitudes and tastes.

Advantages to a business enterprise of segmenting the market

The marketing strategy will focus on customers who are most likely to buy the product.

It will help the business to avoid markets which will not be profitable.

It gives the business a competitive advantage in the market.

Target market

A target market is a particular segment that has been identified as containing likely customers of a product or service.

The target segment will be the one in which the firm has a competitive advantage and in which it believes that it can satisfy customers better than competitors.

Having selected a target market, a business can develop the correct marketing mix (product, price, promotion, place) to reach the target market.

For example, the target market for the *Less Stress More Success* book series is Junior Cycle and Leaving Certificate exam students.

Niche market

A niche market is a specialist market for a particular type of product or service (e.g. *Less Stress More Success* for students).

A niche market is identified through market segmentation.

A business that focuses on a niche market is addressing a need for a product or service that is not being addressed by mainstream providers.

A niche market can be thought of as a narrowly defined group of potential customers.

For example: Instead of offering a general cleaning service, a cleaning business might establish a niche market by specialising in a cleaning window blinds.

Marketing mix

The marketing mix consists of the Four Ps (product, price, promotion and place) used by a firm to implement its marketing strategy.

Marketing Mix

The Four Ps of the Marketing Mix:

- Product – product or service
- Price – price to charge
- Promotion – how to promote a product or service to potential customers
- Place – where to sell the product or service

Product

This is the physical product or service offered to the consumer and includes its distinctive features (form, shape and colour) as well as guarantees and after-sales service.

Product design

The product must be designed reliably to satisfy the needs of the target market.

It must comply with safety standards and perform well.

Its distinguishing feature is its **Unique Selling Point (USP).**

The key elements involved in a product are:

- Product design
- Packaging
- Branding
- Product life cycle

Packaging

Good packaging makes a product attractive and appealing to consumers.

Packaging makes a product recognisable to the consumer.

Attractive packaging demonstrates an image of quality and reliability.

Packaging provides information regarding the product.

Branding

A brand is a distinctive name, symbol or design that identifies the goods or services of a firm, and distinguishes them from those of competitors.

Branding allows immediate recognition by consumers.

The unique mark or name used to brand goods is a form of trademark. By registering the trademark the enterprise has exclusive rights to use the mark. Well-known brands include L'Oréal Paris, Lacoste, Pepsi-Cola, Kellogg's, Microsoft, Sony, Kodak.

Benefits of branding to the business:

- **Marketing**: Having a brand name makes it easier to distinguish the product from competitors' products and instantly recognisable. Can be used as a marketing tool for advertising purposes. (For example, Kellogg's is a well-known brand and they have used a range of promotion strategies to keep the brand to the fore of consumer's minds.)
- **New products are easier to introduce** if the brand name is already well known. (Kellogg's releases different products under the Kellogg's brand.)
- **Pricing**: A well-known brand name can command a premium price. (Kellogg's brands command higher prices than, for instance, own-brand labels and so Kellogg's can charge premium prices.)
- **Sales increase**: Repeat purchases increase sales.
- **Market segmentation**: Individual market segments can be identified and targeted with different products under the brand name (e.g. Kellogg's Rice Krispies).
- **Customer Loyalty**: Over time, consumers become loyal to a particular brand and will not change.

Benefits of branding for the consumer:

- Branding helps the buyer to **identify** a particular supplier's goods and creates and **maintains their confidence** in the performance of the brand.
- Brands help consumers/buyers to judge the quality of a product. Country of origin can influence consumers in making judgements as to whether a product is of value or not (e.g. French perfume, Italian leather, Swiss watches).
- The purchase and use of brands allows a consumer/buyer to fulfil their need for self-expression and also communicate his or her self-image. A consumer/buyer who defines himself or herself as successful and powerful may drive a Mercedes!

Own brands

Large retailers sell goods under their own brand name – e.g. Marks & Spencer (M&S), Dunnes Stores (St Bernard).

The goods are produced by manufacturers to the retailer's specifications and are usually sold at lower prices than other brands.

Product life cycle

1. Product Development

During the development phase there is no cash inflow (sales). There is substantial cash outflow because of the costs associated with the development process.

exam focus

Products follow a life cycle of six distinct stages:
1. Development
2. Introduction
3. Growth
4. Maturity
5. Saturation
6. Decline

2. Introduction

This is a period of slow sales growth and high expenditure on advertising and promotion as the product is introduced to the market. There is very little cash inflow from sales at this stage and no profit.

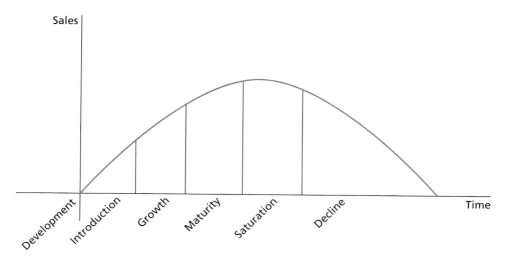

Product Life Cycle

3. Growth

The product is known and is demanded by consumers. There is rapid sales growth, positive cash flow and increasing profit.

4. Maturity

Sales and profit reach a peak and start to level off. Profits stabilise as the product is accepted by most consumers.

5. Saturation

Sales slow down as most consumers have bought the product. The business must cut its price to maintain its market share and/or bring out new and improved versions of the product.

6. Decline

Sales decline and profits fall as more technically advanced products take over the market. The product is eventually withdrawn from the market.

Explain the factors a business should consider when designing a product.

(15 marks)

Source 2017 Higher Level Section 3

Suggested solution

Cost/price

The design of the product must be cost-effective. It should take account of all manufacturing and distribution costs. These costs have to be recovered, together with a profit margin from the price charged to consumers.

Function/legal requirements/safety standards

This factor links into the main clauses of the Sale of Goods and Supply of Services Act 1980, which puts a legislative onus on producers to manufacture goods that are of merchantable quality and fit for the purpose intended. The product must do what it is expected to do.

The product must be practical and comply with safety standards.

Form/appearance/packaging

The product must be aesthetically appealing in terms of shape, size, colour, style, image, etc., e.g. (iPad). Car marketing campaigns emphasise efficiency, reliability and aesthetic appeal in their advertisements.

Marking scheme

3 × 5 marks (2 + 3)

Price

Price is the amount of money charged for the product or service.

Price is an important element in a purchasing decision because the demand for a product or service is influenced by price.

Factors to be considered when deciding on the selling price of a product

The factors which should be taken into account when deciding on the selling price include:

- **Costs** – The price should cover the firm's costs (production, marketing, distribution, etc.) and include a profit margin.
- **Competitor's prices** – The price will have to be similar to that of the competitors to gain market share. If competition is very intense, the price to be charged will be affected.
- **Stage of product life cycle** – If the product is new and at the introduction stage, a high price may be charged to recover costs. Products at end of the life cycle may be sold at a low price to keep sales from falling.
- **Consumers** – The type of buyers will determine the price which can be charged.
- **Demand** – If demand for the product is high, the firm can charge a high price.

Pricing policies

- **Cost plus pricing** – All costs are calculated and a margin for profit is added to determine the selling price.
- **Competitive pricing** – To compete in the market prices must be set at the same level as those of competitors.
- **Penetration pricing** – This involves setting prices lower than competitors in order to gain market share.
- **Premium pricing** – This is charging a high price to reflect the high-quality image of a product or service.

- **Tactical pricing** – This involves the use of discounts, promotional prices and special offers. Cash discounts are often granted to customers who pay immediately by cash. Businesses often offer trade discount to buyer who buys in bulk.

Break-even analysis

Breaking even is when a firm is just covering its costs, making neither a profit nor a loss. The purpose of break-even analysis is to ascertain the sales level, in units and value, that a company must achieve to break even.

1. Costs

> Total Costs = Fixed Costs + Variable Costs

Fixed costs are costs that remain unchanged, irrespective of the level of production (e.g. rent and rates, insurance, management salaries). These costs have to be paid whether or not anything is produced.

Variable costs are costs that change directly with the level of production (e.g. the raw materials used and direct labour). These will tend to double if output doubles.

> Total Variable Costs = Variable Cost per Unit × Number of Units Produced

2. Revenue

Total revenue is the money received by a firm from the sale of its goods or services.

> Total Revenue = Selling Price × Quantity Sold

3. Contribution

This is a measure of the amount of money that each unit sold contributes towards covering the fixed costs of a business. Once fixed costs are covered, all further contribution is profit.

> Contribution = Total Revenue − Variable Costs
> Contribution per Unit = Selling Price per Unit − Variable Costs per Unit

4. Break-even

This is the level of output and sales at which a firm generates just enough income to cover fixed and variable costs, earning neither a profit nor a loss.

If the selling price of a product exceeds its variable cost, each unit sold will earn a contribution towards fixed costs. If total contributions cover fixed costs, the firm breaks even.

5. Break-even point

The break-even point (BEP) is the level of sales at which the firm breaks even, making neither a profit nor a loss.

$$\text{Break-even point} = \frac{\text{Fixed Costs}}{\text{Contribution Per Unit}}$$

6. Margin of Safety

This is the difference between sales volume and the break-even point, and is the amount by which sales can fall before a firm incurs a loss.

$$\text{Margin of Safety} = \text{Sales Volume} - \text{Break-even Point}$$

Break-even chart

All costs (fixed and variable), together with the sales income expected from the product, can be represented on a **break-even chart**, which will show the break-even point.

Uses of a break-even chart:

- It is used to determine how many products a business must sell in order to break even.
- It shows the margin of safety at different levels of output.
- It shows the profit the firm can make if it operates at full capacity.
- It shows the impact of changes in selling price on profitability.
- It shows the impact of changes in costs on profitability.

How to Draw a Break-even Chart

Illustrate by means of a break-even chart the following figures, showing (a) break-even point, (b) profit at full capacity, and (c) margin of safety:

Fixed costs:	€20,000
Variable costs:	€3 per unit
Forecasted output (sales):	12,000 units
Selling price:	€5 per unit
Full capacity:	15,000 units

Calculate break-even point

Calculate the break-even point. This allows you to position the diagram properly on the page.

Break-even Point

$$\text{Break-even point} = \frac{\text{Fixed Costs}}{\text{Contribution per Unit}}$$

Contribution per Unit = Selling Price per Unit − Variable Cost per Unit

$$= €5 - €3$$

Contribution per Unit = €2

$$\text{Break-even point} = \frac{€20,000}{2} = 10,000 \text{ units}$$

This means that 10,000 units must be sold in order to break even.

Break-even in euro (€) = 10,000 × €5 = €50,000

Drawing the break-even chart

Step 1. Draw the axis

Label the horizontal axis as **Output (units)** and the vertical axis as **Costs and revenue**. Decide the scale, making sure the break-even point (BEP) is positioned in the middle of the chart.

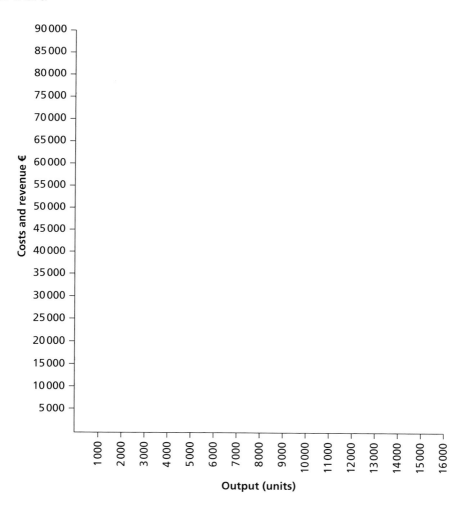

Step 2. Draw the fixed cost (FC) line

Draw the fixed cost line. This will be a straight line parallel to the horizontal axis at the appropriate level (€20,000).

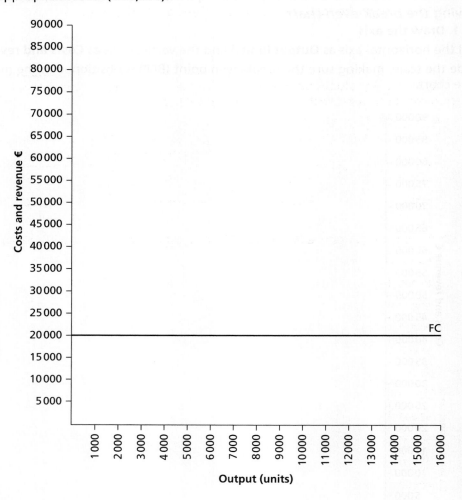

Step 3. Draw the total cost (TC) line

Draw the total cost line (TC = FC + VC). This line starts at the point of intersection of the fixed cost line and the vertical axis and slopes upwards. To draw this line it is necessary to work out the total cost at two different levels of output.

Workings for drawing the total cost line

The total cost line starts at the point of intersection of the fixed cost line and the vertical axis and slopes upwards. We must find two other points on this line and work out total cost at two levels of output.

Units	Variable Costs	Fixed Cost	Total Cost
0	0	€20,000	€20,000
5,000	€15,000	€20,000	€35,000
15,000	€45,000	€20,000	€65,000

Points on line are (0 units, €20,000) (5,000 units, €35,000) (15,000 units, €65,000)

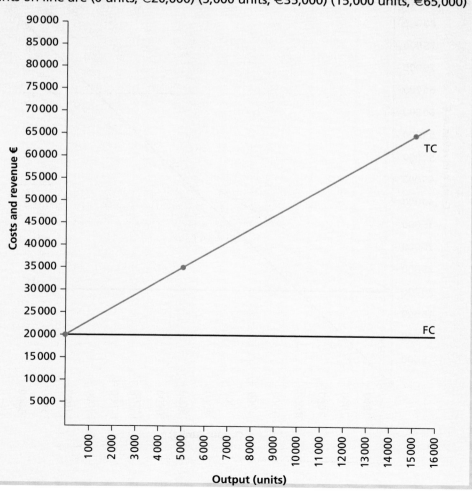

Step 4. Draw total revenue (TR) line

Draw the total revenue line. This line starts at 0 and slopes upwards. To draw this line it is necessary to work out total revenue at two different levels of output.

Workings for drawing the total revenue line

The total revenue line starts at 0 and slopes upwards. Find two other points on this line and work out total revenue at two different levels of output.

Units	Selling Price	Revenue
0	€5	0
5,000	€5	€25,000
15,000	€5	€75,000

Points on line are (0 units, 0 revenue) (5,000 units, €25,000) (15,000 units, €75,000)

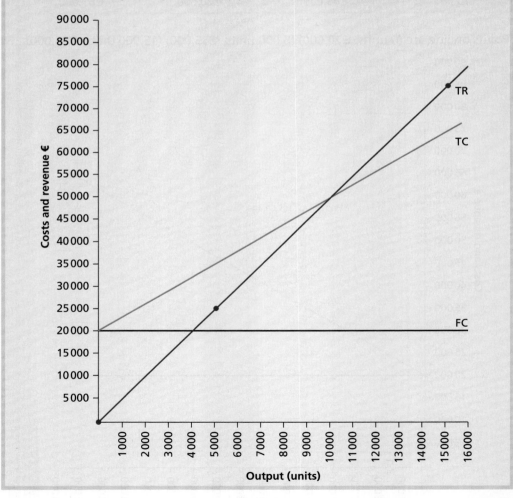

Step 5. Show the break-even point, the margin of safety and the profit at full capacity

Break-even point

Establish the break-even point (BEP), which is where the total cost line and total revenue line intersect. Before this point the business is making a loss; after this point the business is making a profit.

Margin of safety

Show the margin of safety using this formula:

Sales − Break-even Point = Margin of Safety.

12,000 units − 10,000 units = 2,000 units

This means that sales can fall by 2,000 units before a loss is incurred.

Profit at full capacity

Show profit at full capacity by using this formula:

Total Revenue − Total Costs = Profit at Full Capacity.

Sales (15,000 units × €5):	€75,000
Less variable cost (15,000 × €3):	€45,000
Contribution	€30,000
Less fixed costs	€20,000
Profit	€10,000

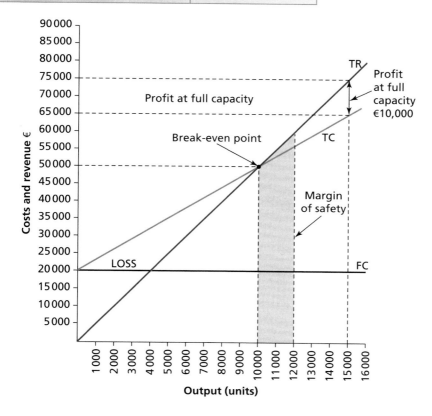

HL

Read the information supplied and answer the questions that follow.

Medron plc has supplied the following financial information for the new medical device:

Forecast Output (Sales)	60,000 units
Selling Price per unit	€30
Fixed Costs	€400,000

(A) Illustrate the following by means of a break-even chart:

(i) Break-even point

(ii) Margin of safety at the forecast output

(iii) Profit at forecast output.   (25 marks)

(B) Following a review of costs, Medron plc decreased its variable costs per unit to €10.

(i) Calculate the new break-even point **and** illustrate on your break-even chart the new total cost line (TC2) and the new break-even point (BEP2).

(ii) Outline **one** limitation of a break-even analysis when making business decisions.   (20 marks)

Source: 2016 Higher Level Section 3

Suggested solution

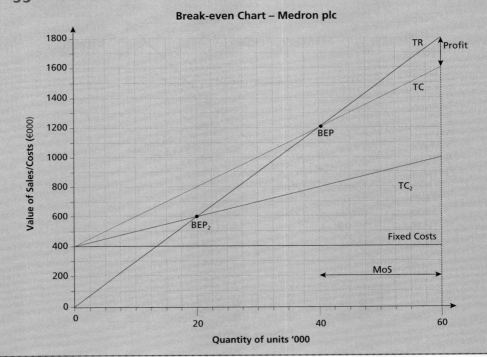

Break-even Chart – Medron plc

Units	Selling Price	Variable Costs	Fixed Costs	Total Costs	Total Revenue	Profit/ loss
0	30	20	400,000	400,000	0	(400,000)
40,000	30	20	400,000	1,200,000	1,200,000	0
60,000	30	20	400,000	1,600,000	1,800,000	200,000

Calculations

(i) BEP = Fixed Costs/Contribution = **400,000/30–20 = 40,000 units**

(ii) Margin of Safety = **60,000–40,000 = 20,000 units**

(iii) Profit at Forecast output = **1,800,000–1,600,000 = €200,000**

Calculations only: 12 marks

BEP 4 marks

MOS 4 marks

Profit at forecast output 4 marks

(B) (i) BEP = Fixed Costs/Contribution = **400,000/30–10 = 20,000 units**

Units	Selling Price	Variable Costs	Fixed Costs	Total Costs	Total Revenue	Profit/ loss
0	30	10	400,000	400,000	0	(400,000)
20,000	30	10	400,000	600,000	600,000	0
60,000	30	10	400,000	1,000,000	1,800,000	800,000

(ii) Break-even analysis assumes fixed costs are constant. Variable costs can vary as output changes.

It assumes that the business knows all its costs and can break them down into fixed and variable.

Variable costs may increase/decrease as output increases – business may be able to purchase larger amounts of raw materials at lower prices (economies of scale from bulk buying).

Assumes that firm sells all its output – in times of low demand, a firm may have difficulty in selling all its products.

Assumes a firm sells all its output at a single price – firms may offer discounts for bulk purchases/may produce more than it can sell and may have to sell the surplus at a discounted price.

Ignores the effect that a change of price may have on sales – price increase causes a fall in demand for the product and vice versa.

Most businesses sell more than one product, so break-even becomes harder to calculate.

Marking scheme

(A) 25 marks (5 × 4 marks + 2 + 1 + 1 + 1):

Title 1 mark

Output in units, '000s 1 mark

Revenue/costs, €'000s 1 mark

FC line 2 marks

TC line 4 marks

TR line 4 marks

BEP 4 marks

MOS 4 marks

Profit at forecast output 4 marks

(B) (i)   15 marks (5 + 5 + 5)

Calculation 5 marks

BEP2 = 5 marks

TC2 = 5 marks

(Calculation only, max. 5 marks)

(ii) 5 marks

Promotion

Promotion consists of all communication used by a business to let customers know about the products on offer and to get them interested in buying them.

Advertising

Advertising is the communication of information to persuade customers to buy a particular product or service.

The methods of promotion are:
- Advertising
- Sales promotion
- Public relations
- Personal selling

Function of advertising

The function of advertising is to:

- Provide information about the product or service
- Persuade consumers to buy the product or service
- Remind consumers that the product is still available
- Increase sales and profits

Advertising media

The medium used will depend on the:

- Market segment
- Type of product or service
- Message
- Cost

Advertising Media

The main locations for advertising include:

- Television
- Newspapers
- Magazines and journals
- Radio
- Cinemas
- Online
- Poster sites/hoardings
- Public transport

Sales promotion

Sales promotion consists of short-term incentives to encourage customers to purchase the product or service.

It is used in addition to normal advertising.

It is ideal for promoting a new product.

The aim is to give an immediate boost to the sales of a product.

It is popular in large multiples (such as Dunnes, Tesco) in an effort to increase market share.

Sales promotion methods include:
- Special offers
- Free samples
- Extra quantities for same price
- Competitions – holidays, cars, etc.
- Tokens for holiday breaks
- Two-for-the-price-of-one offers
- Money-off packs
- In-store demonstrations

Public relations

Public relations is concerned with creating and maintaining a good public image in relation to a company and its products and services.

It aims to generate favourable publicity and a good corporate image of the business amongst its customers and the general public.

Public relations is about building a relationship with the public. It is not directly concerned with increasing sales of products.

The person in business who manages public relations is called the public relations officer (PRO).

Public Relations Officers (PRO)

The role of the public relations officer is to deal with:

- Media relations – through press releases and press conferences
- Customer relations
- Local community relations
- The generation of favourable publicity for firm

Developing public relations

Methods of developing public relations include:

- Press conferences, press releases conveying information to the media
- Sponsorship – A payment made for the right to be associated with an activity or event (the product name will be displayed – e.g. Heineken Champions Cup rugby)
- Donations – to communities, sports clubs, schools
- Open days – to allow the general public to visit the company site

Personal selling

This is the use of personal contact to persuade customers to purchase the product or service.

Face-to-face meetings are useful for the sale of expensive products or products that require a high degree of expertise or technical knowledge and need to be demonstrated to the customer.

Read the information supplied and answer the questions that follow.

Stitch Express

Stitch Express is a business set up by Alex Dunne originally offering clothing alterations, dress restyling and repairs. The business has grown and Alex believes it is time to update his marketing strategy. Following market research, Alex introduced a dry-cleaning service. There are a few competitors in the market, so Alex decided to review his pricing and promotion policies. Alex believes he will need to rebrand the business, as a result of introducing the dry-cleaning service.

Evaluate the effectiveness of sales promotion techniques Alex could consider to boost sales.

(15 marks)

Source: 2016 Higher Level Section 3

Suggested solution

Customer loyalty programmes – offering discounts, cashback, points, etc. to regular customers (through key fob, customer card, etc.).This will reward the loyal customers. One free dry-clean for every five shirts dry-cleaned.

Special offers – free gifts – adding a free gift or extra service for free, e.g. 'dry-clean suit – shirt and tie cleaned for free'. This may encourage the customer to avail of the service more often. (Get suit cleaned every two weeks rather than every month).

OR

Buy One, Get One Free/3 for price of 2 – getting three items dry-cleaned/altered and only paying for two items. This may increase the volume of trade for Stitch Express.

OR

Introductory Offer

Money-off vouchers/coupons – putting coupons in local papers and magazines for reduction in cost of dry-cleaning/alteration service. This may attract new customers to the service.

Competitions on social media – could encourage customers to share posts from Stitch Express on Facebook by offering the winners €100 worth of dry-cleaning, etc. This could be a reward for loyal customers.

(Include evaluation of each technique you have chosen.)

Marking scheme

Name and describe technique	3 × 4 marks (2 + 2)
Evaluation	3 marks (1 + 1 + 1)

Place

This is the process of getting the product to the consumer.
A distribution system is essential to move goods from manufacturer to consumer.

Channels of distribution

The term 'channels of distribution' refers to the movement of goods from manufacturer to wholesaler to retailer to consumer.
The main channels of distribution are:

- **Direct** – Manufacturer sells directly to consumers. For example, furniture manufacturers selling directly from the factory.
- **Modern** – Large retailers (e.g. Dunnes, Tesco) bypass wholesalers and purchase large quantities of goods directly from manufacturer at a discount and sell to consumers.
- **Traditional** – The path through which goods normally pass on their way to the final user. The goods are manufactured by the manufacturer, who sells them to the wholesaler, who distributes them to the retailer, who sells them directly to the consumer.

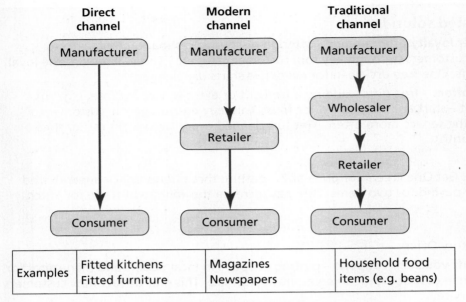

Examples	Fitted kitchens Fitted furniture	Magazines Newspapers	Household food items (e.g. beans)

Main Channels of Distribution

Wholesaler and retailer

Wholesaler – A firm that buys products in bulk from the manufacturer/producer and then resells in smaller quantities to the retailer (e.g. Musgraves Cash and Carry).

Retailer – A firm that sells products directly to the consumers. They normally buy in large quantities from wholesalers. (A newsagent is a retailer.)

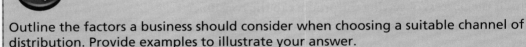

Outline the factors a business should consider when choosing a suitable channel of distribution. Provide examples to illustrate your answer.

(20 marks)

Source: 2012 Higher Level Section 3

Suggested solution

Cost: Cost is a factor in choice of channel of distribution. The more stages in the channel of distribution, the more expensive the product will be for the consumer as each middleman will require a cut or mark-up. Ryanair was motivated by cost factors when it cut travel agents out of its ticket sales distribution network. Tesco and Dunnes Stores purchase directly from manufacturers.

Type of goods/durability: Some goods are bulky, others fragile and more perishable. Perishable goods must be distributed quickly to the market, e.g. fresh fish/flowers are delivered directly to the retailer. High-quality products may be sold directly to consumer.

Market size: If the market is large, then using a wholesaler to break bulk, store goods and transport products to the retailer may be the most economical distribution option. Cadburys distributes their products through wholesalers like Musgrave Group.

E-business: Companies can advertise and sell their products online using a company website. Consumers place orders and goods are delivered using the postal system or a courier delivery service. Dell computers is an example.

Technological developments: Have enabled direct contact between business and the consumer, e.g. direct banking and insurance services. Customers can get quotations over the telephone, pay for services with a credit card, transfer funds, etc. These services were originally carried out in a branch or by an agent or broker.

Marking scheme

2 × 7 marks (3 + 3 + 1) (state/explain/example)
1 × 6 marks (3 + 2 + 1) (state/explain/example)

Getting Started

 Be able to:

- Identify and explain the elements involved in setting up a new business.
- Explain the stages involved in setting up a new business.
- List the main sources of finance available for setting up a new business.
- **HL** Apply the main sources of finance available for setting up a new business.
- Identify the elements of the production processes.
- Illustrate the central role of the business plan.

Why people set up their own business

1. **Independence** – The wish to be independent and have control over their own situation.
2. **Profit** – A belief that they will make more money and enjoy a better standard of living by being self-employed.
3. **Redundancy** – A person is made redundant and has difficulty finding employment.
4. **Spotting an opportunity** – The entrepreneur spots an opportunity in the market or comes up with a new idea.
5. **Ambition** – They want to fulfil a lifelong ambition.

Important start-up decisions
When starting up a business an entrepreneur must make decisions on:

- Finance
- Ownership
- Production

Finance options
The entrepreneur must decide where to get the money from to set up the business. Sources of finance can be divided into three categories, depending on the length of time for which the money is required.

Sources of finance

- Short-term sources – Due for repayment within one year.
- Medium-term sources – Due to be repaid between one and five years.
- Long-term sources – Available for longer than five years.

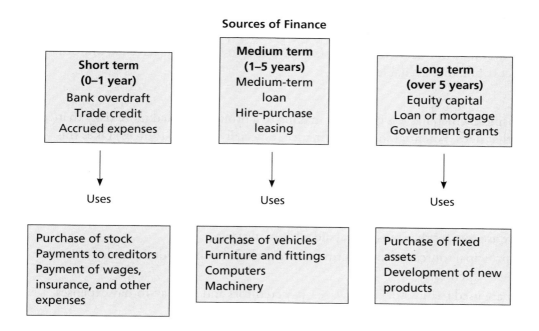

Sources of Finance

Short term (0–1 year)	Medium term (1–5 years)	Long term (over 5 years)
Bank overdraft Trade credit Accrued expenses	Medium-term loan Hire-purchase leasing	Equity capital Loan or mortgage Government grants

Uses → Uses → Uses →

Purchase of stock Payments to creditors Payment of wages, insurance, and other expenses	Purchase of vehicles Furniture and fittings Computers Machinery	Purchase of fixed assets Development of new products

Factors that should be considered before choosing between different sources of finance

Cost

A business should try to obtain the cheapest source of finance available. The rate of interest is of great importance. All loans advertised by financial institutions should quote the **APR**. Close examination of the **APR** attached to each type of loan finance is needed when making the choice.

Purpose/correct match

Sources of finance must be matched with uses (e.g. a long-term business expansion plan should not be financed by a bank overdraft). Assets which are going to last a long time are paid for with long-term finance. Day-to-day expenses are financed or paid for with short-term finance.

Amount

Large amounts of money are not available through some sources. Some sources of finance may not offer flexibility for smaller amounts.

Control

Issuing new voting shares in a company could lead to a change of power. The use of loan capital will not affect voting control, but financial institutions such as the bank may take control of fixed assets or impose conditions as part of the loan agreement.

Collateral

Lenders often seek security before giving finance. This restricts the freedom of the borrower regarding what it wishes to do with these particular assets. Sometimes the borrower may not have enough assets to give as security, which can then limit the sources of finance available.

Risk

A business which has less chance of making to a profit is deemed more risky than one that does. Potential sources of finance (especially external sources) takes this into account and may not lend money to higher-risk businesses, unless there is some guarantee that their money will be returned.

Short-term sources of finance

These are sources that must be repaid within one year.

The principal sources of short-term finance include bank overdraft, trade credit and accrued expenses.

They are used to buy stock, pay wages, pay creditors and pay day-to-day expenses.

Bank overdraft

- A bank overdraft is a short-term source of finance.
- The bank allows current account holders to withdraw more money from the account than the amount in the account.
- A limit is set for the overdraft.

Cost: Interest is charged on overdrawn funds.

Risk: Bank can demand full repayment at any time.

Security: No security is required to obtain a bank overdraft.

Control: The owner keeps full control of the business.

Trade credit

- This involves buying goods on credit and paying for them later.
- It is provided by suppliers rather than by financial institutions.

Cost: It is a free source of finance but interest may be charged on overdue accounts.

Risk: Failure to repay will damage a business's credit rating and make it difficult to buy on credit in the future.

Security: No security required to buy goods on credit.

Control: The owner keeps full control of the business.

Accrued expenses

- Expenses/services incurred by a business but not yet paid for (e.g. telephone and electricity charges).
- By delaying payment the money can be used for other purposes.

Cost: It is a free source of finance – no interest is charged.
Risk: Failure to repay will damage a business's credit rating and reputation.
Security: No security required.
Control: The owner keeps full control of the business.

Medium-term sources of finance

These are sources that must be repaid between one and five years.
The principal sources of medium-term finance are medium-term loans, leasing and hire purchase. They are used to purchase vehicles, machinery, office equipment, etc.

Medium-term loan

- A medium-term loan is negotiated with the bank and repaid in agreed instalments over an agreed period between one and five years.
- The interest on the loan is tax deductible and large amounts of finance can be raised.
- Repayment can be arranged to suit ability to pay.
- The bank may require security or personal guarantees to ensure the loan is repaid.

Cost: Interest is charged on the loan.
Risk: Failure to repay the loan will damage the business's credit rating and may result in the security provided being sold to repay the loan.
Security: Security may be required depending on the amount of the loan.
Control: The owner keeps full control of the business.

Leasing

- Leasing is a medium-term source of finance and involves the renting of an asset from a finance company.
- The business will never own the asset.
- The business has possession and use of the asset during the period of the lease.
- The business does not have to use a cash lump sum to buy the asset.
- No security is required.
- Lease repayments can be set off against profits to reduce tax liability.
- The business may have the option to replace the asset if it becomes obsolete.

Cost: Monthly rentals may be expensive. Rentals are tax deductible.
Risk: Failure to repay rental will damage the business's credit rating and may result in the asset being repossessed.

Security: No security is required to obtain leasing finance.
Control: The owner keeps full control of the business.

Hire purchase

- Purchasing an asset by paying a deposit and paying the balance with interest by regular instalments over an agreed period.
- The asset remains the property of the hire purchase company until the final payment is made.

Cost: The interest charged on hire purchase finance is high.
Risk: Failure to repay will damage the business's credit rating and may result in the asset being repossessed.
Security: No security is required to get hire purchase finance.
Control: The owner keeps full control of the business.

Long-term sources of finance

These are sources that must be repaid after five years.
The principal sources of long-term finance are equity capital, long-term loans and government grants.
Long-term finance should be used to finance the permanent assets of the business.

Equity capital

- A source of long-term finance.
- It is the permanent capital of a company used to finance the permanent assets of the business.
- The money is provided by the shareholders who receive dividends from company profits.
- There is no commitment to equity shareholders that they will receive a dividend each year.

Cost: Dividend paid to shareholder every year.
Risk: Loss of capital if business fails.
Security: No security is required to obtain equity capital.
Control: The owner loses some control to new shareholders. Shareholders must be given shares and votes in return for their investment.

Long-term loans

- These are loans for five years or longer.
- They are provided by financial institutions and repaid by instalments.
- Finance is used for large capital expenditure (fixed assets).

Cost: High interest payments.
Risk: Failure to repay the loan will damage the business's credit rating and may result in the security provided being sold to repay the loan.

Security: Fixed assets are required as security. If the start-up business does not own fixed assets, the owner may be asked to sign a personal guarantee that the loan will be repaid.

Control: The owner keeps full control of the business.

Government grants

- Money from the government which does not have to be repaid.
- There are usually specific conditions attached.
- The grants are expected to create employment and are only given for potentially viable projects.
- Grants are available from Enterprise Ireland and country and city enterprise boards.

Cost: There is no interest to be paid or repayments to be made.

Risk: If the conditions attached are not fulfilled, the grant may be recalled.

Security: No security required to get a government grant.

Control: The owner keeps full control of the business.

Management of working capital

Management of working capital is essential for start-up businesses.

Working Capital is the finance used for the day-to-day running and payment of immediate debts of the business. It is the excess of current assets over current liabilities. If working capital is positive, the business is said to be liquid. If working capital is negative, the business is not liquid and said to be overtrading.

Liquidity is the ability of the business to pay short-term debts as they arise.

If working capital is negative (current liabilities are greater than current assets), the business is said to be **overtrading**.

Overtrading arises when a firm increases production and sales too much or too quickly and runs short of cash.

How to manage working capital

To manage working capital, a business must exercise:

- Credit control
- Stock control
- Cash flow management

Credit control

Credit control is exercised over trade debtors to ensure customers who buy goods on credit pay their debts on time to minimise the risk of bad debts.

Good working capital management involves good credit control, which improves cash flow.

Stock control

Stock control is an important part of working capital management.

It ensures that the firm has the correct amount of stock at all times to satisfy customer demand – never too much, never too little.

Cash flow management

Management of cash flow is another vital element of working capital management.

A cash flow forecast is an estimate of a firm's future cash inflow and cash outflows.

It draws attention to periods of negative cash flow so that arrangements can be made to ensure that finance is available.

It also draws attention to periods of surplus when excess funds can be invested.

Read the information supplied below and answer the questions which follow.

Marie Nolan is the owner of Marie's Pizzas, a successful pizza restaurant with a home-delivery service. Demand for takeaways has increased, as more people are eating at home due to the economic downturn. Marie is planning to expand her business through franchising, and her accountant recommends that a business plan should be prepared before going ahead.

(i) Discuss the factors that should be considered when choosing between different sources of finance.

(ii) Analyse **two** appropriate sources of finance for acquiring an additional delivery van at Marie's Pizzas.

(30 marks)

Source: 2010 Higher Level Section 3

Suggested solution

(i) **Cost:** a business should try to obtain the cheapest source of finance available. The rate of interest is of great importance. All loans advertised by financial institutions should quote the **APR**. Close examination of the **APR** attached to each type of loan finance is needed when making the choice.

- **Purpose/Correct match:** Sources of finance must be matched with uses, e.g. a long-term business expansion plan should not be financed by a bank overdraft. Assets which are going to last a long time are paid for with long-term finance. Day-to-day expenses are financed or paid for with short-term finance.

- **Amount:** Large amounts of money are not available through some sources. Some sources of finance may not offer flexibility for smaller amounts.

- **Control:** Issuing new voting shares in a company could lead to a change of power. The use of loan capital will not affect voting control, but financial institutions such as banks may take control of fixed assets or impose conditions as part of the loan agreement.

- **Collateral:** Lenders often seek security before giving finance. This restricts the freedom of the borrower regarding what it wishes to do with these particular assets. Sometimes the borrower may not have enough assets to give as security, which can then limit the sources of finance available.

- **Risk:** A business which has less chance of making a profit is deemed more risky than one that does. Potential sources of finance (especially external sources) take this into account and may not lend money to higher risk businesses, unless there is some guarantee that their money will be returned.
- **Status of the business:** Private Limited or Public Limited companies will find it easier to obtain finance than a sole trader as they are required to prepare far more detailed financial information, which can assist the finance-raising process by the banks.

(ii) Medium-Term Loan

- A medium-term loan is obtained for a period of one to five years.
- Interest must be paid, but it is tax deductible.
- The loan is repaid in agreed instalments.
- The bank may require security or personal guarantees to ensure the loan is repaid.

Leasing

- This involves renting rather than purchasing the asset.
- The business will never get to own the asset.
- Payments may be offset against tax.
- No security is required.
- While it costs more than cash purchase, it helps a business's cash flow.
- The business may have an option to replace the asset if it becomes obsolete.

Hire Purchase

- This is purchasing an asset in instalments and ownership passes with the final payment.
- It is expensive and carries a high rate of interest.
- No security is required, but the lender may repossess the asset if you default on repayments.
- It is not as tax-efficient as leasing.

Marking scheme

(i) 3 factors when choosing between sources of finance	3 × 5 marks (2 + 3)
(i) **2 medium-term** sources of finance	8 marks (2 + 3 + 3)
	7 marks (2 + 3 + 2)
	State, explain, explain

30 marks total

Ownership options

When starting a business, an entrepreneur has a choice of many different types of business structures through which to conduct business.

There are three basic structures to choose from:

- Sole trader
- Partnership
- Private limited company

Sole trader

A sole trader is a person who owns and runs his/her own business.

The key features of a sole trader are:

- Owner makes all the decisions – complete control
- Owner keeps all the profits
- Easily set up – few regulations
- Unlimited liability – sole trader is responsible for all debts of the business and may have to sell personal assets to pay business debts
- A lot of pressure and work for one person

Partnership

A partnership is when between two and 20 people form a business together in order to make profit.

The key features of a partnership are:

- Risks and responsibilities and decision-making are shared
- More capital is available to run the business
- Different skills and expertise of partners
- Easy and inexpensive to form
- Profits and losses are shared
- Unlimited liability

Private limited company

A private limited company is a business set up by between one and 149 people called shareholders.

The key features of a private limited company are:

- Shareholders have limited liability – this means that if the business fails, the shareholders can only lose the amount they have invested in the business. They cannot lose their private property to pay business debts.
- Shareholders buy shares in the company and this forms its share capital. Profits are divided among shareholders through dividends.
- A limited company is a legal entity separate from its owners.
- A board of directors is elected by shareholders to run the company.

Production options

Having decided what products to produce, a firm must choose a method of production. There are three main methods of production:

- Job production
- Batch production
- Mass production

Job production

- This is the production of a product to a specific customer order.
- It is a one-off production unit – a unique product.
- It is not produced to be held in stock.
- Highly skilled, direct labour is required.
- The product is expensive.

Examples of job production products include:

- Customised kitchen
- Wedding dress
- Specially produced pieces of crystal for presentations
- Hand-crafted furniture
- Shipbuilding

Batch production

- This is the production of certain quantities of identical products in one production run, and then production switches to a different batch.
- Skilled or semi-skilled labour is used.
- Uses a lot of flexible machines (e.g. ovens).
- The products produced are of average price and held in stock in anticipation of a customer's demand.

Examples of products produced using batch production:

- Bread baked in different sizes
- Production of clothing in different sizes, colours and designs
- School textbooks
- Paint and wallpaper manufacturing
- Carpet manufacturing

Mass production

- This is the production of large numbers of identical products.
- There is non-stop, continuous production.
- Items are produced for stock and then sold – large demand is essential.
- High degree of automation, resulting in low labour costs.
- Unit costs are reduced as the firm benefits from large-scale production.

Examples of products produced using mass production:

- Golf balls
- Ballpoint pens
- Cars
- Toilet paper
- Cornflakes
- Chocolate bars

Read the information supplied and answer the questions that follow.

Sarah Fleming is a wedding dress designer and has worked for over 20 years in the bridal and clothing industry. She specialises in creating unique wedding dresses with an emphasis on personal service.

Business is good and Sarah has applied for a bank loan of €10,000 to finance expansion.

(i) Name the type of production process used by Sarah.

(ii) Outline **two** challenges for Sarah of this type of production process.

(iii) Discuss two implications for Sarah of changing to another type of production process.

(25 marks)

Source: 2014 Higher Level Section 3

Suggested solution

(i) **Job Production**

(ii) The product involved, i.e. the designer wedding dress, requires highly skilled labour. Sarah will have to continue her professional development to keep up with new production techniques, IT developments, and changes in fashion and style.

Highly skilled labour will mean a higher wages bill. This type of work is very labour-intensive and the high salaries will increase the running costs of the business.

Raw materials, equipment, tools and machinery are expensive for this specialised production. In addition, it is generally a small-scale operation and does not benefit from economies of scale. It is a very slow process.

Quality standards have to be very high. There is no room for error. The slightest fault with the product will have to be corrected in an efficient manner to prevent the loss of the sale and business's reputation.

Once-off production to a specific order: If the customer ordering the product is unable to pay (goes bankrupt), it may be difficult to find an alternative buyer.

(iii) Discuss **two** implications for Sarah of changing to another type of production process.

Both batch and flow (mass) production are heavily automated production processes. Substantial investment in machinery, equipment, IT, premises, etc. will be required.

Finance will be required to fund the necessary investment. Sarah will have to look carefully at her finance options. Are her reserves adequate? If not, long-term loans for capital investment and finance for increased working capital needs will have to be sourced.

Sarah will have to review the ownership structure and maybe change to a private limited company in order to be able to raise finance through selling shares and benefit from limited liability. This involves a loss of control of the business.

Sarah will no longer be making goods to order. She will be creating goods for stock. A stock control system will have to be developed, leading to increased costs. A marketing plan will have to be implemented.

Marking scheme

(i) 5 marks

(ii) 2 × 5 marks (3 + 2)

(iii) 2 × 5 marks (3 + 2)

Business plan

A good business plan is essential for all start-up businesses.

Benefits for a business of preparing a business plan

Guide to future action

A plan provides a focus for the business and guides the actions of individuals.

A **business plan** sets out how a business is going to achieve its aims and objectives. It outlines the marketing, production and financial plans for the proposed business.

Finance/Grants

A business plan can be used when seeking finance for a business venture from a financial institution or grants from government agencies.

No financial institution/government agency will give finance to a business without being convinced that the investment has a good chance of being recovered.

Assessing performance

A plan provides a benchmark against which performance can be measured. If targets are not reached, then action to fix the problem can be implemented.

Viability

In preparing a business plan, all aspects of a business are analysed. A SWOT analysis may be carried out, problem areas can be identified and steps taken to deal with them. By planning ahead, the business can foresee difficulties and take steps to address the problems.

Read the information supplied below and answer the questions that follow.

Zac Computing Ltd, an innovative new technology business, considers its business plan to be an essential document in the context of a business start-up and future growth.

(i) Explain the term 'business plan'.

(ii) Evaluate the importance of a business plan to an innovative new technology business.

(20 marks)

Suggested solution

(i) A business plan is a written statement/proposal about the business and its objectives (where it wants to go) and strategies in areas such as marketing, ownership, production, finance and the identifying of opportunities. It is important in the context of business start-ups.

(ii)

- It sets out both short- and long-term strategies/plans over agreed time periods, e.g. one year, five years, ten years, etc. It plans how to get where the enterprise wants to go and, as such, gives the entrepreneur a focus.

  E.g. 'Achieve healthy gross margin in the first year of operation. Maintain just-in-time (JIT) inventory levels. Increase sales modestly but steadily in the second and third year.'

- It is a vital document when approaching any financial institution, grant agencies or other investors seeking funds (capital) for the enterprise. No financial institutions will give funds to an enterprise without being convinced that the investment has a good chance of being recovered. The business plan markets the enterprise; it sells the business ideas to others and encourages them to seriously consider the project.

  E.g. 'Managing the business by implementing and consistently measuring and adjusting goals/targets and actual results, i.e. financial goals vs. results'.

- The nature of the business plan is such that targets are set in figures wherever possible. By having these figures available, they can be used as the benchmarks or standards against which the operations and performance of the enterprise can be measured. If the standards are not reached, then the action to fix the problem can be implemented.

  E.g. 'Managing the business by implementing and consistently measuring and adjusting goals/targets and actual results, i.e. employee learning and growth goals vs. results, customer satisfaction goals vs. results'.

Evaluation: A business plan will enable the business to determine if it can be commercially viable. It may support the business when seeking sources of finance from potential investors.

Marking scheme

(i)   6 marks (3 + 3)

(ii) 2 × 6 marks (3 + 2 + 1) + 2

(State/explain/reference to Zac Computing Ltd/evaluate)

Example of a Business Plan

MICHELLE MORAN CATERING SERVICE LTD

Company ownership and management structure

Name of company:	Michelle Moran Catering Service Ltd
Formed:	1 January 2019
Shareholders:	Michelle Moran, Audrey Griffin
Registered office:	45 O'Connell Street, Killarney, Co. Kerry
Solicitors:	Keane and Irwin, Killarney
Accountants:	Ferguson and Keegan Ltd, Killarney
Bankers:	Allied Irish Bank, Main Street, Killarney
Managing Director:	Michelle Moran
Education:	Business Studies degree, University of Limerick
Work experience:	Ten years' experience in catering industry

Product or service

Salad rolls, sandwiches, sausage rolls, soup, scones, cakes
Unique selling points: Home-made products, prompt delivery, personal service and quality

Marketing and marketing strategy

Target market:	300 small businesses, including factories and schools without canteen facilities requiring supplies
Market niche:	Schools, colleges and factories
Competition:	Confectioners, bakeries and delicatessens
Targets:	100 customers after six months
Pricing policy:	10 per cent lower than competitors

Sales and distribution

Advertising and promotion: Brochures, newspapers, leaflets, local radio
Distribution: Local morning delivery service

Financing

<u>Requirements:</u>

Ten-year lease of premises		€20,000
Equipment		€10,000
Motor vehicle		€15,000
Working capital		€5,000
		€50,000

<u>Finance available:</u>

Own investment (equity)	€10,000	
Grant (CEB)	€5,000	€15,000
Finance required:		€35,000

<u>Financial projections</u>

See projected profit and loss accounts and balance sheet (three years), cash flow forecast and break-even charts (three years) enclosed.

Michelle Moran
_____

Michelle Moran

(i) Outline the main sections contained in a business plan.

(ii) Explain the importance of a business plan for **two** different stakeholders.

(20 marks)

Source: 2017 Higher Level Section 3

Suggested solution

(i) **Production**

Reference to:

- Type of production
- Machinery required
- Targets
- Production plan, lead times

Development of points required.

Marketing

Reference to:

- Marketing mix
- Results of market research

Development of points required.

Finance

Reference to:

- Forecasted Revenue and Costs
- Cash Flow Forecast
- Production Budgets
- Projected Profits

Development of points required.

Business details (company registration, etc.)

Reference to:

- Details of directors
- Details of shareholders
- Legal organisation (company/sole trader/partnership)

Development of points required.

(ii) **Employees**

Employees are interested in a business plan to confirm if the business is going to survive so they can have **employment security**.

They may also be interested to see if the business is going to expand and possibly offer opportunities for promotion in the future.

Investors (the profitability)

Investors will be interested in a business plan to see if the business is **capable of making a profit and offering a good return on their investment**. Projected sales and market research results may persuade investors to provide capital to a business.

Financial institutions (the cash position)

Financial institutions require business plans from a business when they are seeking loan capital. It helps finance providers to make a decision regarding **finance approval** as they can see the experience of the owners/management and analyse their ideas. It is the primary tool to convey the potential viability of the business to finance providers.

Management/employer

Management will use a business plan as a source of control. They will use it to **measure actual performance against goals and see if the business has progressed satisfactorily.** The management have goals to be reached, and the business plan provides benchmarks which they can use to monitor actual business performance against the set targets in the business plan.

Suppliers

Suppliers will be interested in a customer's business plan to ensure that the business is viable and **can sustain any line of credit** that is offered to them.

Government agencies

Government agencies will be interested if finance or other assistance is sought by a business.

Marking scheme

(i) 3 × 4 marks (2 + 2)

(ii) 2 × 4 marks (2 + 2)

Read the information supplied and answer the question that follows.

Having been made redundant, Lia O'Brien has decided to set up her own enterprise manufacturing individually designed disposable tableware and paper cups for small coffee shops and restaurants.

She recognises, however, that having an idea and having the will to succeed will not be enough to ensure success.

Discuss the key issues Lia will have to address before setting up her business enterprise.

(15 marks)

Source: 2015 Higher Level Section 3

Suggested solution

Raising finance/capital: Lia will decide how much debt capital and equity capital she is going to use as sources of finance for the growth and expansion of her business. Debt capital carries the risks associated with being highly geared. Fixed interest repayments on debt capital must be made regardless of profitability.

Production method: A firm must choose an appropriate method of production that suits the type of goods being manufactured and the potential demand for the product. Job or batch production have different demands in terms of automation, staffing and storage. Lia will have to opt for job or batch production in order to manufacture the different range of products she is selling.

Ownership options: An ownership structure has to be decided upon. Different structures have different demands in terms of risk, control, ownership, liability, tax implications, etc. It would be advisable for Lia to choose a private limited company structure because of the benefits of limited liability, incorporation and raising finance, etc.

Marketing her business: Finding customers/market research/deciding on brand/USP/advertising, etc.

Availability of services: (Infrastructure/utilities/labour, etc.)

Marking scheme

3 × 5 marks (2 + 2 + 1)

18 Business Expansion

Reasons for expansion

1. Economies of scale

The general cost of running a large enterprise rather than a smaller one may be reduced due to rationalisation and cutting down expenses. Large-scale production arising from expansion reduces the unit cost of production.

2. Increased financial strength and security

A large business enterprise commands prestige, influence and power with banks, other businesses and government departments. A larger business will survive better in a recession.

3. Eliminate competition

Competition can be eliminated by a merger or takeover of a competitor that is a threat to the business.

4. Protect sources of raw materials

A business might want to control a source of raw materials on which its future depends by taking over the supplier.

5. Diversification

Growth allows a business to branch into different product ranges. This reduces risk, since a diversified business does not depend on any one product type.

6. Synergy

This is the theory that the sum of two amalgamated businesses is higher than the sum of the two enterprises if they remained separate. It allows for the closure of the inefficient plant and the sale of the assets that may not be required.

Finance for expansion

Expansion is a long-term activity, so appropriate long-term finance should be sought for it.

There are three long-term sources of finance for expansion:

- Equity capital
- Retained earnings
- Debt capital

Equity capital

The company raises finance by selling ordinary shares.

Shareholders receive a share of the profit of the business in the form of a dividend.

Shareholders have voting rights and a say in policy-making.

In the event of the business being wound up, ordinary shareholders only get what remains after all other debts are paid.

Benefits of using equity capital to finance expansion

Equity finance allows a business to obtain finance without incurring debt.

Equity capital is a cheap source of finance as there is no guarantee to equity shareholders that they will receive a dividend each year.

Share capital does not have to be repaid to shareholders except on the winding up of the company.

Equity capital does not create any cost for the business except the payment of dividends.

Disadvantages of using equity capital to finance expansion

Issuing shares to new shareholders reduces the control of the existing shareholders in the decision-making process.

Issuing shares is expensive as there are various legal formalities and professional fees to be met.

Retained earnings

This is the amount of profit reinvested in the business for expansion rather than distributed as dividends.

The use of retained earnings is very suitable to finance expansion as there is no cost involved and there is no loss of control.

Debt capital

This is a long-term loan from a financial institution to finance expansion.

Interest on the loan must be repaid to the lender irrespective of profitability.

Taking out a loan does not affect the control of the owners in the decision-making process in the business.

Benefits of using debt capital to finance expansion

Debt capital is easy to get. There are many different types of business loans available from banks.

Interest payments are an allowable expense in the profit and loss account, reducing the tax liability of the business.

Disadvantages of using debt capital to finance expansion

All loan interest and capital repayments must be made to the bank, irrespective of business performance.

Repayments of interest and capital may affect the liquidity of the business.

Debt capital and equity capital as sources of finance for expansion

> Equity Capital = Ordinary Share Capital + Reserves
> Debt Capital = Long-term Loans

Debt capital and equity capital may be compared as follows:

	Equity Capital	Debt Capital
1. Cost/Interest/Dividends	There is no obligation to pay dividends to shareholders.	Interest payments must be made.
2. Risk	Low – The business is lowly geared. The business has no long-term debt and no interest repayments.	High – The business is highly geared. Interest payments must be made regardless of profitability.
3. Control	The issue of shares may dilute the control of the existing shareholders.	Debt capital will not impact on control of business.
4. Security	No security required.	Security is required.
5. Tax implications	Dividends to ordinary shareholders are not tax deductible.	Interest payments are tax deductible.

Evaluation

Generally companies will use a combination of both debt capital and equity capital to finance their business.

Equity capital is low risk and does not require security. However, loss of confidence in the stock market is a challenge to raising equity capital.

Debt capital is high risk. Interest must be paid, irrespective of profitability. However, the current economic climate poses challenges in obtaining finance from financial institutions.

Implications of business expansion

For	Short Term	Long Term
Share price	Share price should increase because of increased demand for shares in a bigger company.	Successful expansion will lead to an increase in the value of the business in the long term, leading to an increase in share price.
Products	Larger businesses will have a wider range of products.	Because of continuing market research and product development, there will be a wider range of products in the long term.
Company structure	A formal management structure with a clear chain of command must be set up to deal with a wider range of activities.	As business grows larger, more delegation is necessary to successfully manage the business.
Finance	Finance in the form of equity capital and debt capital must be raised to finance expansion.	As the business grows, it should be easier to raise equity capital and debt capital in the future.
Profits and dividends	The high cost of expansion and possible redundancy payments may lead to a reduction in profit and dividends in the short term.	Increased efficiency and the success of expansion will lead to increased profits and dividends in the long term.
Employees	Expansion may lead to uncertainty about the future, poor motivation, cost-cutting and possible job losses.	As business grows, employees can be provided with better wages, better working conditions, training and promotion opportunities.
Customers	Economies of scale should provide customers with more competitively priced products.	Customers benefit from a wider range of products and lower prices, but lose personal contact with the owner.

Methods of expansion

Internal growth (organic growth)

This is growth generated from within the business using its own resources. Internal growth occurs when a firm:

- Retains its profits
- Uses its retained profits to invest in additional fixed assets and resources

Internal growth is achieved by:

- Increasing sales in existing home markets
- Developing new markets – new markets can be entered by:
  - **Exporting** – Selling products into foreign markets.
  - **Franchising** – The granting of a licence by the franchiser to the franchisee allowing the sale of their product or service (e.g. McDonald's, Subway, Domino's Pizza, Supermac's, Eddie Rocket's).

External growth (inorganic growth)

Business alliance

An agreement between two or more businesses to pool resources and expertise to work together over a specified period of time or to complete a specified project while all parties maintain their separate identities.

A business can expand externally by:
- Business alliance
- Merger
- Takeover

The partners benefit from the sharing of:

- Expertise/skills
- Business networks and markets
- Increased resources

The **advantages of an alliance** as a form of business expansion are that it:

- Is a cost-effective method of expansion. Resources are shared and costs are divided between partners.
- Reduces the risks associated with expansion for each partner as risks are shared.
- Provides access to extended business network and markets.

Example: North Cork Business Alliance

A group consisting of sole traders, small businesses and companies who 'share knowledge and expertise to better serve their customers and to develop and enhance business by exchanging quality referrals'.

Merger

A merger occurs when two companies voluntarily agree to come together to run their business as one single company.

'A merger is an agreement between two companies to bring both firms together under a common board of directors.'

Example: British Airways and the Spanish carrier Iberia merged to create the world's third-largest airline.

Takeover

A takeover is the purchase of one company by another with or without its consent.

Example: The Pfizer Pharmaceuticals takeover of drug maker Hospira Inc. The value of the takeover was $15 billion.

Advantages of mergers and takeovers

- Economies of scale – they can make savings from being bigger.
- They can compete better with larger firms.
- They can invest more finance in research and development, leading to better quality goods for consumers.

Importance of business expansion

Importance of business expansion in Ireland

- Employment is created, which reduces the numbers unemployed.
- Increased tax revenue for government.
- Better quality goods and services as more money is spent on research and development by bigger businesses.
- Bigger firms can compete better on international markets.

Importance of Irish business expansion in foreign markets

- Economies of scale – selling into foreign markets means large-scale production, reducing unit cost.
- Increased sales and profit for firms exporting into foreign markets.
- Expanding into foreign markets means the business is less dependent on home market.
- Exporting improves balance of payments. Money comes into the country.

HL

'For a business to survive it needs to grow and expand.'

(i) Evaluate **two** methods of business expansion. (20 marks)

(ii) Discuss the short-term and long-term implications of business expansion using the following headings:

Organisation structure; Product mix; Profitability; Employment

(20 marks)

Suggested solution

(i) A merger:

- A **friendly or voluntary** amalgamation or joining together of two or more firms for their mutual benefit, trading under a common name.
- A **single new legal entity** is formed once it is approved by shareholders.
- E.g. Irish Permanent and Trustee Savings Bank merged to form Permanent TSB. Avonmore Co-op and Waterford Foods merged to form Glanbia plc.
- It is a defensive strategy as the merger may involve diversification into new product areas, which reduces the risk of the firm 'having all its eggs in the one basket'.
- Costs will be lower because of economies of scale and the sharing of costs and resources.

Evaluation: **Own judgement required**

A takeover:

- This occurs when one company purchases 51% or more of the shares in another company, in either a hostile or friendly manner.
- The acquiring company absorbs the other company, which loses its identity after the acquisition and becomes part of the acquiring company.
- The cost of the takeover can be very expensive.
- Eircom took over Meteor mobile phone company for €420 million. Google bought the popular online video site YouTube for $1.65 billion. Google also acquired Motorola Mobility, a mobile device manufacturing company, for $12.5 billion.

Evaluation: **Own judgement required**

A strategic alliance:

- When two or more independent firms agree to co-operate and share resources and expertise with each other for the mutual benefit of all parties involved.
- The firms remain completely independent legally and each firm maintains its own separate trading identity.
- Google has worked with several corporations in order to improve production and services. For example, in January 2013, Google announced a partnership with Kia Motors and Hyundai. The partnership integrated Google maps and placed it into new car models, which were released later in 2013.
- The firms benefit from the sharing of resources and talent that otherwise they wouldn't have access to. Either party can end the arrangement easily if they choose to do so.

Evaluation: Own judgement required

A franchise:

- is a business arrangement whereby the franchisor (the existing business with the proven business model) grants a contractual licence/permission to the franchisee (person setting up the business) to use its name, logo and business idea in return for a fee or a percentage of profits or sales.
- franchisor can expand his/her business without having to invest further capital or take additional risks as these are passed onto the franchisee in the contractual arrangement.
- franchises in Ireland include: The Zip Yard, Gloria Jean's Coffees, McDonald's and GEMS.
- is a cost-effective form of expansion for the franchisor. It can also be risky for a franchisor as, if standards are not maintained by the franchisee, the image of the franchisor could be affected.

Evaluation: **Own judgement required**

(ii) *Organisation structure:*

Short-term implication

- As the business expands, a new structure may be required as more activities may need to be organised. The business needs a formal organisation structure such as a functional structure, which clearly identifies the chain of command and span of control within the business.

Long-term implication

- This functional organisation structure may be replaced by a geographic structure to facilitate expansion into new geographic regions or a product structure to facilitate the increased range of products.
- As businesses grow, they rely more on specialist support functions and personnel. An IT Department and/or a HR Department may be introduced to assist line managers and thereby increase efficiency.

Product mix:

Short-term implication

- As the business begins to expand, the product mix and portfolio of products available for sale will increase to suit the wider range of market segments targeted by the business.
- Any products acquired during growth that do not fit the company's business model may be sold off.
- Wider product range makes the management of the marketing mix more difficult.

Long-term implication

- Mergers and acquisitions will allow the business to satisfy the various niche markets. This will result in further investment in R&D and product development in order to satisfy the wide range of market segments the business is selling into.
- Different marketing mixes may have to be put in place for the wider range of products.

Profitability:

Short-term implication

Short-term restructuring costs. Initially, profits may fall as a result of the increased expenditure on assets such as machinery, buildings, IT and R&D, premises, etc.

Diseconomies of scale due to lack of proper management and duplication of work.

Long-term implication

- As the business consolidates its position during business growth and maturity, sales and revenues should increase leading to greater profitability.
- The business may develop economies of scale such as bulk buying, increased market power, automation and elimination of duplication leading to efficiencies and greater profitability.
- Greater profits will allow for higher dividends to shareholders, encouraging further investment and the build-up of reserves.
- Profits could also fall in the long term due to diseconomies of scale (poor management, lower employee motivation resulting from very big business).
- Disconnection between management and employees.

Employment:

Short-term implication

- Initial expansion may result in rationalisation as the business attempts to remove wasteful duplication of roles. This can lead to compulsory redundancies. The uncertainty/fear about the future can demotivate staff and management and cause industrial relations problems (different pay and reward systems).
- Work relationships could be stressful, due to uncertainty.
- More training required for staff.

Long-term implication

As the business consolidates its position during business growth and maturity, its HR department may be able to engage in a recruitment drive for new employees as part of its manpower planning.

The business may be able to motivate workers through higher wages and better working conditions.

Staff training and development opportunities could open up promotion possibilities for staff, improving staff morale and industrial relations.

Bigger businesses could attract highly qualified personnel.

Marking scheme

(i) Two methods @ 10 marks each (2 + 3 + 3 + 2)

(Name explain/explain/evaluate)

(ii) 4 × 5 marks (4 + 1)

Applied Business Question (ABQ) (Higher Level)

Based on Units 3, 4 and 5

This is a compulsory question for Leaving Certificate 2021/2026

Digibrand

Ryan Cullen studied Marketing, Innovation and Technology as part of his degree at Dublin City University (DCU). In his third year of study, he set up Digibrand, a digital marketing agency developing marketing campaigns for businesses, using various forms of digital and electronic media such as internet, Facebook, and Twitter to reach consumers. Initially, Ryan carried on his business in TechSpace, a co-working office space in a building in Dublin. Ten other like-minded tech entrepreneurs shared the office space, each paying €300 a desk per month. Ryan had instant and affordable access to facilities such as high-speed broadband, security and meeting rooms.

In the second year of business, Ryan obtained more projects than he could handle, so he teamed up with two classmates, Jane McDaid and Mark Reilly. Ryan offered them a percentage commission on each project they worked on, and he consistently praised the high standard of their work. Decisions were made democratically. Ryan actively encouraged their suggestions on designs and always obtained their point of view before finalising a website design, marketing content for social media or a logo for clients in different industry sectors. In the evenings after college, Ryan used Skype to share opinions with the team, and used email to send design and graphics between each member of the team. Ryan gave responsibility for a major project to Jane, as he believed she had the potential to create a very innovative marketing campaign. Upon graduation, Ryan decided to completely focus on the business and Jane and Mark began working for him full-time.

Digibrand was gaining more clients. Ryan needed to relocate as he wished to expand his office space and build the business. He researched renting an office in a business park rather than buying a premises. He discovered he would need finance to pay three months' rent in advance, and he would need equipment and office furniture.

Like most new start-ups, cash was scarce, and Ryan wished to avoid huge debt. He had to ensure that he managed his working capital. He had to work hard at getting paid quickly for work carried out for clients to ensure he could pay wages and various day-to-day expenses. Profits were increasing by an average of 20% annually, and Ryan reinvested them in the business.

After four years in business, Ryan remained very passionate about Digibrand, which had built up a strong client base in Ireland. Ryan was keen to keep up this pace and momentum. He continued to avail of various supports, including Enterprise Ireland's grant scheme towards R&D costs. At the Dublin Web Summit 2015, Ryan was approached by MediaMania, a leading London-based digital marketing agency, which focuses exclusively on the retail sector in the UK. MediaMania was planning to expand its business outside the UK and was interested in merging with Digibrand. Ryan was unsure of the consequences of merging with another business at this stage, so he held a meeting with Jane and Mark to find out their views on the offer.

(A) Ryan Cullen has developed effective management skills. Would you agree with this statement?

Outline reasons for your answer, with reference to the text of the ABQ. (30 marks)

(B) (i) Identify and describe the most appropriate sources of finance for Digibrand's relocation. (Refer to short-, medium- and long-term sources of finance in your answer.)

(ii) Outline the importance of preparing a cash flow forecast for Digibrand. (30 marks)

(C) (i) Discuss **one** possible opportunity and **one** possible threat for Digibrand of **merging** with MediaMania.

(ii) Evaluate **one** other method which Ryan could consider to grow his business. (20 marks)

(**80 marks**)

Suggested solution

(A) Yes.

Leadership is the act of inspiring/influencing people to perform and engage in achieving goals.

Leadership involves directing and assisting/guiding people on the right course so that everybody works together to achieve the goals of the enterprise. Leaders know how to achieve goals and inspire people along the way.

Delegation involves the assignment of authority and responsibility to another person, generally from a leader to a subordinate, to undertake a specific project as he/she trusts the staff to do the work. Ryan delegates responsibility to staff.

There are various types of leaders/leadership styles including Autocratic, Democratic and Laissez-faire. Ryan displays a Democratic leadership style where power is shared with employees: he includes employees in decision-making, and intrapreneurship is encouraged. Ryan consults and seeks opinions.

Link:

'Ryan actively encouraged their suggestions on designs and always obtained their point of view before finalising a website design, marketing content for social media or a logo for clients in different industry sectors.'

OR

'In the evenings after college, Ryan used Skype to share opinions with the team, and used email to send design and graphics between each member of the team.'

OR

'Ryan gave responsibility for a major project to Jane, as he believed she had the potential to create a very innovative marketing campaign.'

OR

'Decisions were made democratically.'

Motivation

Motivation in management is the process through which managers encourage employees to be productive and effective. Managers put certain factors in place that cause employees to behave in certain ways for the benefit of the business. A culture of empowerment within a business motivates employees. Employees' behaviour can be influenced by motivating them to meet their unsatisfied needs.

Two widely used theories of motivation are Maslow's Theory of Motivation/ McGregor's Theory X and Theory Y. Ryan has adopted Mc Gregor's theory Y approach to motivation.

Theory Y: Employees are interested in their work and are given interesting and challenging jobs. Employees are motivated to change when they are consulted. Employees want to achieve their best and gain respect and recognition.

According to Maslow's theory, employees are motivated by a desire to satisfy five specific needs: physical needs; safety and security needs; social and acceptance needs; esteem needs and self-actualisation needs.

Link:

'Ryan offered them a percentage commission on each project they worked on ...' (Maslow's physical needs)

OR

(and) '... he consistently praised the high standard of their work.' (Maslow's esteem needs)

OR

'Ryan gave responsibility for a major project to Jane, as he believed she had the potential to create a very innovative marketing campaign.' (Maslow's esteem needs)

Communication

Communication involves people exchanging information in order to better understand each other. Consultation implies that good two-way communication exists. Feedback is required to ensure the message has been understood and acted upon.

Communicating the goals/objectives allows the activities of all to be co-ordinated. Upward/downward/horizontal channels of communication are necessary so that everyone understands what tasks they have to perform.

There are a variety of methods of communication used in a business depending on the nature of the message – written, oral, visual and electronic.

Link:

'... obtained their point of view before finalising a website design, marketing content for social media or a logo for clients in different industry sectors.'

OR

'In the evenings after college, Ryan used Skype to share opinions with the team, and used email to send design and graphics between each member of the team.'

OR

'Ryan was unsure of the consequences of merging with another business at this stage, so he held a meeting with Jane and Mark to find out their views on the offer.'

> **Note:**
> You cannot repeat links within a section. Theory has to be relevant to the ABQ. Links for leadership, motivation and communication can overlap, but if a specific link is used to explain one management skill, it cannot be repeated for another management skill.

Marking scheme

(A)	Ryan Cullen has developed effective management skills. Would you agree with this statement? Outline reasons for your answer, with reference to the text of the ABQ.	Yes 3 marks 3 × 9 marks (3 + 3 + 3) (Name/explain/link)

(B) Short-term finance

Bank overdraft

A bank overdraft is a common source of finance for small businesses. It is a facility that allows the business to 'overdraw' on their business current account. The length of time that account is 'overdrawn' has to be negotiated with the bank. The advantage is that the business only needs to borrow when and as much as it needs. A high rate of interest and a facility fee are attached to an overdraft, and the bank can insist on being repaid quickly. It can be used as a form of working capital to aid in the day-to-day running of the business.

Link:

'He discovered he would need finance to pay three months' rent in advance.'

Short-term finance

Accrued expenses (unpaid bills)

Expenses that do not have to be paid until after the service is provided. Service is provided, and, during that time, the money due can be used as a short-term source of finance. No cost involved provided the bill is paid on time.

Link:

'... to ensure he could pay wages and various day-to-day expenses.

Short-term finance

Credit card.

Medium-term

Leasing:

Leasing involves renting an asset from a finance company rather than purchasing it. The business will never own the asset, and, at the end of the leasing period, the owner may start a new leasing agreement with new assets. There is no security required, payments are tax deductible and ownership is not affected. As no lump sum is required, it may improve the cash flow position.

Medium-term

Medium-term loan:

Business can avail of medium-term loans at quite competitive interest rates. The loan is repaid in equal instalments over the period of the loan (one to five years) allowing the business to cash purchase and negotiate the best cash prices available. Interest paid is tax deductible, and control of the business is not affected. Security or personal guarantees may be required to ensure the loan is repaid.

Medium-term

Hire purchase:

Hire purchase involves buying assets over a period of time. A deposit is paid at the beginning, followed by equal instalments and a final payment, after which the buyer now owns the asset. Interest is extremely high, no security is required, however, the assets may be seized if there is a default in repayments.

Link:

'... he would need (to invest in) equipment and office furniture.'

Long-term

Retained profit/ Reserves

The profits of the business can be ploughed back into the business to help it grow. The advantage of reinvested profits is that it does not have an associated cost. The disadvantage is that it may be limited and so could constrain the rate of business expansion.

Link:

'Profits were increasing by an average of 20% annually and Ryan reinvested them in the business.'

Government grants
Grants are available to businesses that create employment, from various government agencies such as Enterprise Ireland and LEOs (Local Enterprise Offices) for start-up, expansion, research and development, etc. Grants normally are interest-free and do not have to be repaid if used for the intended purposes.

Link:
'He continued to avail of various supports, including Enterprise Ireland's grant scheme towards R&D costs.'

(ii) Outline the importance of preparing a cash flow forecast for Digibrand.
Ryan will be able to improve his financial control by comparing actual receipts and payments with cash flow forecast; it will help him to see if he is meeting his targets. A cash flow forecast will have to be prepared if Digibrand intends to borrow finance. The cash flow will help to identify if the business can afford to make repayments on a potential loan. It will also help Ryan to identify times of high expenditure. Digibrand is a new company, and availability of cash is more important than profit in the early years of a business. Without adequate cash to pay its bills, Digibrand could fail.

Link:
'Like most new start-ups cash was scarce and Ryan wished to avoid huge debt.'

OR
'He had to ensure that he managed his working capital.'

OR
'He had to work hard at getting paid quickly for work carried out for clients to ensure he could pay wages and various day-to-day expenses.'

Marking scheme

(B) (i)	Identify and describe the most appropriate sources of finance for Digibrand's relocation. (Refer to short-, medium- and long-term sources of finance in your answer.)	3 × 8 marks (3 + 3 (2 + 1) + 2) (Name/correct source/link)
(ii)	Outline the importance of preparing a cash flow forecast.	6 marks (3 (2 + 1) + 3 (for link))

(C) (i) Opportunities
Quick method of business expansion – improved chance of survival/increased level of power in the market.
Shared resources and expertise – quick access to new technologies/new skills and expertise/economies of scale/sharing of costs.
Diversification to new product areas and access to new markets – merging with another firm will allow both firms to access each other's markets/export market/reduced dependence on one market. Share strengths in different areas, e.g. different regions of

the world/different sectors of industry.

Link:

'MediaMania is planning to expand its business outside the UK.'

OR

'... MediaMania, a leading London-based digital marketing agency, which focuses

> **Note:**
> Links from the ABQ could be presented as either an opportunity or threat depending on how the theory is developed by the candidate.

exclusively on the retail sector in the UK.'

Threats

Sharing of profits – all shareholders are entitled to a share of profits from newly merged firm.

Loss of personal touch with customers – the larger a business gets, the harder it becomes to retain relationships with existing customers.

Different organisational cultures may lead to conflict; change can be difficult for both owners and employees to adapt to.

Proprietary knowledge may be taken; the intellectual property of Digibrand could be taken by MediaMania.

Potential loss of control.

Potential redundancies.

Link:

'... Digibrand, which had built up a strong client base in Ireland.'

OR

'MediaMania is planning to expand its business outside the UK ...'

OR

'... MediaMania, a leading London-based digital marketing agency, which focuses

> **Note:**
> If link is given as an opportunity, a different link needs to be given as a threat.

exclusively on the retail sector in the UK.'

(ii)

Strategic Alliance – this involves two firms coming together (voluntarily) to work on a particular project or to develop a specific product/service, but there is **no change in ownership and both remain separate corporate entities.**

Evaluation***

This type of expansion may be suited to Digibrand as it could enable it to work with other firms who may have more expertise in particular areas of marketing. Access to new markets/contacts. Digibrand can easily withdraw from the activity. Both firms benefit from shared skills and expertise and costs are shared.

Takeover – A takeover is where **51% of the shares in another company have been purchased** in either a hostile or friendly manner. The acquiring company absorbs the other company, which loses its identity after the acquisition and becomes part of the acquiring company.

Evaluation*****

This is unlikely as Digibrand is a very small company and MediaMania is a leading London-based company. It would be very costly for Digibrand.

Organic Growth – this is the natural expansion of a business/growth from within the business using its own resources. Digibrand could sell more of its services or develop new services.

Growing the domestic market/enter the international market/licensing/franchising.

Evaluation*****

This type of expansion would allow Ryan to retain ownership of his business and avoid any costly acquisitions. However, it is a slow gradual process as it takes time to build up reserves.

Marking scheme

(C) (i)	Discuss one possible opportunity and one possible threat of merging with MediaMania.	2 × 5 marks each (3 (2 + 1) + 3 (for link))
(ii)	Evaluate one other method which Ryan could consider to grow his business.	10 marks (2 + 3 + 3 + 2) (Name/explain/explain/evaluate)

UNIT 6

Domestic Environment

Business does not operate in a vacuum. It is part of the wider economic system. This unit looks at the different types of industry and business in the local and national economy. It also examines the relationship between business and the government.

Objective

To enable pupils to understand the interaction between businesses, the local community, the government and the economy.

- **Chapter 19:** Categories of Industry
- **Chapter 20:** Types of Business Organisation
- **Chapter 21:** Community Development
- **Chapter 22:** Business and the Economy
- **Chapter 23:** Government and Business
- **Chapter 24:** The Social Responsibility of Business

19 Categories of Industry

aims Be able to:

● Recognise and illustrate the categories of industry and their contribution to the economy.

Categories of industry

● Primary Sector – extractive industries (agriculture, forestry, fishing, mining)
● Secondary Sector – manufacturing and construction
● Tertiary Sector – service industries

key point

Primary Sector – extractive industries are:
● Agriculture
● Forestry
● Fishing
● Mining

The primary sector

The importance of the primary sector to the economy

1. Employment
Many people are employed directly and indirectly in agriculture, fishing, forestry and mining.

2. Raw materials for industry
The primary sector supplies raw materials for much of the manufacturing and construction sectors:

● Ingredients for the food-processing industry
● Timber, sand and gravel for the building and construction industry
● Energy (coal, gas, turf), which is very important in the economy.

3. Food for the country

Agriculture supplies meat, milk, fruit and vegetables. Fish is an important source of protein, vitamins and fats.

4. The market for products

Farmers buy farm machinery, fertilisers and farm chemicals. Fishermen and foresters buy equipment and materials.

5. Exports

Exports from the primary sector bring money into the country, which improves the standard of living for those involved in the primary sector and improves our balance of payments. This also reduces the country's need to import goods and services.

6. Development of natural resources

This includes mining, quarrying, etc.

Trends in the primary sector

1. Diversification

Because of falling farm incomes and production quotas, many farmers are moving away from traditional farming to enterprises such as organic farming, production of biofuels, agritourism. They are also changing land use to tree production, where there is a grant scheme in operation.

2. Declining numbers in the primary sector

The number of people employed in the primary sector has declined due to fluctuating prices and mechanisation. Many farms are too small to be viable, forcing many farmers to take part-time employment to increase income.

3. Declining EU payments

Traditionally, farmers received many EU grants and payments. Farmers now receive a single EU payment per annum, regardless of output.

4. Consumer confidence

Consumer confidence and concerns about the quality of food – particularly the issues of animal disease and chemical and pesticide residues in food – has led to a growth in the demand for organically produced food. The growth in organic food sales in Ireland is broadly attributed to people who are making food choices based on health and wellbeing.

These customers are essentially looking for high-quality, natural food.

5. Policy reforms such as milk quota abolition, CAP reform and export growth

Given the removal of milk quota, there remains an opportunity to expand for the first time in 30 years, particularly in the dairy sector. Nevertheless, there remain challenges to expansion, including land access, elderly age profile, the uptake of technologies, the financial strength of this sector, increasing price volatility and environmental constraints.

6. Developments in the area of wind energy and solar power.

The secondary sector

PFIZER IRELAND
PHARMACEUTICALS

exam focus

Manufacturing industry in
Ireland is carried out by:
- Indigenous firms
- Transnational companies
- Agribusinesses

The secondary sector includes the manufacturing industry and construction businesses. They take raw materials produced by the primary sector and process them into finished products.

Manufacturing industry

1. Indigenous Firms
- Indigenous firm are set up, owned and managed by people living in Ireland, with their principal place of business in Ireland.
- The state body Enterprise Ireland has the responsibility for developing indigenous Irish industry.
- Examples of indigenous Irish firms: Glanbia, Dawn Meats.

2. Transnational Companies
- Transnational companies are foreign firms with manufacturing plants in Ireland.
- Example: Pfizer is an American pharmaceutical company with plants in Ireland.

3. Agribusinesses
- Agribusiness refers to those firms involved in food production.
- They use agriculture materials in the production of finished goods.
- Example: The Kerry Group is a major food company.

Construction industry

The construction industry is involved in building the country's infrastructure (roads, schools, hospitals), industrial buildings and private housing.

The importance of the secondary sector to the economy

1. Employment
Manufacturing and construction provide a great deal of employment, increasing the wealth of people living in Ireland and contributing tax revenue to the government.

2. Uses Irish raw materials

Manufacturing and construction use Irish raw materials and natural resources in helping build the country's infrastructure.

3. Exports

Much of the output of manufacturing industry is exported, which contributes positively to the balance of payments.

Trends in the secondary sector

1. Increased competition

Challenges faced by the agribusiness sector in food markets for foreign retailers (e.g. Aldi and Lidl).

2. Increased wages

Increased wages over the last few years have resulted in a loss of competitiveness, forcing the relocation of some manufacturing businesses to low-cost economies (e.g. some manufacturing businesses such as Dell have relocated to lower-cost economies, such as Poland).

The tertiary sector

The tertiary sector (or **services sector**) provides services to individuals and to other businesses.

Examples: financial, communication, distribution, leisure, tourism, professional and personal services, educational.

The importance of the tertiary sector to the economy

1. Employment

The sector is labour intensive and creates many jobs.

2. Support services

The sector provides support services for the efficient running of all other sectors of the economy.

3. Tax revenue

Many small, indigenous businesses are involved in providing services, contributing large amounts of tax to the government through pay, VAT and corporation tax.

4. Tourism

Tourism is a very important service industry and a big employer.
Tourists spend large amounts of money in Ireland.

Discuss the challenges facing businesses in the tertiary (services) sector in Ireland.

(15 marks)

Source: 2017 Higher Level Section 3

Suggested solution

Access to technology/e-commerce
- Poor access to broadband especially in rural areas.
- Poor use of websites for selling to consumers.

Commercial Rates
- Commercial rates charged to business by local authorities.
- They have placed small local retailers under huge pressure as they try to compete with larger retailers.

Brexit uncertainty
- The uncertainty caused by the UK's planned exit from the EU will have a negative impact on the exporting of goods and services.

Rents
- The increase in the cost of rental accommodation in cities such as Dublin will increase demands for higher wages. This reduces the profits of service firms and makes it more difficult for them to remain competitive.

Wage demands
- Successful wage demands in the transport sector such as Dublin Bus and Luas have led to knock-on claims in the services sector. This reduces the profits of service firms and makes it more difficult for them to remain competitive.

Retailer closures
- The huge growth in online purchasing has led to the closure of many retail outlets.
- Growth of discount retailers, e.g. Aldi, Lidl, TK Maxx.

Additional points could include:
- Poor infrastructure
- Lack of skilled workers in certain areas
- Cost of utilities
- Demographic changes
- Automation of services leading to unemployment (i.e. banking sector).

Marking scheme

3 × 5 marks (2 + 2 + 1)

(Specific reference to industry/business in the tertiary (services) sector required for 1 mark)

20 Types of Business Organisation

 Be able to:

- Recognise the types of business organisation.
- Compare and contrast the types of business organisation.
- Explain why businesses change their organisational structure over time.

Types of business organisation

There are nine main forms of business organisation:

1. Sole trader
2. Partnership
3. Company
4. Business alliance
5. Franchise
6. Transnational company
7. Co-operative
8. State-owned enterprise
9. Indigenous firm

1. Sole trader

A sole trader is a business owned and controlled by one person.

Advantages and Disadvantages of Being a Sole Trader

Advantages	Disadvantages
1. Owner keeps all profit.	1. Unlimited liability – if the business fails, the owner could be sued for personal assets.
2. Owner makes all decisions – complete control.	2. Lack of capital for expansion.
3. Independence – freedom and flexibility.	3. Lack of continuity of existence.
4. Confidentiality of accounts.	4. Difficulty of raising finance.
5. Personal service to customers.	5. One person responsible for a range of tasks and decisions.
6. Easy to set up – few regulations.	6. Suffers all losses made.
	7. A lot of pressure and work on one person.

2. Partnership

- A partnership is an agreement between two or more people to conduct business with a view to making a profit.
- Membership of a partnership is between two and 20.
- Partnerships are common among doctors, solicitors and accountants.

- Partners draw up a Deed of Partnership, which is a legal agreement setting out the rights, responsibilities and duties of each partner.
- A business must register its name with the Companies Registration Office if the name is different from the names of the partners.

Advantages and Disadvantages of a Partnership

Advantages	Disadvantages
1. Extra capital is available.	1. Partners have unlimited liability.
2. Shared decision-making.	2. Disagreements among partners.
3. Risk and responsibility is shared.	3. Profit shared among partners.
4. Different skills and expertise of partners.	4. Decision-making is slow.
5. Confidentiality of accounts.	5. Business does not have a separate legal existence distinct from partners.
6. Easy to form.	

HL

Discuss the opportunities **and** challenges of partnership as a form of business ownership.

(20 marks)

Source: 2013 Higher Level Section 3

Suggested solution

Opportunities
- Partnerships have access to greater amounts of **capital** as up to 20 partners can bring financial resources to the business.
- Partnerships have access to **different skill sets** as new partners may bring new skill sets and expertise to the business, e.g. IT or marketing skills.
- Partnership can lead to **more effective decision-making** as the decision-making process is shared, eliciting different points of view and opinions from a range of talented people.
- Ability to achieve **economies of scale**.
- Financial information can remain **confidential**.

Challenges
- Partners, in the main, have **unlimited liability**. This means that they are responsible for the debts of the business if it goes bankrupt and may have to forfeit their personal assets in order to pay business debts.
- The partners are **jointly and severally liable** for the debts of the business which means that they have a collective responsibility for each other's debts and their personal assets can be used to clear the debts of their partners.
- Shared decision-making could lead to differences of opinion, disagreements, arguments between the partners and lost opportunities. This could, at best, lead to **delayed decision-making** or, at worst, lead to the dissolution of the partnership.

- The profits of the business have to be **shared** according to the ratio set out in the Deed of Partnership.
- Not a separate legal entity, therefore **partners and not the business can be sued in law**.
- If one partner dies or resigns, the partnership must be **dissolved**.

Marking scheme

Discuss the opportunities and challenges of partnership as a form of business ownership.   4 × 5 marks

2 opportunities @ 5 marks each (2 + 3)

2 challenges @ 5 marks each (2 + 3)

3. Company

A company is a legal form of business organisation. It is a separate legal entity and, therefore, is separate and distinct from those who run it. The company (and not the individual shareholders) is the appropriate party to be sued in the event that debts are incurred by the company which remain unpaid despite demand.

Companies Act 2014

This Act came into effect on 1 June 2015. Its main function is to simplify the rules that companies have to comply with.

Under the Act, there is provision for two new types of private limited company:

(a) A Private Company Limited by Shares (CLS) – these companies are the most widely utilised companies.

(b) A Designated Activity Company (DAC) – this most closely resembles the private limited company structure in existence prior to the Act.

These two types of private companies replaced the previous private companies limited by shares structure.

Features of a Private Company Limited by Shares (CLS)

- It only requires one director.
- It has a single document constitution in place of the memorandum and articles of association. This document will have no objects clause so the company will not be restricted in what it can do.
- The maximum number of shareholders is 149.
- The shareholders can decide not to hold an AGM by passing a written resolution to that effect.
- No authorised share capital is required. No limit on the number of shares it can issue.
- The title of Ltd applies to every CLS.

Designated Activity Company (DAC)

A company established for a very specific purpose will be a Designated Activity Company.

This type of company retains an obects clause, a minimum of two directors and a two-part constitution comparable to the existing memorandum and articles of association. It must have an authorised share capital and, unless it has just one shareholder, it must hold an AGM each year. The title of DAC will apply instead of Ltd.

The main differences between the two company types are:

	Company Limited by Shares (CLS)	Designated Activity Company (DAC)
1	Must end in the suffix Limited or Ltd.	Must end in the suffix Designated Activity Company or DAC.
2	Minimum of one director.	Minimum of two directors.
3	1–149 shareholders.	1–149 shareholders.
4	Articles of association only. No objects clause – full and unlimited capacity – company will not be restricted in what it can do.	Memorandum and articles of association. Capacity limited to the objects clause in the Memorandum.
5	May dispense with holding the AGM.	Cannot dispense with holding the AGM.
6	No requirement for an authorised share capital. No limit on the number of shares it can issue.	Must have an authorised share capital.

Constitution: A private company limited by shares (CLS) has a one-document constitution. This consists of the articles of association. This document sets out the conditions upon which the company is granted incorporation. It must contain provisions dealing with certain matters, e.g. the name of the company.

A designated activity company (DAC) has a two-document constitution consisting of both a memorandum and articles of association.

AGM: Provisions relating to shareholder meetings have been greatly simplified with the requirement to hold an annual general meeting being optional for a CLS and the delivery of notice of an annual general meeting by electronic means being permitted.

Directors: Private limited companies will be entitled to have a single director, but all companies must retain the office of the company secretary. DACs must have at least two directors. The existing common law duties of directors are codified into eight principle duties, which will apply to all directors, including shadow directors.

Shareholders: The maximum number of shareholders in both a CLS and a DAC is 149.

Limited liability: A company is a legal form of business organisation. It is a separate legal entity and, therefore, is separate and distinct from those who run it. The company (and not the individual shareholders) is the appropriate person to be sued in the event that debts are incurred by the company, and which remain unpaid despite demand.

The shares in a company are owned by its shareholders. If the company is a limited liability company, the shareholders' liability, should the company fail, is limited to the amount, if any, remaining unpaid on the shares held by them.

Registration: Companies can be registered with the Companies Registration Office (CRO). The CRO is the central repository of public statutory information on Irish companies. It operates under the aegis of the Department of Jobs, Enterprise and Innovation (DJEI).

Company names: there are restrictions on the choice of company name. The CRO may have to refuse a name if:

- It is identical to or too similar to a name already appearing on the register of companies
- It is offensive
- It would suggest state sponsorship

Forming a company

Who may form a company?

The Companies Act generally allows one or more persons to form a private company for any lawful purpose by subscribing to a constitution. A private company may have a maximum of 149 members and there is no limit on the number of members of a public company.

How to form a company?

Send the following documents, together with the registration fee, to the Companies Registration Office (CRO).

1. Constitution

This document sets out the conditions upon which the company is granted incorporation. It must contain provisions dealing with certain matters, e.g. the name of the company and, if it is a company with limited liability, that fact must be also stated. The constitution will not state any objects if the company is a LTD – a private company limited by shares. This document sets out the rules under which the company proposes to regulate its affairs.

2. Form A1

This form asks for details of the company name, its registered office, its email address, details of its secretary and directors, their consent to acting as such, the subscribers and details of their shares (if any). It incorporates a declaration that the requirements of the Companies Act have been complied with, and as to which activity the company is being formed to engage in.

3. Form A1 is completed and submitted together with a constitution (a one-document constitution if the company is a LTD company, a memorandum and articles of association for all other company types). Company incorporation can be completed online.

4. The Companies Registration Office then issues a certificate of incorporation, which is the birth certificate of the company.

Articles of Association	Form A1
This document sets out the internal rules and regulations for the running of the company.	*This document is the application for registration.*
It contains:	It contains:
• Details of share capital (the different classes of shares)	• Company name
• Details of shares (voting rights of shares, issue of shares, transfer of shares)	• Company's registered address
• Regulations regarding meetings (procedures at meetings, procedure for calling meetings)	• Details of secretary and directors
• Signature of each subscriber	• Declaration of compliance with Companies Acts
• Details regarding directors (how directors are to be elected, powers and duties of directors)	• Statement of capital authorised and issued
• Procedure for winding up the company	

Advantages and Disadvantages of a Private Limited Company

Advantages	Disadvantages
1. Shareholders have limited liability.	1. Difficult to set up as there are many regulations to be followed.
2. The company is a separate legal entity from the shareholders.	2. Expensive formation and running costs.
3. More capital can be raised from up to 149 shareholders.	3. Business affairs are public in that the annual accounts are sent to the CRO. The books are audited and presented to the AGM.
4. Better credit rating with lenders.	4. Profits are shared among shareholders in the form of dividends.
5. Continuity of existence.	5. The law is very strict on the operation and control of companies.
6. Risk and responsibility are shared.	

Public limited company

- A public limited company is a business owned by at least seven shareholders with no maximum requirement.
- Shares are quoted on the stock exchange so they can be bought and sold by members of the public.
- Shareholders have limited liability.
- A public limited company has the initials plc after its name.
- Before a public limited company commences business, it must hold a Trading Certificate issued by the Registrar.
- All accounts and an annual report must be published and audited each year and returns made to the Registrar of Companies for filing and access to the public.

Advantages and Disadvantages of a Public Limited Company

Advantages	Disadvantages
1. Shareholders have limited liability.	1. High formation expenses.
2. Access to large amounts of capital.	2. Accounts must be audited and published.
3. Higher credit rating with financial institutions – easier to borrow money.	3. Many legal requirements to be followed.
4. Continuity of existence.	4. Owners may have little say in the running of the company as most decisions are made by management.
5. Top-quality management can be recruited.	

People involved in a public limited company

Shareholders

- They are the individuals or institutions who invest money in a company in return for shares.
- They are the owners of the business.
- They provide the capital of the company.
- They receive dividends if the firm makes profit.
- Ordinary shareholders have one vote per share, and they elect a board of directors at the AGM.

Board of Directors

- A board of directors is elected by the shareholders at the company AGM to run the business.
- The board elects a managing director to run the business on a day-to-day basis.

Managing Director

- Elected by the board of directors to run the company.
- Manages the company on a day-to-day basis on behalf of the shareholders and the board of directors.
- The managing director delegates areas of responsibility to departmental managers.

Auditors

- Auditors are accountants who are appointed to check the accuracy of the company accounts.
- They present an annual report to the shareholders on whether the accounts present a true and fair view of the company.

Company Secretary

A company secretary is an officer of a company with responsibility for:

- Notifying shareholders of the AGM.
- Organising the AGM of the company and keeping the minutes of the meeting.
- Sending annual returns to the Registrar of Companies.
- Maintaining an up-to-date register of shareholders.

4. Business alliance

- A business alliance is an agreement formed between two or more businesses to work together in particular commercial matters, while at the same time retaining their separate identities independent of each other.
- The alliance involves sharing of expertise and skills, shared costs and risk and improved service for the customer. (For example, Oneworld is one of the world's largest airline alliances and has among its members American Airlines, British Airways and Qantas.)

Advantages and Disadvantages of a Business Alliance

Advantages	Disadvantages
1. Easy to establish – few legal formalities.	1. Agreement must be negotiated between the businesses on how the alliance will work.
2. Each firm benefits from the skills and expertise of the other.	2. Ownership and control is shared – any conflict between the firms could lead to the alliance closing.
3. Firms can develop new markets for their products and services.	
4. Economies of scale – bigger is cheaper, costs are reduced.	3. A legal contract may be difficult to get out of should one firm wish to withdraw.

5. Franchise

- This is the granting of a licence by the franchisor (existing business) to the franchisee (person setting up the business), allowing the right to use the franchisor's trade name, logo and business system, and to sell their product or service.
- The licence is expensive and a percentage of sales/royalties must be paid annually.
- Examples of franchises: McDonald's, Supermac's, Kentucky Fried Chicken, Pizza Hut, Subway, Dunkin' Donuts.

Advantages and Disadvantages of a Franchise

Advantages	Disadvantages
1. Business has the use of an established trade name, logo and style.	1. Little freedom for franchisee to be creative – must observe rules in contract.
2. Product/service will have public acceptance.	2. Cost – the initial franchise fee and ongoing royalties make franchising a costly business operation.
3. Franchisee has lower costs and so benefits from economies of scale.	
4. Faster start – support provided in start-up by franchisor.	
5. Low-risk business name and idea is proven.	
6. National advertising is undertaken by franchisor.	

6. Transnational company

A company with its headquarters in one country and branches in a number of different countries. Examples include the Smurfit Kappa Group, Ford, Intel, Coca-Cola, Nestlé, Toyota, Nokia.

Advantages	Disadvantages
1. They provide employment – employees spend their income locally.	1. Lack of loyalty – they may close a plant causing local unemployment and move to a developing country to avail of cheaper raw materials and labour.
2. They provide revenue for the government in the form of corporation tax and VAT.	2. They provide intense competition for local firms, forcing closure of some firms with job losses.
3. Much of transnational output is exported, contributing favourably to the balance of payments.	3. Most of the profits made are repatriated to their head office in another country.
4. They buy their raw materials and supplies from local Irish businesses.	4. Some transnationals have great size and power and may exert pressure on governments in host countries to achieve their objectives.

7. Co-operative

- A co-operative is a business owned and controlled by its members, all of whom share a common interest.
- They are democratically run – one person/one vote.
- They are run by an elected management committee.

Advantages and Disadvantages of a Co-operative

Advantages	Disadvantages
1. Members have limited liability.	1. Difficulty of obtaining external finance.
2. Each member has an equal say in the running of the business – one member/one vote.	2. Rules and regulations place a large burden on smaller co-operatives.
3. There is a great incentive for members to do business with the co-operative, as the amount of dividend depends on the business transacted.	3. Co-operative must submit audited accounts annually.
	4. Limited management expertise.
	5. Members receive a limited return on their investment.
4. Producer co-operatives provide a market for the output of the agricultural and fishing industries.	

8. State-owned enterprise

- State enterprises are set up, owned, financed and controlled by the government.
- Capital to finance the enterprise is provided by the government.
- Commercial state enterprises produce goods and services that are sold to the public (e.g. CIE, Bord na Móna).
- Non-commercial state enterprises are state-funded (e.g. Environmental Protection Agency [EPA]).

Advantages and Disadvantages of a State-Owned Enterprise

Advantages	Disadvantages
1. Employment – they employ large numbers of people.	1. Some state firms suffer losses, which are borne by the taxpayer.
2. Provide essential services, including non-profitable services (e.g. Bus Éireann).	2. The absence of a profit motive may lead to inefficiency.
3. Promote industrial development (e.g. IDA, Enterprise Ireland).	3. Many state enterprises lack adequate capital, which may lead to heavy borrowing.
4. Development of the country's natural resources (e.g. Bord na Móna, Bord Gáis).	4. Directors may lack management expertise.
5. Provide important infrastructure for the development of the country.	

9. Indigenous firm

- Indigenous firms are firms that are set up in Ireland and owned and managed by people living in Ireland.
- They produce goods and/or provide services in Ireland. Their principal place of business is in Ireland.
- Enterprise Ireland is the state agency responsible for the development of indigenous firms in Ireland.
- Examples of indigenous firms: O'Flynn Construction, based in Cork, is one of the biggest construction companies in Ireland. Other are *The Irish Times*, Supermac's and Eason.

Advantages and Disadvantages of Indigenous Firms

Advantages	Disadvantages
1. Employment – provide a lot of employment.	1. Many indigenous firms are heavily assisted by grants.
2. Profits remain in Ireland and may be re-invested here.	2. They must have an internationally recognised brand to sell abroad.
3. They export much of their output, which has a positive effect on balance of payments.	3. It is difficult for them to compete with transnationals and competition from abroad.
4. They purchase materials and other goods and services from Irish suppliers.	
5. They contribute a great deal of revenue to the government in the form of PAYE, VAT and corporation tax.	

Reasons why a business enterprise might change its organisational structure

Businesses change their structure over time to adapt to changing circumstances and market demands.

1. Business Wants to Increase in Size

The business may wish to grow larger, and growing larger requires more people with skills and expertise. Specialisation is necessary in areas such as finance, marketing and production.

Examples:

- Changing from sole trader to a partnership or to a private limited company will mean the inclusion of new partners/shareholders who bring new skills, experience and expertise to the company.
- A private company converting to a public limited company will attract top management with new skills and expertise.

2. Limited Liability

The desire for the protection of limited liability is another reason for changing structure. A business person may wish to protect family members and personal assets from business risks.

Example: If a sole trader or partnership converts to a private limited company, all the owners get the protection of limited liability.

3. Raising Finance

If more capital is needed for the development of the business, then changing the business's status will bring in extra finance.

Examples:

- A sole trader changing to a partnership will allow the business to raise finance from new partners.
- A sole trader changing to a private limited company will allow capital to be raised from up to 149 shareholders.
- A private limited company or a co-operative converting to a public limited company can raise large amounts of finance by selling shares on the stock exchange. (Some producer co-operatives in the agricultural sector have become public limited companies, such as Kerry Group plc.)

4. Privatisation

The state may wish to sell some of its businesses. It could therefore convert its state-owned enterprises into public limited companies.

5. Marketing

The expansion of markets may be better served by joining a business alliance with another enterprise, either abroad or in Ireland. Forming an alliance allows the firm to share skills and resources.

Example: An Irish firm forming an alliance with a foreign firm allows the Irish firm to market and distribute goods abroad.

'There are currently over 315 active franchise systems in Ireland, employing more than 42,000 people.' (The Irish Franchise Association)

Outline the reasons why a person who wishes to open a business might choose the franchise model of business.
(20 marks)

Source: 2014 Higher Level Section 3

HL

Suggested solution

Less risk of business failure: Franchising provides a person who wishes to open a business with the opportunity of replicating a proven, well-established business model. The franchisee (person setting up the business) pays the franchisor (existing business) for the right to use the franchisor's trade name and business system. The business name is well known in the market so it is low risk.

Economies of scale: The new franchisee benefits from economies of scale generated by the franchisor. Bulk discounts, gained by the franchisor as a result of bulk purchasing, are passed on to individual franchisees, allowing them to charge lower prices and generate larger profits.

Training and on-going support is provided in the start-up and development by the franchisor. The franchisor may pay for a national advertising campaign and create a marketing strategy for the franchisee. New product development is undertaken by the franchisor, business start-up advice and training programmes will help the new franchisees in their businesses.

Banks are more likely to lend money: Failure rates for franchises are far lower than the failure rates for new independent businesses and, for that reason, banks are more willing to lend money.

Marketing campaigns are conducted nationally, etc.

Marking scheme

2 × 7 marks (4 + 3) and 1 × 6 marks (4 + 2)

(Statement and explanation)

aims Be able to:

- Identify the importance of community initiatives in the development of the local economy.

Community development

Benefits/importance of community development

1. Employment

Creates employment and thereby increases spending in the local economy; 'spin-off jobs' are also created among suppliers and support services (e.g. transport, entertainment, etc.).

2. Promotes a culture of enterprise

Promotes an enterprise culture which encourages new ideas, attracts new businesses and motivates entrepreneurs to set up business in the area.

3. Empowering the local community

Empowers local community and generates a sense of pride within the community. A community spirit is created, which generates growth and prosperity in the local area.

4. Skills development

Creates opportunities for personal and skills development (e.g. youth training, training for long-term unemployed).

5. Improves **physical appearance** of the area

(e.g. TidyTowns initiative).

exam focus

Community development is 'a voluntary effect to support and develop the social and economic activity of a local community for the benefit of the local community'.

exam focus

The agencies available to assist communities with community development projects are:

- Local enterprise office
- Rural development (Leader) programme
- Area partnership companies

Community initiatives

There are many agencies available to assist communities with community development projects.

Local Enterprise Office

The Local Enterprise Office is a first-stop shop for anyone seeking information and support on starting or growing a business in Ireland.

Local Enterprise Offices (LEOs) were established following the dissolution of the County and City Enterprise Boards (CEBs).

With 31 dedicated teams across the local authority network in Ireland, Local Enterprise Offices offer a wide range of experience, skills and services.

The Local Enterprise Office is for people interested in starting up a new business or already in business including: entrepreneurs, early-stage promoters, start-ups and small businesses looking to expand.

The LEOs are about promoting entrepreneurship and self-help and are now a first-stop shop for those beginning a new business as well as those wishing to expand their existing one.

First-Stop Shop

Local Enterprise Offices are a local first-stop shop for new entrepreneurs and existing microenterprises and small business owners. They are the front door through which all information on state supports for small and microbusinesses can be accessed and signposted, and through which other supports and bodies with programmes relevant to small business, as well as important local services and compliance requirements can be provided.

The LEOs are the business connection to the local authority, Enterprise Ireland and all state agencies that can help grow the business. This includes the following key agencies to ensure the business will have access to all Government supports: Revenue, Department of Social Protection, Education and Training Boards, Credit Review Office and Fáilte Ireland.

Services Provided by the Local Enterprise Office

1. Business Information and Advisory Services

The Local Enterprise Offices (LEOs) provide an extensive range of supports to local business communities. The confidential advisory service is open to anyone exploring self-employment as an option or for those who are currently operating a business.

2. Mentoring

The Mentor Programme is designed to match up the knowledge, skills, insights and entrepreneurial capability of experienced business practitioners with small business owner/managers who need practical and strategic one-to-one advice and guidance. The mentor contributes independent, informed observation and advice to aid decision-making.

Role of Mentor

- Listen, advise and provide direction
- Help the entrepreneur identify problems and suggest areas for improvement

- Discuss solutions and innovative ways of improving business activity
- Help with the decision making process
- Share experience and knowledge
- Provide structure and context for discussion
- Offer assistance in compiling a business plan

Areas of involvement typically include:

- Website Planning & Design
- Production Planning
- Distribution
- Market Research
- Marketing & Promotion
- Business Strategy
- Financial Planning

3. Financial Supports

Local Enterprise Offices (LEOs) provide a range of financial supports designed to assist with the establishment and/or growth of enterprises (limited company, individuals/sole trader, co-operatives and partnerships) employing up to ten people.

These include:

Feasibility Study Grants

Feasibility Study Grants are designed to assist the promoter with researching market demand for a product or service and examining its sustainability. It includes assistance with innovation including specific consultancy requirements, hiring of expertise from third level colleges, private specialists, design and prototype development.

The maximum Feasibility Study Grant payable shall be 50% of the investment or €15,000, whichever is the lesser.

Priming Grants

A Priming Grant is a business start-up grant, available to microenterprises within the first 18 months of start-up.

The maximum grant payable shall be 50% of the investment or €150,000, whichever is the lesser.

Expenditure may be considered under the following headings: capital items, salary costs, general overhead costs, and consultancy/innovation/marketing costs.

Business Expansion Grants

The Business Expansion grant is designed to assist the business in its growth phase after the initial 18 month start-up period.

The maximum Business Expansion Grant payable shall be 50% of the investment or €150,000 whichever is the lesser.

A business that had availed of a Priming Grant will be ineligible to apply for a Business Expansion grant until 12 months after approval/drawdown date of Priming Grant, whichever is the later.

4. Training Programmes

To assist the small business community in meeting the challenges of the business world, LEOs provide a wide range of high-quality training supports, which are tailored to meet specific business requirements.

Whether it is starting a business or growing a business, there is something suitable for everyone.

Rural Development Programme (LEADER)

Since its launch, LEADER has provided rural communities, across the EU, with the resources to fund the local development of their area.

LEADER Programme 2014–2020

Funding of €250 million will be distributed to entrepreneurs and community groups throughout Ireland, by local action groups, which are made up of people from the local community as well as from the local public and private sector.

The programme is co-financed by the European agricultural fund for regional development .

The priority of the new LEADER Programme 2014–2020 is to 'promote social inclusion, poverty reduction and economic development in rural areas.'

The LEADER Programme supports local and community projects across a diverse range of themes including:

1. Economic development, enterprise development and job creation

Rural tourism

Rural tourism provides a stimulus for enterprise and job creation. Actions that may be supported include:

- Feasibility studies to explore the tourism potential of an area
- The provision of amenity and leisure facilities
- Actions that promote the development of cultural/heritage infrastructure.

Enterprise development

LEADER can support micro, small and medium enterprises. The areas that might benefit from LEADER support include:

- Artisan and other food businesses
- Renewable energy
- Social enterprises
- Industries.

Rural towns

LEADER supports the regeneration of rural towns and seeks to promote them as attractive places to visit, live and do business in. Actions might include town renewal schemes that renovate derelict buildings with incentives to attract businesses to vacant properties.

Broadband

LEADER supports local actions that complement national initiatives aimed at developing a comprehensive rural broadband infrastructure. Actions might include: basic ICT training to priority groups, for example, to enable older people and young people to stay connected, skills development for installing broadband, funding small-scale equipment to allow local businesses to access broadband.

2. Social Inclusion

Provision of basic services targeted at hard to reach communities

LEADER focuses on improving access to basic services for people living in rural and remote areas and groups who are at risk of social exclusion.

Rural youth

The promotion of youth entrepreneurship and training can provide improved pathways for young people to access economic opportunities in rural areas. Actions might include:

- The provision of youth club/cafés
- Improved access to ICT
- Sports/recreation activities
- Arts-based projects
- Youth development programmes

3. Rural Environment

Protection of sustainable use of water resources

Greater protection of local water resources is important for sustaining rural communities.

Actions funded may include:

- Raising general awareness of water conservation
- Water recycling schemes
- Rainwater harvesting

Protection and improvement of local biodiversity

The protection of biodiversity is a growing concern with the loss of various species of wildlife, flora and fauna, as well as their natural habitat. Factors that impact on local biodiversity include population growth, cutting hedgerows and changes in land usage. Actions that promote local biodiversity include:

- Feasibility studies and action plans that protect aspects of biodiversity, for example, upgrading of parks and river walks, habitat creation and planting.

Development of renewable energy

Clean sources of energy have a lower environmental impact than conventional technologies.

The programme seeks to mitigate the impact of recent environmental trends including climate change. Renewable energy technologies may also generate new employment opportunities in rural areas. Actions might include:

- Awareness raising on environmental issues and feasibility studies relating to green technologies.
- Installation and use of renewable energy technologies.
- Local projects, for example, biomass heating, solar power, community wind farms and community-based heating systems.

Area Partnership companies

Area Partnership works with disadvantaged communities and identifies target groups with the objective of overcoming barriers to them. It shares equally in the economic, cultural and social life of the area, helping people to bring about positive changes in their own lives and the life of the community.

Area Partnership works with a variety of agencies and organisations so that individuals, groups and communities can find ways to bring about positive changes and create more hopeful prospects for people who experience unemployment, poverty and social exclusion.

Area Partnership offers a range of programmes and services and supports including:

1. Education and Training Programme

Area Partnership provides information, advice and supports to people, access to educational opportunities that include:

- Information and advice on educational opportunities and career progression
- Support to access education and training
- Opportunities to take part in lifelong learning and educational courses

2. Enterprise and Employment Programme

Area partnership aims to support individuals interested in self-employment. Enterprise support staff guide people through the steps required to turn an idea into a business venture by providing the following:

- General advice and support for clients considering self-employment
- Training supports such as start your own business courses and bookkeeping and accounting for small businesses
- Assistance and advice on company and tax registration
- Assistance with the preparation of a business plan
- Business mentor support

3. Local Development Programme

Area partnership works with key organisations to enhance and develop these areas and communities that continue to experience poverty and disadvantage.

One example of this is the Green View Community Garden in Finglas South where North West Area Partnership in conjunction with Dublin City Council brought the community together with key stakeholders to reclaim a disused piece of waste ground and turn it into a valuable community asset.

In addition to the funding under the Local Community Development Programme, Dublin North West Area Partnership also assigned a small team of men from the TÚS Community Workplace Programme to help with the physical development of the site.

4. TÚS Programme (Community Work Placement Initiative)

TÚS is a Community Placement Initiative providing quality, short-term suitable work opportunities for people who are unemployed. It also provides services that benefit local communities. The Department of Social Protection is responsible for the TÚS Programme nationally and Area Partnership is responsible for the roll out of the programme locally.

Outline **two** benefits of local business for a local community.

(10 marks)

Source: 2014 Higher Level Section A

Suggested solution

Employment/jobs – direct employment in the community (in the business itself).

Spin-off businesses – employment in spin-off businesses such as transport, suppliers, cleaning services, etc.

Increased disposable incomes leading to an improved standard of living, leading to increased spending in the local community, thereby encouraging other businesses.

Growth in local services to meet the needs of local businesses (taxi services, banks, credit unions, etc.) Local people in the community can avail of these services.

Community spirit and quality of life – successful local business improves community spirit and social interaction between citizens.

Taxation – local rates, taxes and service charges contribute to the development of local infrastructure.

Culture of enterprise – encourages more businesses to develop.

Marking scheme

6(3 + 3) + 4(2 + 2)

22 # Business and the Economy

Economy

An economy is a system that uses the four factors of production to produce goods and services demanded by consumers.

Factors of production

Land – Natural resources available for production (e.g. land, forests, rivers, etc.). The payment for land is rent.

Labour – The human input in the production process. The payment for labour is wages/salaries.

Capital – Anything which is man-made and used in the production process (e.g. machinery, buildings, factories used to produce goods and services). The payment for capital is interest.

Enterprise – Entrepreneurs organise the other factors of production to produce goods and services. Entrepreneurs are risk-takers who set up a business. The payment for enterprise is profit.

Impact of economy on business

The performance of the economy affects business. The economy is affected by a number of economic variables.

Inflation

Inflation is defined as the 'sustained' increase in the general level of prices of goods and services in the economy as measured by the consumer price index.

exam focus

Important **economic variables** include:

- Inflation
- Interest rates
- Taxation
- Unemployment
- Exchange rates
- Grants/subsidies

Impact of High Inflation on Business	Benefits of Low Inflation on Business
1. Increase in the cost of production (e.g. raw materials).	1. Improved competitive position on international trade – more goods sold abroad.
2. Increased wage demands to keep up with rate of inflation.	2. Costs and wages will be more stable – lower wage demands.
3. Increase in selling price of goods/ services may lead to a fall in demand. Decline in sales/reduction in profit.	3. Higher consumer spending, increasing sales and profits.
4. Exports become less competitive because of increase in prices. Exports decrease.	4. Increased tax revenue for government – more VAT from increased spending.

Interest rates

The interest rate charged by a financial institution for a loan is the price that has to be paid for the use of the money by the borrower.

Impact of Increasing/High Interest Rates on Irish Business	Impact of Low Interest Rates on Irish Business
1. Increased cost of borrowing – expensive for people and business to borrow.	1. Businesses can borrow more easily – economic activity will increase.
2. Less investment/borrowing for expansion will be more expensive.	2. Encourages new investment as borrowing for expansion will be cheaper.
3. Reduced consumer spending means reduced sales and reduced profits.	3. Increased consumer spending means increased sales and increased profits.

Taxation

Tax is a compulsory contribution of money to the government and is paid by individuals and businesses.

Impact of High Taxes on Business	How Low Taxation Rates Can Help Business
1. Income tax (PAYE) has the effect of reducing wages/salaries – people have less disposable income, leaving them with less incentive to work.	1. Lower PAYE/PRSI rates – employees have more incentive to work/more take lesser pay.
2. An indirect tax such as VAT increases the cost of goods and services business sales/ profits fall.	2. Lower VAT rates – selling prices will be lower – more demand/more sales/more profits.

3. Corporation tax reduces company profit. Company has less money for investment/expansion. Less money for dividends to shareholders.	3. Lower corporation tax rates – companies will make more profit/more money for expansion/investment.
4. PRSI increases the cost of employing staff for business.	4. Lower PRSI rates/cost of employing staff is reduced.

Unemployment

Unemployment is the percentage of people in the labour force who are unable to find employment.

Impact of Rising Unemployment on Irish Economy	Impact of Low Unemployment on Irish Economy
1. More social welfare to be paid out by the government.	1. Wealth creation – more people have jobs and income.
2. Government revenue from taxation decreases, less PAYE/VAT.	2. Increased demand for goods and services – increased consumer spending.
3. Decrease in consumer spending/reduced sales/reduced profit.	3. More tax revenue for the government – PAYE, PRSI, VAT.
4. Possible higher taxes in the future to pay for increased government spending on social welfare.	4. Demand for labour may push up wages as firms must compete to attract skilled staff.
5. Workers become deskilled if unemployed for a long time.	5. Greater immigration into the country.
6. Easier for businesses to find employees to fill job vacancies – wages will be lower.	

Exchange rates

The exchange rate is the price at which a currency can be exchanged for another (i.e. the price of the currency of one country in terms of the currency of another).

Impact of Exchange Rate on Business

Exchange rates have a significant impact on companies that export large amounts of their output and on companies that import large quantities of raw materials.

Impact of Increasing Value of Euro Against Other Currencies (If euro increases against other currencies)	Impact of Decreasing Value of Euro Against Other Currencies (If euro decreases against other currencies)
(A) EXPORTS Irish exports abroad will be more expensive and less competitive. Irish exporters will find it more difficult to sell goods abroad. Sales and profits decrease.	**(A) EXPORTS** Irish exports abroad will be cheaper. Irish exporters will find it easier to sell goods abroad. Sales and profits increase.
(B) IMPORTS Price of imported goods will decrease. Irish people will buy more foreign goods. Irish firms will pay less for raw materials from abroad – reducing business costs.	**(B) IMPORTS** Price paid for imports will increase. Irish people will buy more Irish goods. Irish firm will pay more for raw materials from abroad.

Grants and subsidies

Grants

Grants are non-repayable amounts of finance provided by the government and the EU to a business to promote enterprise and expansion.

Grants are often given to businesses to encourage them to locate in areas of greatest need (e.g. Gaeltacht areas or particularly underdeveloped areas with high unemployment).

Subsidies

A subsidy is a price support given by the government to a business to allow it to sell its products at a price below the market price.

Subsidies are designed to increase the production of (or reduce the price of) goods or services that are deemed to be essential.

Example: A subsidy to CIÉ to help provide a reasonably priced public transport system.

Impact of business activity on the development of the Irish economy

By providing goods and services , business affects the economy at local and national level.

It affects employment, tax revenue and the environment.

Employment

Business creates jobs in all sectors of the economy, which means less unemployment and reduced social welfare payments.

Tax revenue

There will be an increase in tax revenue:

- PAYE – because more people are employed
- VAT – because extra goods and services are purchased
- Corporation tax – because increased business leads to increased profit

Environmental costs

An increase in business may have a negative impact on the environment, including industrial pollution, illegal dumping, water and air pollution.

Creation of wealth

Business activities create profit for entrepreneurs and wages for employees. This wealth builds up into assets over time and living standards are greatly improved.

Profit reinvested

Much of the profit of business is reinvested for expansion, eventually leading to more jobs and increased output. New premises, plant and machinery are provided for the future development of the business.

(a) Explain the term **'exchange rate'**.

(b) Describe two possible risks which exchange rates could present for businesses in Ireland.

(10 marks)

Source: 2015 Higher Level Section 1

HL

Suggested solution

(a) This is the price of one currency expressed in terms of another currency.

(b) If the euro increases in value relative to $/£, Irish exports are more expensive abroad and are less competitive, which is bad for Irish business as sales and profits decrease.

If the euro falls in value relative to the $/£, imports will become more expensive, increasing costs for businesses, e.g. imports of oil, which is a raw material for businesses, may result in businesses increasing their prices or reducing their profit margins.

Marking scheme

(a) 6 marks (3 + 3)

(b) 4 marks (2 + 2)

Discuss the economic effects on the Irish economy of the growth in employment in recent times.

(20 marks)

Source: 2015 Higher Level Section 3

Suggested solution

- As people have more discretionary income, people will spend more on luxury items leading to, e.g. more new cars and foreign holidays being purchased.

- Business confidence/growth of enterprise: Rate of unemployment in Ireland has declined from 14.2% in 2011 to 5.8% in May 2018. The demand for goods and services has increased, and new businesses open or expand due to increased business profits. There is more enterprise in the economy as people's self-esteem and confidence increases.

- Government current expenditure should decrease as the unemployed become employed, thereby reducing social welfare claims. This may allow the government to increase expenditure in other areas of the economy, e.g. health and education.

- The government revenue/tax take will increase as receipts from major sources of taxation, e.g. VAT receipts, will rise as there will be more consumer expenditure and PAYE receipts will rise as more people are working and paying income tax. There will be more government finance to invest in the Irish economy.

- Emigration should fall and the 'brain drain' (exporting of skilled labour) should reverse.

Marking scheme

4 × 5 marks (2 + 3)

Be able to:

- List the ways in which the government creates a suitable climate for business.
- Explain the ways in which the government affects the labour force.

Why does the government intervene in business?

The government intervenes in business for a number of reasons:

1. Essential services

Provides essential services to all parts of the country irrespective of profitability (e.g. health, education, security).

2. Government regulations

Sets down rules and regulations to be observed by business and society (e.g. Companies Act 2014) and regulates the formation and operation of companies.

3. Protects consumers and employees

Through legislation, the government protects consumers (e.g. Sale of Goods and Supply of Services Act 1980) and employees (e.g. Employment Equality Acts 1998–2015).

4. Provides infrastructure

Government capital expenditure provides the state's infrastructure (roads, railways, airports) so that the economy can operate efficiently.

5. Promotes enterprise and employment

Government promotes enterprise and employment through state agencies (e.g. Enterprise Ireland is responsible for the development of indigenous industry).

6. Develops natural resources

State companies have been set up to develop the natural resources of the country (e.g. Bord na Móna, Bord Gáis).

Government's role in creating a suitable climate for business

Businesses in the economy need a suitable climate in which they can operate. It is the role of the government to create this climate by providing the right conditions.

1. Taxation system

The tax system could be used to create a positive climate for business.

PAYE

- Reduction in PAYE rates should increase spending and stimulate demand for goods and services.
- An increase in PAYE rates could fund business supports (e.g. grants or a reduction in employer's PRSI).

Tax credits

- An increase in tax credits will reduce people's tax liability and may stimulate demand for goods and services.

VAT/excise duties

- Reduction in VAT, reduces cost of goods and services, stimulates demand – makes the Irish economy more competitive.

Corporation tax

- A reduction in corporation tax may improve company profits and the ability to fund future growth of business.

Stamp duty

- Changes may restimulate demand in the construction sector.

2. Government expenditure

- **Capital spending** on roads, hospitals, communications improves the infrastructure of the country, boosts the construction sectors and allows business to function more efficiently.
- **Current spending** on goods and services creates business for firms supplying these goods and services.

3. Government agencies

Government agencies play an important role in encouraging a climate for business through the many services they provide. These agencies include:

- **Local Enterprise Offices** – provide grants and supports to microenterprises.
- **Enterprise Ireland** – provides grants and incentives to indigenous firms.
- **IDA Ireland** – provides grants and incentives to encourage foreign firms to locate in Ireland.
- **SOLAS** – provides training to ensure a skilled workforce is available to meet the future needs of business.

4. Government planning

National pay deals agreed between the government and the social partners create a suitable climate for business in the following ways:

- **Reasonable wages** – controls increases, ensures that business costs are controlled.
- **Industrial relations** in the country are improved.

Businesses can plan ahead because they know their future wage costs.

5. Economic policies

- **Low interest rates** will allow business and individuals to borrow more easily. Demand for goods and services will increase.
- **Low inflation** keeps prices down, leading to increased demand for goods and services.
- **Low unemployment** will increase demand for goods and services.

Government's role in regulating business

The government must regulate business in order to ensure that employees' and consumers' rights are safeguarded and the environment is protected. It regulates business through legislation and state agencies, including:

1. Health and Safety Authority (HSA)

Responsible for ensuring health and safety at work.

2. Competition and Consumer Protection Comission (CCPC)

Ensures that all businesses obey consumer legislation.

Informs consumers of their rights.

3. Data Protection Commissioner (DPC)

Protects the public against misuse of data in manual or electronic format.

4. Environmental Protection Agency (EPA)

Monitors businesses to ensure that they do not damage the environment and prosecutes offenders.

5. Companies Act 2014

Governs the operation of all companies in Ireland.

The Irish government and the labour force in Ireland

The Irish government affects the labour force in Ireland in a number of ways:

- **As an employer** – The Irish government is the single largest employer, employing 300,000 public servant workers (civil service, state bodies).
- **Taxation policies** – Low rates of **income tax** will result in consumers having more disposable income, therefore spending more money on goods and services. This creates a demand for these goods and services, leading to increased production and job creation.
- **Corporation tax** – Corporation tax remaining at 12.5% means that more foreign companies may locate/remain in Ireland and offer employment. It also encourages Irish entrepreneurs to set up in Ireland and create jobs.
- **Infrastructure** – Government investment in the country's infrastructure (building of new motorways, schools, hospitals, etc.) leads to an increase in the number of workers employed in the construction industry. It encourages other businesses to operate here in Ireland and thereby increases employment.

- **Increased spending on education/training** – Government investments in the education of the Irish labour force through training schemes, short-term courses, and upskilling programmes will result in a more skilled, educated and employable work force.
- **Grants and incentives** – Given to foreign companies to locate in Ireland, they will result in foreign industry providing employment to the Irish labour force.
- **Entrepreneurship** – The Irish government encourages the development of enterprise through supports provided by Local Enterprise Offices, Business Innovation Centres, etc.

Privatisation

Privatisation is the sale of shares in a state-owned enterprise to the private sector (i.e. selling state businesses to private investors on the stock exchange).

The business would then be owned and controlled by shareholders, just like any other business enterprise.

Arguments in favour of privatisation of state enterprises

1. Government revenue

Selling off a state company provides the government with a large amount of money.

2. Reduced government expenditure

The sale of a loss-making enterprise means it will no longer have to be subsidised on a yearly basis by the government, which means less borrowing.

3. Access to finance

Privatised firms are able to take out loans and sell shares and generally have greater access to sources of finance than state enterprises. This makes it easier to finance expansion.

4. Efficiency

State-owned firms are often perceived as being inefficient because they can rely on government funding and have little competition. Private firms are driven by profit motives and should therefore be more efficiently run.

5. Competition

The elimination of a state monopoly can result in open market competition and can lead to greater choice and lower prices for consumers.

Arguments against privatisation of state enterprises

1. Loss of state assets

Privatisation results in a loss of state assets and a loss of future profit to the state.

2. Increased unemployment

There may be a loss of jobs through rationalisation of services leading to higher social welfare spending.

3. Loss of essential services

Non-profit-making essential services may be discontinued by the private business in an effort to reduce costs (e.g. postal, electricity, gas and water, and transport services to remote areas).

4. Profit motive

Privatised companies must maximise returns to shareholders and this could result in increased prices for consumers.

5. Loss of control

The share of privatised firms may end up with foreign investors. Profit from successful enterprises may end up in foreign hands instead of being available to the citizens of Ireland.

The national minimum wage for an experienced worker was increased on 1st January 2018 to €9.55 per hour.

Discuss the different ways in which the Irish government affects the labour force in Ireland.

(20 marks)

Suggested solution

- The setting of a legal national minimum wage may protect workers on low pay; however, some workers may be worse off as employers may not employ them due to rising costs (employers demand less labour at the higher wage rate so employment will fall). Labour supply should increase as more workers will be willing to offer themselves for employment at the higher wage.

- The government sets rates for PAYE/PRSI/USC, etc. These rates of tax may act as an incentive/disincentive to work.

- A low corporation tax rate of 12.5% encourages foreign direct investment, thereby increasing businesses in Ireland and increasing the labour force. Low personal taxation in the form of lower PAYE and lower tax on interest earned (DIRT) gives employees and consumers more disposable income, which increases the demand for the goods and services, thereby increasing the labour force.

- The government investment in third level education for all students in Ireland through tax relief on tuition fees ensures a steady supply of highly skilled labour. Training provided through organisations such as SOLAS for unemployed people allows for upskilling and helps the unemployed to re-enter the labour force.

- Government agencies, such as Enterprise Ireland and LEOs, are tasked with the responsibility of helping businesses set up, grow and develop, which creates employment, thereby improving the labour force. LEOs give up to €15,000 in feasibility/innovation grants, where entrepreneurs match at least 50% of the costs. Business expansion grants of up to €80,000 are available for sole traders, partnerships, community or limited companies. SEED and BES schemes are available for companies exporting or companies having export potential.

- IDA Ireland, a state body, attracts multinational companies into Ireland through grant aid, etc. and creates large employment around the country.

- The existence of regulations such as employment law, health and safety law, competition law, etc. A better regulatory environment encourages the growth and expansion of business, leading to increases in the labour force.

- Spending on new and improving infrastructural projects, such as roads, airports, ports, telecommunications and broadband, increases employment during the construction phase and also encourages more business as a result of improved infrastructure, thereby creating additional employment.

- The Irish government is a major employer – almost 250,000 people work in the public sector, making the Government the largest single employer. Pay cuts and an embargo on recruitment introduced in the public sector in recent years impacted negatively on the labour force.

Marking scheme
4 × 5 marks (2 + 3)

Outline the role of the Irish government in encouraging **and** in regulating business in Ireland.

(20 marks)

Source: Higher Level Section 3

Suggested solution

Irish government role in encouraging business:

- Through **decreases in taxation** business activity is encouraged. A reduction in PAYE rates would increase spending power and stimulate demand for goods and services. A reduction in corporation tax may improve company profits, and the ability to fund future growth of the business. A reduction in VAT reduces cost of goods and services, stimulates demand and makes the Irish economy more competitive.

- Through **increases in state expenditure** business activity is encouraged. The government could increase capital expenditure on infrastructure, schools, hospitals, etc. This will create jobs and consumer demand.
- Through a **network of state agencies** that give business advice, training and guidance, mentoring services and grant aid to facilitate growth and expansion. Examples include:
  - Fáilte Ireland (developing and promoting tourism)
  - Enterprise Ireland (grant aid to indigenous industry, e.g. R&D and marketing)
  - SOLAS (provides industrial training for workers)
  - IDA Ireland (provides grant aid to attract FDI)
  - Local Enterprise Offices to encourage entrepreneurship.
- Through government planning. Forward planning reduces uncertainty for business.

National wage agreements involving the social partners allow businesses to predict their future wage costs, as well as decreasing significantly the risk of industrial relations problems during the length of the agreement.

Government role in regulating business:

- The government regulates business in order to protect the **environment**. It established the EPA (Environmental Protection Agency) whose role it is to protect the environment through its licensing, enforcement and monitoring of business activities.
- The government regulates businesses in order to protect the **consumer**. The Sale of Goods and Supply of Services Act 1980 gave rights to the consumer in relation to goods or services bought or hired. The Competition and Consumer Protection Act 2014 enforces consumer protection law.
- The government regulates business in order to protect the **employees** in the workplace with legislation on unfair dismissal, equality and industrial relations.
- It established the Health and Safety Authority, which works to create a national culture where all stakeholders commit to a safe and healthy workplace.
- The government regulates business in order to protect the **general public** against misuse of information in manual or electronic format through the Data Protection Act of 2018. Data protection is the means by which the privacy rights of individuals are safeguarded in relation to the processing of their personal data.

Marking scheme

The role of the Irish Government in encouraging **and** in regulating business in Ireland. At least one of each required. 4 @ 5 marks (2 + 3)

 Be able to:

- Identify important environmental issues in business.
- Define ethical business practice.
- Describe the characteristics of an environmentally conscious company.
- Analyse the impact of environmental issues on business.
- Discuss the social responsibilities of business.
- Evaluate the effects on a firm's costs of meeting its ethical, social and environmental responsibilities.

Business ethics

Business ethics are moral principles that govern the actions of individuals or groups of business people. They are the guiding principles, like honesty and fairness, on how to act in business situations.

Ethical business practice involves conducting business guided by a set of moral principles that govern the actions of an individual or group in certain circumstances.

A **code of ethics** is a formal written statement setting out the behaviour expected from a business in its dealings with employees, customers and the community in which it operates.

 ## Social responsibility of business

The social responsibility of a business is its duty and obligation to treat all those with whom it comes into contact with justice, fairness and honesty.

Social responsibilities of business

Corporate Social Responsibility refers to how businesses interact with their stakeholders on a daily basis including investors, employees, suppliers, customers and government.

Discuss the social responsibilities of a business to any four stakeholders referred to above.

(20 marks)

Source: 2016 Higher Level Section 3

Suggested solution

Investors:

Do not conceal information – be honest and transparent with investors at all times; act ethically at all times; present a true and fair view of the financial performance and standing of the business; and maintain a proper set of accounts.

Use investment capital appropriately – investors' funds must be spent in the manner for which they are given.

Give a reasonable return on investment – investors are taking a risk when providing capital and should be given a fair return if profits are made.

Employees:

Pay a fair wage – employees must be paid at least the minimum wage and must be given wages which reflect the work which has been done and the qualifications and skills of the employees.

Ensure a safe and healthy working environment – the workplace should be maintained to meet legal and moral standards.

Treat all employees fairly – respect all employees equally and treat them in a fair and dignified manner. Obey employment legislation and do not discriminate.

Maintain employment/job security – business must strive to keep the business in a good financial position to keep employees in their positions.

Customers:

Provide quality products at reasonable prices – produce products which are safe and unlikely to cause harm and charge prices which are fair.

Do not mislead consumers regarding products/service. Advertising and information must be truthful and appropriate to the audience targeted.

Deal with complaints in a fair manner – provide customers with an adequate complaints procedure.

Provide an after-sales service – customers should be given adequate assistance if required after purchase.

Suppliers:

Honour the contracts agreed.

Make payments within the time agreed.

No pressure/duress.

Follow tendering procedures where applicable.

Government:

Pay all taxes when due, e.g PAYE, VAT and corporation tax.

Comply with various legislation (i.e. employment law, environmental law, company law, consumer law, etc.)

Use government finance provided as intended (grants).

Co-operate with government departments and agencies.

Marking scheme

2 × 6 marks (3 + 3)

2 × 4 marks (2 + 2)

How business can be socially responsible

1. Making it an objective

Business should make social responsibility an objective when preparing their mission statement.

2. Code of ethics

Develop and promote a code of ethics within the company, setting out guidelines for management and staff about the standards of behaviour expected of them when acting on behalf of the company.

3. Obeying legislation

Working closely with the EPA and obeying regulations regarding pollution, etc.

4. Consultation with stakeholders

When developing policies that affect the environment.

5. Community involvement

Getting involved in the community (e.g. by sponsoring clubs, providing facilities for schools, etc.)

Environmental issues facing businesses

1. Pollution

Pollution means introducing into the environment chemical substances that endanger human health and harm the environment.

Business must minimise polluting the air and water.

2. Climate change

The burning of fossil fuels in factories and businesses and emissions from vehicles causes greenhouse gases such as carbon dioxide to be released into the atmosphere. This traps heat and causes the Earth's temperature to rise, leading to hurricanes, melting glaciers, rising sea levels, floods and drought.

Businesses and individuals can contribute to the solution of this problem by using cleaner fuels, recycling waste, reducing car emissions and using renewable forms of energy to reduce 'greenhouse gases'.

3. Waste management

Business has a responsibility to minimise the amount of waste it produces.

Business and individuals must find ways to reduce, reuse and recycle as much of their waste as possible.

Example: A company in County Cork recycles waste rubber tyres into shredded rubber for use in a variety of markets, including equestrian surfaces, garden/landscaping markets, playgrounds, sports facilities.

4. Sustainable development

This refers to a form of development that meets present-day needs without compromising the ability of future generations to satisfy their own needs.

Example: Using renewable energy resources (such as wind and solar power) instead of fossil fuels (such as coal, oil, and gas), which are not renewable.

Characteristics of an environmentally conscious business

Consultation
Engages in consultation with all the interested parties when developing and implementing policies that affect the environment.

Honesty
Tells the truth and is above-board in all matters affecting the environment. Environmentally conscious businesses are not afraid to have their affairs examined, as they generally have nothing to hide (e.g. they do not hide industrial accidents).

Awareness of environmental issues
Promotes environmental issues among its employees, customers and the business community and spends money on these issues. Regular communication and engagement with staff to increase awareness and promoting positive behaviours with regard to the environment.

Openness to development of new product design/clean manufacturing processes/recycling
Designs products that are durable and capable of maximum possible lifespan; helps to reduce energy consumption/waste.
Uses parts that can be recycled/safely disposed of and avoids environmentally sensitive materials – pollution prevention. Continually reducing the impact of its products on the environment through improved recycling and reuse programmes.

Sensitive to all environmental considerations in its policy-making
Conducts environmental audits (environmental impact statements) to assess the impact of its business on the environment.

Compliant with the law
Conducts business with integrity and complies with the environmental laws and regulations. Seeks advice from the EPA to ensure compliance.

Engages in sustainable development
Takes into account the needs of future generations when using national resources. Businesses should adopt an environmentally-friendly approach when using natural resources. This is especially important because of the potential for climate change. Greater use could be made of wind and sunshine to create energy, and businesses should use this energy more efficiently (e.g. CFC/LED light bulbs).

Effects of meeting ethical, social and environmental responsibilities on a firm's revenue and costs

Effects on revenue
- A firm's revenues should increase as a result of being socially responsible.
- Environmentally conscious customers will always support businesses that are socially responsible, so sales and profits will increase.

- Firms that market their products using ethical business practices as their unique selling point are likely to attract more customers, increasing sales and profits.

Two examples:

- The Body Shop's unique selling point is that its products are not tested on animals.
- Food companies that sell organic products attract more customers, thereby increasing sales and profits. Glenisk Ltd, Tullamore, Co. Offaly, produce a range of organic dairy products where raw materials are processed without the use of pesticides or synthetic fertilizers.

Effects on costs

Costs may be **increased** initially due to:

- Higher wages and better conditions for employees – proper training, etc. will increase labour costs.
- Using environmentally friendly raw materials and packaging may be more expensive, leading to increases in the cost of production.
- The cost of installing special equipment to reduce noise, pollution and emissions will increase costs.
- Developing codes of practice and compliance with legislative requirements will increase costs.
- The safe disposal of dangerous and toxic waste has a cost.

In the long term, costs may be **reduced** due to:

- Using cleaner technologies and systems will reduce costs and insurance premiums.
- Using renewable energy rather than non-renewable energy may reduce costs over time.

(i) Explain the term 'code of ethics'.

(ii) Outline the benefits **and** challenges for a business of introducing a code of ethics.

(20 marks)

Source: 2017 Higher Level Section 3

Suggested solution

(i) A set of **guidelines/formal written statement** drawn up by a business, which sets out the **expected moral behaviours** for a business. The rules provide a set of norms, which guide or govern relationships with stakeholders. It is concerned about right and wrong, fairness, honesty and respect in a business context.

(ii) **Benefits of a code of ethics:**

Decision-making

A code of ethics can provide a foundation on which to base all decisions that affect internal and external stakeholders, such as employees or residents in the local community.

Having a solid code of ethics in place from the beginning can help to guide a business as it expands.

Day-to-day decisions

A code of ethics helps employees to fully understand the expectations of the company and the ethical guidelines by which to make decisions when dealing with customer complaints. This will ensure that customers are treated fairly.

Business reputation/good brand image

Displaying the business code of ethics on its website or in press releases, while taking care to ensure that the business's actions are always in line with the words on the code, can create a positive brand image among consumers and jobseekers, creating a loyal customer base and a positive attitude among employees and prospective employees.

Encourages whistle-blowing

A code of ethics may include a whistle-blowing clause, which encourages any wrongdoing to be reported to management.

Staff are encouraged to report unethical behaviour by creating an environment where whistle-blowing is rewarded.

Encourages ethical behaviour

It helps encourage ethical behaviour of senior management and employees at all levels. This will reduce losses due to theft and fraud.

Clearly defined offences

The code of ethics will clearly define the behaviours that are not acceptable. This makes it easier to identify these behaviours and to deter them from happening.

Challenges of introducing a code of ethics:

Culture

Often, newly implemented codes of ethics may not immediately gain the respect or support of employees or management. They may see it as a critique of their personal morals.

Senior management may not treat it as a working document or may choose to ignore it. They may not 'walk the talk'.

The code of ethics **must be updated regularly** and kept up-to-date to include new behaviours, which are considered unethical. E.g. improper use of the company social media account/company emails.

Enforcement

Enforcing a code of ethics can also present challenges. Sanctions given to employees may damage the industrial relations climate in the business and reduce morale.

Staff training must be provided on an ongoing basis to ensure the code is understood and is not ignored. This will involve financial costs for the business.

Marking scheme

(i)   5 marks

(ii) 1 × 7 marks (4 + 3) + 2 × 4 marks (2 + 2)

At least **one** benefit and **one** challenge required.

'Protecting and managing Ireland's environment is a shared responsibility. It involves government and public bodies; businesses and industry; as well as members of the public, working in partnership.'

Environmental Protection Agency (EPA)

Discuss how a business could operate in an environmentally conscious way.

(20 marks)

Source: 2015 Higher Level Section 3

Suggested solution

- Cleaner production methods/materials substitution/energy efficiency (this can include switching to renewable energy sources). The product itself can be designed to reduce consumption of resources (e.g. reduce reliance on natural resources – use of rainwater tanks, solar hot-water systems), and to prolong its useful life. By reducing the environmental impact of business, it will improve the sustainability of the business. This helps achieve the goal of sustainable development.

- Minimise waste/safe disposal of waste: The business could adopt the Four Rs: reduce, reuse, recycle and recover. If waste is produced, every effort should be made to reuse it, if practicable.

- Maximisation of recycled content: Recycling will conserve resources and reduce waste, while it may be possible for a business to recover materials or energy from waste which cannot be reduced, reused or recycled.

- Pollution prevention: The use of processes, practices, materials, products or energy sources that avoid or minimise the creation of pollutants and waste, and thereby reduce the risk to human health and the environment.

- The idea is pollution prevention rather than pollution control. Code of ethics: The business could establish a code of ethics which is a formal written statement setting out the modes of behaviour expected from a business in its dealings with the environment and the wider community in which it operates, encouraging a culture of openness, consultation, honesty and awareness of environmental issues, etc.

Other acceptable points:

Regular environmental audits; advice from the EPA (Enviromental Protection Agency); promotion of environmental issues (rewarding 'Green' initiatives), etc.

OR

(Focus on qualities of an environmentally conscious business)

- Consults stakeholders before introducing policies that might affect the environment.

- Honest – does not cover up environmental accidents/compliant with the law.

- Aware – promotes environmental awareness among staff through adequate training, which will require resources.

- Open to the development of new product design; to new environmentally friendly manufacturing processes; better product end of life solutions/recycling.

- Sensitive to needs of society as a whole and has such safeguards as an environmental audit to ensure that it operates in an environmentally friendly manner. To achieve this it should have policies such as: Reduction of air pollution/Recycling of waste/Energy conservation/Tree planting on premises/ Acceptable disposable methods/Reject excess packaging/Have sustainable development as a top priority, etc.

Marking scheme
4 × 5 marks (2 + 3)

(i) Define the term 'business ethics'.
(ii) Outline how ethical behaviour in business can be encouraged.

(15 marks)

Suggested solution

(i) It is a set of moral rules and standards that provide guidelines for right and truthful behaviour in business situations with various stakeholders such as employees, customers, suppliers and the community in which the business operates.

Business ethics is concerned with right and wrong, fairness, honesty and respect in a business context.

(ii) **Establishing a code of ethics:** A code of ethics is a formal written statement setting out the modes of behaviour expected from a business in its dealings with employees, customers and the community in which it operates; it encourages a culture of openness.

Encouraging 'whistle-blowing': This involves encouraging staff to report unethical behaviour by creating a climate where whistle-blowing is rewarded.

Modelling ethical behaviour: When senior staff members are highly ethical and display ethical behaviour, it will encourage subordinates to behave in a similar manner.

Staff training: A code of ethics should be presented to staff at induction training and further reminder training should include modules on ethical behaviour.

Discipline procedures should be in place for staff guilty of behaving unethically. This could typically include fines, demotion or dismissal. At the same time, ethical behaviour should be encouraged through rewards such as bonuses or promotion.

Marking scheme
(i) 5 marks (2 + 3)
(ii) 2 × 5 marks (2 + 3)

Applied Business Question (ABQ) (Higher Level)

Based on Units 4, 5 and 6

This is a compulsory question for Leaving Certificate 2022/2027

Riverport Indoor Market (RIM) Ltd

Riverport is a scenic town in the West of Ireland. In 2009, a large multinational company, the town's biggest employer, closed down. This loss motivated a group of enthusiastic local residents and business people to do something to revive their local community.

They saw the multinational's empty factory warehouse as a potential resource and believed its location, easy access and ample parking would assist local development projects. They consulted widely, gathering information from as many local interests as possible.

Arising from the consultation process, local farmers, producers and crafts people identified the provision of an indoor farmers' market as being a unique opportunity to sell their produce directly to the consumer. A small group of local business people formed a private limited company, Riverport Indoor Market (RIM) Ltd. It set about identifying the financing options available to purchase the factory warehouse for the agreed price of €400,000. An additional €50,000 was required to refurbish the warehouse into 50 stall units, which could then be rented out to farmers and crafts people. The stallholders had to initially purchase a transport vehicle, equip their stall and pay the agreed stall rent of €50 a day to RIM Ltd. On an ongoing basis, the stallholders would have to manage cash flow effectively and control essential costs such as raw materials, stock, transport operating costs, wages and insurance.

The farmers' market proved a major success. At the end of its second year, the number of stallholders had increased from its original seven to 30. Due to the increasing numbers visiting the market, RIM Ltd was able to lease out units within the warehouse to an indoor children's play and activity centre and a car valeting centre. Many local services in Riverport such as B&Bs, restaurants and petrol stations reported increased year-end profits. The market provided opportunities for locals and visitors to meet informally and interact with each other. The local town council donated a nearby green area for the construction of a public park.

Given that many of the new stallholders travel from neighbouring counties, there are plans now to promote RIM Ltd as a regional market, serving the Connacht area.

RIM Ltd has developed an interactive website, which includes a video clip capturing a day in the life of the market. This website has impressed tour operators so much that they have included the market as part of their visitor tour route. Sales representatives from RIM Ltd use mobile display booths within the region to attract visitors to the area. In addition, RIM Ltd runs monthly competitions to win a prize of a weekend break in Riverport. RIM Ltd continues to build on its good relationship with the local community by providing financial support to the local GAA club, in return for having the RIM Ltd brand name and logo appear on the club's jersey.

(A) Identify and describe the most appropriate sources of finance to meet the needs of:

    (i) RIM Ltd

    (ii) Individual stallholders.   (20 marks)

(B) Discuss the benefits for the local community, arising from the success of RIM Ltd.   (30 marks)

(C) Evaluate the promotional techniques undertaken by RIM Ltd.   (30 marks)

        (80 marks)

Suggested solution

(A) (i)

Long-Term Finance:

Mortgage/Long-Term Loan/Debenture: It is taken out for more than five years. If the bank lends €400,000 to RIM Ltd, it will hold the deeds to the factory warehouse as security against the repayment of the loan. It is paid in agreed instalments, including interest, which is tax deductible. If RIM Ltd defaults on the repayment, then the bank can recover their money through the repossession and sale of the warehouse.

Equity/Share Capital/Owner's Capital: RIM Ltd is a private limited company and the €400,000 needed to purchase the warehouse could be raised by selling ordinary shares to new or existing shareholders. No security or repayments are required for RIM Ltd.

Government Grants: Government agencies such as Enterprise Ireland or County Enterprise Boards could be approached for grant aid assistance to help purchase the factory warehouse for €400,000. Normally, they are interest free and do not have to be repaid if used for their intended purpose.

Link: *'It set about identifying the financing options available to purchase the factory warehouse for the agreed price of €400,000.'*

Medium-Term Finance:

Medium-Term Loan: RIM Ltd could get a medium-term bank loan with a fixed rate of interest that would be repaid in equal monthly instalments up to a five-year period, allowing the company to cash purchase and negotiate the best cash prices available for heating equipment, fixtures and fittings, etc. The bank may require security or personal guarantees. Interest paid is tax deductible. RIM Ltd will know in advance the amount and number of repayments and can budget accordingly.

Link: *'An additional €50,000 was required to refurbish the warehouse into 50 stall units which could then be rented out to farmers and crafts people.'*

(ii) Medium-Term Finance:

Hire Purchase: This is a method of finance that would allow the individual stallholders to purchase an asset, such as a transport vehicle, over a five-year period or less. The stallholder will get immediate possession of the transport vehicle; however, ownership doesn't transfer until the last instalment is made. HP is an expensive source of finance. No security is required, but the HP Co. may repossess the asset if there is a default in repayments.

Leasing: This would involve the renting of an asset by the individual stallholder from a finance company. The stallholder will not have to come up with a lump sum and would have the full use and possession of an asset, provided he/she makes fixed and regular payments to the company. While leasing costs more than cash purchase, it can help the cash flow of a business.

Link: *'The stallholders had to initially purchase a transport vehicle, equip their stall ...'*

Short-Term Finance:

Bank Overdraft: This is a facility offered by a bank that allows current account holders to withdraw more money from their account than they actually have in it. Interest is charged on the outstanding balance on a daily basis. It can be recalled by the bank at any time. The individual stallholders could use their overdraft facility to purchase stock or pay the wages of part-time staff. It can be used as a form of working capital to aid in day-to-day business operations.

Accrued Expenses: This source of finance frees up money by delaying the payment of regular bills such as utilities, rent or insurance. This would free up cash to pay for supplies which, in turn, could be sold allowing these bills to be paid later.

Trade Credit: Stallholders may buy stock for resale on a 'buy now and pay later' basis. The amount of credit available is influenced by the creditworthiness of the stallholder. There is no direct charge, but cash discounts may be forgone.

Link: *'... the stallholders would have to manage cash flow effectively and control essential costs such as raw materials, stock, transport, operating costs, wages and insurance'.*

OR

Link: *'The stallholders had to ... equip their stall and pay the agreed stall rent of €50 a day to RIM Ltd'. (Candidate treating 'equip stall' as a purchase of 'stock'.)*

Marking scheme

(A) (i)	Sources of Finance for RIM Ltd. (Name type, explain, relevant link)	Long-Term 7 marks (2 + 3 + 2)	20 marks
	Medium term source can only be given once either: RIM Ltd or Stallholder	Medium-Term 6 marks (2 + 2 + 2)	
(ii)	Sources of Finance for the individual stallholders. (Name type, explain, relevant link)	Short-Term 7 marks (2 + 3 + 2)	

(B) Discuss the benefits for the local community, arising from the success of RIM Ltd.

<u>Economic Benefits:</u>

Direct employment/Job creation. Jobs are directly created in the community reducing unemployment.

Link: *'At the end of its second year, the number of stallholders had increased from its original seven to 30.'*

Spin-off employment. With increased employment and increased visitor numbers, more income is being spent in the community increasing spin-off jobs in the retail and services businesses.

Link: *'Many local services in Riverport such as B&Bs, restaurants and petrol stations reported increased year-end profits.'*

Enterprise culture. New enterprise is encouraged and promoted. Other new businesses ('start-ups') have set up in the market as confidence grows from the success of RIM Ltd.

Link: *'... lease out units within the warehouse to an indoor children's play and activity centre and a car valeting centre.'*

Local Produce. Goods are provided to local consumers by local producers. Locals do not have to shop outside their local area (i.e. shop local).

Link: *'... unique opportunity to sell their produce directly to the consumer.'*

Income for local authorities. Commercial rates are an important source of income for local authorities and, as new businesses are established, revenue from commercial rates increases, allowing the local council to improve amenities.

Link: *'The local town council donated a nearby green area for the construction of a public park'.*

<u>Social Benefits:</u>

Community spirit/Sense of pride/Improved quality of life. The success of RIM Ltd has facilitated an improvement in community spirit and social interaction between the different community stakeholders. With prosperity comes a sense of pride in the community as the town's appearance and amenities improve.

Link: *'The market provided opportunities for locals and visitors to meet informally and interact with each other'.*

OR

'The local town council donated a nearby green area for the construction of a public park.'

OR

'RIM Ltd was able to lease out units within the warehouse to an indoor children's play and activity centre ...'

Depopulation is prevented and the social fabric maintained. When an area is being developed, people tend to stay there and not leave. The population does not decrease and life stays in the community (schools, health centres, etc.).

Link: *'RIM Ltd was able to lease out units within the warehouse to an indoor children's play and activity centre ...'*

Marking scheme

(A)	Three benefits. (Name type, explain, relevant link)	3 × 10 marks (3 + 4 + 3)	30 marks

Note: At least one of each economic/social required.

(C)

There are four promotional techniques undertaken by RIM Ltd. They are direct advertising, sales promotion, public relations and personal selling.

Direct/Advertising:

- Advertising is the communication of information to a target market/audience using the advertising media such as press, publications, posters, radio, TV, cinema, internet.
- Advertising includes the publication of facts or opinions concerning goods/ services to awaken the public's interest and persuade them to purchase.
- It is a very public form of communication and suitable for a wide audience. It creates an awareness of the product in an attempt to convince consumers to purchase. Advertising encourages repeat purchasing, consumer loyalty and increased sales.
- Individual goes through a number of stages. Advertising must create attention, interest, desire and action (AIDA) to be effective.
- Advertising offers the consumer a reason to buy.

RIM Ltd uses the internet to advertise the indoor market.

Link: *'RIM Ltd has developed an interactive website, which includes a video clip capturing a day in the life of the market'.*

OR

Link: *'The website has impressed tour operators so much that they have included the market as part of their visitor tour route'.*

Personal Selling:

- This occurs when a salesperson is in direct contact with the customer and tries to verbally persuade customers to buy a product or service.
- Sales representatives must have good personal and communications skills. They must have detailed knowledge of the product or service being sold.
- They provide feedback to the company on customers' reactions to the product/ service.
- They attract new customers as well as retaining existing customers.

RIM Ltd uses personal selling by employing sales representatives to visit various locations and promote the market.

Link: *'Sales representatives from RIM Ltd use mobile display booths within the region to attract visitors to the area.'*

Sales Promotion:

- Sales promotion involves the use of short-term incentives and gimmicks/short-term temporary activities to encourage purchase. It is designed to create a sense of immediacy by offering reasons to purchase in the short-term, thereby increasing sales.
- Forms of sales promotion include coupons, vouchers, loyalty cards, free samples, banded offers, competitions, etc.
- May be useful when launching a new product/service or relaunching an existing product or service.
- The purposes of sales promotion include: attracting new users for the product; rewarding loyal users; increasing purchasing frequency among occasional users.
- Sales promotion can be used to complement direct advertising and encourage repeat business.
- Sales promotion offers the consumer an incentive to buy.

Link: *'... RIM Ltd runs monthly competitions to win a prize of a weekend break in Riverport.'*

Public Relations:

- The aim of PR is to generate good will and positive customer relations for the business; to achieve favourable publicity and a positive image for the product, service or firm.
- Specific tools/methods for communicating the message include press statements to the media, speeches by management, conferences, photo opportunities, newsletters, annual reports, company brochures, social/charitable activities.
- Sponsorship: A company pays money so that their name/logo – RIM Ltd – can be associated with an event/sports team (e.g. Fáilte Ireland sponsored the Irish Open Golf Tournament). The company will then be tied to any publicity of the event/sports team. Businesses enhance their reputation by making positive contributions to the local community.
- The business benefits from the indirect advertising generated by the event/sports team.

Link: *'RIM Ltd continues to build on its good relationship with the local community by providing financial support to the local GAA club, in return for having the RIM Ltd brand name and logo appear on the club's jersey.'*

Evaluation required.

Marking scheme

(C)	Three promotional techniques (Name type, explain, relevant link) Evaluation	3 × 9 marks ((2 + 4 + 3) + 3)	30 marks

UNIT 7

International Environment

Ireland is open to economic, social and cultural trends from abroad, and the international environment has a significant impact on Irish business. This unit introduces the international trading environment and describes developments in international business. It also deals with Ireland's membership of the European Union.

Objective
To enable students to understand the opportunities and challenges facing Irish business in the international environment.

- **Chapter 25:** Introduction to the International Trading Environment
- **Chapter 26:** The European Union
- **Chapter 27:** International Business

25 Introduction to the International Trading Environment

Be able to:

- Explain the significance of international trade to the Irish economy.
- Discuss the changing nature of the international economy and its effects on Irish business.
- Discuss the opportunities and challenges facing Irish business in developed and developing markets.

Ireland as an open economy

An open economy is an economy that engages in international trade and is importing and exporting. Ireland has a small open economy that engages in international trade. Nearly 80% of what is produced in Ireland is exported.

This impacts on Ireland's economic development as follows:

- Creates employment.
- Earns foreign currency for the country.
- Generates revenue for the government.
- Helps economic growth.
- Enables essential raw materials and finished goods to be imported.
- Offers wider choice and lower prices to consumers.

International trade

This is trade between countries. It involves exporting and importing goods and services.

Exporting

Exporting is producing goods and services in one country and selling them to another country.

- **Visible exports** are **physical goods** sold to other countries and resulting in an inflow of cash (e.g. agricultural products produced in Ireland and sold abroad, such as beef exported to the UK and lamb exported to France).
- **Invisible exports** are **services** sold by one country to other countries. These are activities that bring money into the country. In the case of Ireland, this includes:
  - Foreign students coming to Ireland to learn English during the summer.
  - Irish musicians performing abroad.

Importing

Importing is buying goods and services from a foreign country, which means money goes out of the country.

- **Visible imports** are **physical goods** bought from other countries, such as:
  - Cars from Germany.
  - Wine from South Africa.
  - Leather shoes from Italy.
- **Invisible imports** are **services** bought from other countries, which means that Irish money goes to a foreign country:
  - Irish people going on holiday to Spain.
  - Foreign musicians performing in Ireland.

International trade is measured by:
- Balance of trade
- Balance of payments

Measuring international trade

- **Balance of trade**
  - If visible exports are greater than visible imports, there is a **surplus** in the balance of trade.
  - If visible exports are less than visible imports, there is a **deficit** in the balance of trade.

Balance of trade = visible exports − visible imports

- **Balance of payments**
  - The balance of payments is the difference between the value of **total exports** (visible and invisible) and the value of **total imports** (visible and invisible). It is expressed as a surplus or deficit.

Balance of payments = total exports − total imports

  - It is the amount of money coming into a country minus money going out of a country during the course of a year.

Balance of trade/balance of payments calculation

Using the following information, calculate:
(i) Balance of trade
(ii) Balance of payments

Total imports	€16 billion
Invisible imports	€9 billion
Invisible exports	€11 billion
Total exports	€19 billion

(i) Balance of trade: **€1 billion**
(ii) Balance of payments: **€3 billion**

> *Workings*
> Visible exports = €19B − €11B = €8 billion
> Visible imports = €16B − €9B = €7 billion
> Balance of trade = visible exports − visible imports
> = €8 billion − €7 billion
> = €1 billion
> Balance of Payments = Total exports − Total imports
> = 19 billion − €16 billion
> = €3 billion

Reasons for exporting

1. Domestic market is too small: Irish firms have to export to expand, to increase sales and profits and survive.
2. To spread the business risk by not relying on local markets only.
3. Irish firms can avail of economies of scale from large-scale production by going into the export market. This means a lower cost of production and a more competitive price, resulting in increased sales and more profits.

Reasons for importing

1. There is a lack of raw materials for industry (e.g. oil).
2. The climate is unsuitable for the production of certain products (e.g. bananas).
3. Customers want choice and variety (e.g. Italian shoes, French wines).
4. Certain finished goods demanded by consumers cannot be produced here (e.g. Japanese cars).

The significance of international trade to Irish economy

1. **Comparative advantage**: Some countries have an advantage and a tradition of certain skills in producing goods and services (e.g. food production in Ireland). Surpluses of these products can be exported in exchange for imports of essential raw materials required for production (e.g. oil).
2. **Variety and choice**: Trade allows consumers to enjoy a wide choice and variety of goods that cannot be produced here because of climate or lack of essential factors of production (e.g. fruit, food products).

3. **Economies of scale**: Large-scale production through exporting allows for economies of scale. This means lower costs of production and a more competitive price with increased sales and profit.

4. **Economic growth**: International trade allows countries like Ireland with small home markets to achieve growth through exports. It provides foreign markets for Irish produce. By selling abroad, foreign currency is earned, which is used to pay for the imports people in Ireland need.

5. **Increased efficiency**: International trade increases competition. Production is more efficient, which means lower prices for consumers.

Free trade and protectionism

Free trade

This means there are no barriers to the movement of goods and services between countries. Free trade exists between EU member countries.

Protectionism

This is setting up **barriers to trade** to reduce imports to the country, to protect home industry from foreign competition, and to protect jobs. Barriers to trade include:

- **Tariffs** – Taxes or duties on imported goods to make them more expensive so they will be less competitive on the domestic market.
  - They encourage consumers to buy more home-produced goods.
- **Quotas** – A limit on the quantity of goods that can be imported/exported.
  - Quotas discourage imports and/or encourage sales of domestically produced goods.
- **Embargos** – A ban on importing of specified goods from particular countries.
- **Subsidies** – Payments by governments to firms to reduce cost of production, allowing them to sell goods at a more competitive price on export markets.
- **Administrative regulations** – Such as customs delays and excessive paperwork designed to exclude exports.

Changing trends in the international economy and their impact on Irish businesses

1. **Deregulation** has increased competition in the marketplace and reduced protectionism, i.e. removal of trade barriers. Irish businesses now need to be more competitive as they face competition from larger foreign companies. They need to produce top-quality goods and services at competitive prices in order to survive. In Ireland, deregulation allows new business to enter the marketplace and offer Irish consumers value for their money.

> **Impact:** Deregulation of the **electricity** and **airline** sectors has offered choices and value for money for Irish businesses.

2. **The growth in trading blocs and agreements**: The EU is an example of a trading bloc which allows free trade among its members. Being a member, Ireland can trade freely with other countries in the EU without any barriers or restrictions.

> **Impact:** This offers a wider marketplace (512 million) for Irish goods and services due to the growth in membership.

3. **The World Trade Organisation** is the body responsible for promoting fair trade between countries. It negotiates between member states by encouraging deregulation and the removal of barriers to trade.

> **Impact:** This allows for huge sales opportunities abroad for Irish businesses.

4. **The European Union/enlarging the European Union**: As countries in Eastern Europe join the EU, opportunities arise for Irish business to promote their goods and services abroad.

> **Impact:** There is a huge population in these countries and a demand for Irish products and services.

5. **Emerging countries/new market opportunities**: Due to the growth of economies in the Pacific Rim (South Korea, China, Japan, Taiwan, Singapore, Thailand, Malaysia, Indonesia), new markets have emerged. These economies are developing rapidly; the Pacific Rim is the fastest-growing economic region in the world.

> **Impact:** The Pacific Rim countries have provided both markets and competition for Irish businesses.

6. **The influence of transnational corporations (TNCs)**: Some TNCs are more powerful than the country in which they operate. Ireland attracts these companies by offering tax incentives. (Ireland has a very low corporation tax rate of 12.5%.) TNCs often lobby governments and the EU to accept their conditions of trade. This enables them to trade with fewer restrictions.

> **Impact:** There could be major consequences for the Irish economy if TNCs choose not to locate in Ireland as they are very large and employ significant numbers of workers (e.g. Pfizer, Boston Scientific).

7. **Technology**: The information and communications technology (ICT) sector has shown remarkable growth in recent years. ICT companies in Ireland are engaged in a range of activities (networks, software development, etc.)

> **Impact:** E-commerce/business has enabled Irish businesses to advertise what they do worldwide. Developments in technology have allowed this to take place. Businesses are now in constant contact with companies around the globe.

8. **Competition**: Eastern Europe countries such as the Czech Republic, Hungary and Slovakia have opened up their economies to market forces.

> **Impact:** This presents a particular challenge for Ireland as these countries are excellent producers of agricultural products and can offer quality at a lower price to the European consumer.

9. **Growth in globalisation**: Treating the world as one single marketplace for standardised products is seen in Ireland today. The use of the internet and TV has helped businesses to develop global brands by advertising and promoting them around the world (e.g. Sony, McDonald's, Toyota, Coca-Cola).

> **Impact:** Irish firms need to be able to compete in the world markets.

Opportunities and challenges in international trade

International trade – opportunities for Irish businesses

1. **Access to larger markets**

   EU membership gives Irish firms access to a market of 512 million consumers. This large market allows Irish firms to expand and grow, which would not be possible within the small Irish home market.

2. **Economies of scale**

   Because of large-scale production for many markets, Irish firms can benefit from economies of scale, which allow us to compete with products from low-cost economies.

3. **Earn foreign currency**

   International trade allows Irish businesses to export into foreign countries and earn foreign currency. This money can be used to pay for imports of essential raw materials and finished goods required by the Irish economy.

4. **Highly skilled workforce**

   Ireland possesses a well-educated and highly-skilled workforce. Many Irish people have obtained valuable experience through engaging in international trade. This creates opportunities for Irish businesses as they have a pool of experienced people from which to recruit.

5. **Ireland's 'green' image**

   Ireland's image abroad as a green, healthy and environmentally friendly country is particularly helpful when marketing abroad, particularly in relation to Ireland's tourism and food industries.

6. **English – a language of trade**

   English is an important international trading language and gives Ireland an advantage when doing business internationally.

7. **Free trade and markets**

As trade restrictions are abolished and as access to new and existing markets emerges, Ireland is finding that international trade provides huge opportunities for increased sales and profit.

International trade – challenges faced by Irish businesses

1. **Competition**

International competition requires companies to acquire greater efficiency and to improve quality and standards in order to survive in domestic and export markets.

2. **High-cost base**

Ireland is an economy with a high-cost base for raw materials, labour and insurance. This makes it difficult for Irish firms to compete against businesses from low-cost economies. Irish firms must produce high-quality products in order to compete on international markets.

3. **Distribution costs**

Because of Ireland's location on the edge of Europe, distribution costs for exports are high, making Irish products less competitive. A similar problem exists in relation to raw materials imported into Ireland.

4. **Different language, customs, cultures in other countries**

Possessing competency in multiple languages is important for firms that want to successfully engage in international trade. Firms must also consider the customs and cultures of different countries when marketing products abroad.

5. **Payment difficulties**

There may be problems getting paid for exports. Problems collecting debts are more difficult when dealing in foreign markets.

6. **Cost of adapting products to meet international standards and regulations**

Products being exported from Ireland may have to be adapted to satisfy safety laws and other international standards and regulations in foreign markets. Different climates around the world may require products to be adapted before being exported.

The role of information and communication technology (ICT) in international trade

1. **Marketing and access to global markets**

The internet allows Irish firms to market and sell their products through their websites to customers worldwide. For example, customers can place orders and make payments by credit card. This is called e-commerce.

2. **Instant communication**

Instant communication with customers all over the world is made possible through the use of e-mail and mobile phones.

3. **Market research**

The internet allows Irish firms to carry out research and acquire up-to-d information on markets and size of populations, which hel decisions regarding individual markets.

4. Reduced costs – videoconferencing

Videoconferencing allows managers of international businesses to be in touch with people in different locations around the world in order to hold meetings and exchange up-to-date information to aid their decision-making. Videoconferencing is one tool that eliminates the need for staff to make expensive and time-consuming trips to attend meetings around the world.

The Irish economy is 'performing well', but Brexit poses a threat.

Source: *Financial Times*, December 2016

Invisible Exports: €101,750 million	Invisible Imports: €109,376 million
Total Exports: €194,366 million	Total Imports: €171,534 million

(i) Calculate the **Balance of Trade** using the figures above. (**Show your workings.**)

(ii) Define the term 'tariff' and explain the possible effect on the Irish economy if the UK Government was to impose a tariff on Irish goods in the future.

(25 marks)

Source: 2017 Higher Level Section 3

Suggested solution

(i) (194,366–101,750) – (171,534–109,376) = €30,458 million **Surplus**

(€92,616–€62,158) = €30,458 million (surplus)

If either the € symbol or million is omitted award 3 marks out of 4 marks.

(ii) Tariff is a charge/tax applied to **imported** products to persuade consumers to purchase domestically produced goods and to restrict goods from another country. Ireland will sell **fewer exports** to the UK.

AND Balance of Trade should decrease/Loss of profits/Unemployment in the Irish export-oriented companies/Products less competitive in the UK so reduction in Irish exports to the UK/May have to seek out new markets.

Marking scheme

(i)   Calculation: Visible exports: 4 marks

      Visible imports: 4 marks

      Answer: 5 marks (4 + 1) (answer/surplus)

(ii) Tariff 6 marks (4 + 2)

      Effect 6 marks (4 + 2)

Explain the following international trade terms:

(i) Open economy

(ii) Trading bloc

(iii) Protectionism

(iv) Deregulation

(20 marks)

Source: 2016 Higher Level Section 3

Suggested solution

(i) Open Economy

An open economy is an economy which engages in international trade – goods and services are traded in the international community. Funds can also be transferred across borders allowing countries to borrow from another country if necessary. A measure of a country's openness is the fraction of GDP devoted to imports and exports. Nearly 80% of what is produced in Ireland is exported.

(ii) Trading Bloc

A trading bloc is a group of countries that organise a free trade area, common market or customs union in order to reduce or eliminate barriers to trade, e.g. European Union, NAFTA (an agreement between the United States, Canada and Mexico). Trading blocs agree a common set of tariffs on imports from countries outside the trading bloc.

(iii) Protectionism

Protectionism involves governments protecting their home industries from foreign competition by erecting barriers to trade, e.g. tariffs, quotas, embargoes, paying subsidies to home industries. Protectionism measures are put in place to reduce imports and/or make them more expensive, to protect jobs, protect specific industries and to improve the balance of payments.

(iv) Deregulation

The reduction or elimination of government power in a particular industry. It involves removing legal barriers to entering an industry.

It usually creates more competition within the industry. An increase in competition should lead to an increase in efficiency and lower prices.

The EU deregulated the airline industry to allow more competition due to the removal of monopolies and more choice for consumers/value for money. It resulted in the emergence of low-cost airlines such as Ryanair.

Marking scheme

2 × 6 marks (3 + 3)

2 × 4 marks (2 + 2)

HL

(a) Read the information below, supplied by the CSO and answer the questions which follow:

	Balance of Trade	Balance of Invisible Trade
	€m	€m
Quarter 2, 2012	10,004	(6,769) deficit
Quarter 2, 2011	9,660	(9,192) deficit

(i) Explain the terms 'Balance of Trade' and 'Balance of Payments'.
(ii) Calculate the Balance of Payments figures for both years from the above data.
(iii) Illustrate what is meant by the term 'invisible exports' with reference to the Irish economy.

(20 marks)

(b) Discuss the opportunities **and** challenges for large indigenous companies, such as Kerry Group plc, in exporting to non-EU countries.

(20 marks)

Source: 2013 Higher Level Section 3

Suggested solution

(a) (i)

The Balance of Trade
- The difference between **visible exports and visible imports**.
- Visible exports are physical goods sent out of the country and money comes in, e.g. Apple computers, beef exported to UK, lamb exported to France.
- Visible imports are physical goods coming in to the country and money goes out, e.g. wine from France, leather shoes from Italy.

Balance of Trade
Visible Exports > Visible Imports = Surplus
Visible Exports < Visible Imports = Deficit

The Balance of Payments
- The difference between **Total Exports (Visible and Invisible) and Total Imports (Visible and Invisible)**.
- The total amount of money entering and leaving a country during the course of a year.
- It includes the balance of trade plus the balance of invisible trade.
- Invisible exports, e.g. American tourists holidaying in Ireland.
- Invisible imports, e.g. Irish people holidaying in Spain.

Balance of Payments
Total Exports > Total Imports = Surplus
Total Exports < Total Imports = Deficit

(ii) Balance of Payments = Balance of Trade plus the Balance of Invisible trade
Quarter 2 2012 BOP = 10,004 €m + (6,769) €m = 3,235 €m surplus
Quarter 2 2011 BOP = 9660 €m + (9,192) €m = 468 €m surplus

(iii)

- The purchase of an Irish service by a foreigner.
- Invisible exports are Irish services sold abroad by Irish firms.
- Money coming into Ireland from Irish services sold abroad to foreign customers.

(b) **Opportunities**

- *Changes in technology* have had a positive impact on Irish exporters, making communications easier and instantaneous worldwide.
- The internet allows Irish exporters to market their goods internationally.
- Videoconferencing allows meetings to be held at a fraction of the cost of a traditional meeting. E-mail allows for instant, cheap and reliable communication.
- *The opening of new emerging markets.* China which is now the second biggest economy in the world, overtaking Japan, has created new opportunities for Irish exporters, especially in the food and drinks area.
- Africa's fast-growing middle class and associated spending power has created a need for high-end goods, presenting a significant opportunity for Ireland.
- *Business risks are reduced* because of reduced dependence on the Irish (domestic) market. Economies of scale are made possible in the context of larger markets, which should increase the competitiveness of business.
- *Culture and Green image.* Ireland's ancient Celtic culture and unspoilt pollution-free image provides a unique selling point for companies like Kerry Group plc when marketing food products abroad.

Challenges

- *The growth in globalisation* and global companies with their quality produce at competitive prices are a challenge for Irish exporters. Irish exporting companies will have to become more efficient and invest in R&D in order to provide products with a unique selling point (USP) to survive the competitive threat from global companies.
- Kerry Group invested €100 million in a new R&D facility in Ireland to serve customers in EMEA (Europe, Middle East & Africa).
- *Currency/Exchange rate fluctuations.* If the euro(€) strengthens, for example, against the US dollar($), Irish exports become more expensive leading to a decline in sales to these very important international markets.
- Goods traded between EU and non-EU countries are subject to certain *customs duties*, which increases the selling price of exports making them less competitive.

- Trading outside the EU is often subject to restrictions and may require, for example, additional export licenses.
- *Language and cultural differences* may be an obstacle in exporting to non-EU countries. It is important to gain knowledge of customs, culture and language in order to market products without causing offence. An adapted marketing mix may be needed; for example, a British DIY chain Kingfisher's launch in China encountered serious difficulties because the home improvement market in that country was not yet developed enough.
- *Distribution costs* will be higher as Ireland is geographically located on the peripheral of Europe, which may lead to higher transport costs and less competitive prices.

Marking scheme

(a) (i) 2 explanations @ 5 marks each (3 + 2)

(ii) 6 figures @ 1 mark each

(iii) 4 marks (2 + 2)

(b) 4 × 5 marks:

2 opportunities @ 5 marks each (2 + 3)

2 challenges @ 5 marks each (2 + 3)

26 The European Union

Importance of European Union membership to Ireland

1. Large market

The EU is a trading bloc made up of 27 countries with a population of half a billion people. On 23rd June 2016 Britain voted to leave the EU. This is due to officially come into effect in March 2019. Irish firms have huge opportunities for exporting and expansion.

2. Free-trade area

The EU is a free-trade area where there is free movement of goods, services, capital and labour.

3. Economies of scale

The EU provides a huge market for the products of Irish firms. Economies of scale can be achieved through expansion into these markets.

4. EU grants and supports

The EU has given Ireland many grants to build infrastructure such as roads, airports, etc. Supports to Irish agriculture under the Common Agricultural Policy have increased farm incomes and improved living standards in Ireland.

5. Common currency

Countries in the eurozone – including Ireland – have a single international currency, the euro. This has made trade and travel easier and has eliminated the cost of currency conversion.

European Union institutions

European Commission

The Commission deals with the day-to-day administration of the EU.

The Commission consists of one member from each EU country.

Each Commissioner has responsibility for a particular EU policy area.

The Commission must act in the best interests of the EU and independently of member states.

Functions of the European Commission

- Drafts proposals for new EU laws.
- Makes sure existing EU laws are implemented and obeyed.
- Implements agreed policies of EU (e.g. Common Agriculture Policy, Competition Policy).
- Manages and supervises the EU budget.
- Represents the EU internationally.

European Parliament

Members of European Parliament (MEPs) are elected by the citizens of the EU to represent their interests.

Functions of the European Parliament

- Discusses proposed new laws and proposes amendments.
- Approves the annual EU budget and monitors spending.
- Supervisory powers over other European institutions – vets members of the European Commission and votes on whether to accept the new Commission or not.

Council of European Union/Council of Ministers

The EU's main decision-making body – the Council must adopt all legislation before it becomes law.

The Council is comprised of ministers from the governments of each EU member state. The topic on the agenda determines which minister attends.

Most decisions are made by majority voting. However, unanimous agreement is required for certain issues (e.g. decisions affecting taxation or the entrance of new countries to join the EU).

Functions of the Council of Ministers

- To decide on legislation/to pass European laws – most EU laws are passed jointly by the Council and the Parliament. (This is called 'co-decision'.)
- To approve the EU's budget – the EU annual budget is approved or rejected jointly by the Council and the Parliament.
- Officially signs a number of international agreements with international organisations.

European Court of Auditors

The Court of Auditors is based in Luxembourg. It has one member from each country appointed for a term of six years.

Functions of European Court of Auditors

- Checks that the EU budget is spent according to the regulations of the EU and for the purpose intended.
- Carries out spot checks on the budget to ensure that no fraud is taking place.
- Prepares an annual report certifying that the accounts are reliable and that the money has been properly used.

European Court of Justice

The Court of Justice is based in Luxembourg. It has one judge per member state.

Functions of the European Court of Justice

- Ensures that EU legislation is interpreted and applied in the same way in all EU countries so that the law is equal for everyone.
- Ensures that EU member state and institutions obey the law. It can impose fines on member states if they break the laws.
- Rules on disputes that come before it.

The decision-making process in the European Union

PROPOSAL STAGE

Proposals for a new law are drafted by the Commission.

CONSULTATION STAGE

Parliament debates the proposed new law and may propose amendments. The proposal is returned to the Commission for consideration.

REDRAFTING STAGE

If the Commission accepts these amendments, it will send the redrafted law to the Council of Ministers and the Parliament.

APPROVAL STAGE

The Council of Ministers and Parliament jointly decide whether the proposal will become law. This is called ordinary legislative procedure. If both accept the proposal, it becomes an EU law.

IMPLEMENTATION STAGE

EU laws are implemented by:
- Regulation
- Directive
- Decision

The decision-making process in the European Union

EU regulations

A regulation is an EU law which becomes immediately enforceable as law in all member states. They take precedence over national laws. They are self-executing and do not need any implementing measures.

Example: The General Data Protection Regulation (GDPR) is a regulation in EU law on data protection and privacy for all individuals within the EU and the European Economic Area (EEA).

EU directives

A directive provides an outline to member states of legislation to be achieved in a specific area by a given date.

It obliges member states to change their national laws to allow for EU rules within a time limit.

The directive is binding on each state, but the choice as to how to incorporate it into national legislation is left to the authorities in the member states.

Some directives that have on impact on business in Ireland include:

- The Nitrates Directive – directing the levels of fertilizer to be used on land by Irish farmers.
- The Waste Electrical and Electronic Equipment Directive – this directive states that retailers, when supplying a new product, must accept back waste electrical and electronic equipment from households free of charge.

Decisions

Decisions are directed at specific member states' organisations or individuals. They are binding and must be carried out by the party involved.

The role of interest groups in EU decision-making

Interest groups or pressure groups protect the interests of their members and try to influence the decision-making of the EU.

They are not part of the EU's political framework, but they use methods such as lobbying, information campaigns and public protests in an attempt to influence EU decisions.

Example: The IFA has an office in Brussels to promote and defend the interests of Irish farmers in Europe.

European Union policies and their impact on business

Common policies have been adopted by the EU in many different areas:

Common Agricultural Policy

The Common Agricultural Policy (CAP) was introduced to make the European Union self sufficient in food and to improve farm incomes.

Since Ireland joined the EU, the Common Agricultural Policy has had a huge impact on Irish farming and agriculture, and, through those industries, it had a massive influence on the Irish economy.

The most important policies are:

- Common Agricultural Policy (CAP)
- Common Fisheries Policy (CFP)
- Competition Policy
- European Union Social Charter
- Economic and Monetary Union (EMU)
- Single European Market (SEM)

Impact of Common Agricultural Policy on Ireland

The objectives of the common agricultural policy were:

1. To make the EU self-sufficient in food

CAP aids the provision of safe, traceable food and ensures farmers continually improve their production standards.

Impact on Ireland: Because of CAP, food production has been assured. Ireland is self-sufficient in food products, and it is also a major exporter of food products to world markets. This also makes an important contribution to the balance of payments because of the big export market.

2. To improve farm incomes and to ensure a fair standard of living for the agricultural community

Impact on Ireland: Through a series of payments to Irish farmers, CAP has supported the Irish agricultural industry. There are about 130,000 farmers in Ireland. CAP introduced a system of direct payments to farmers through an annual single payment called the 'single payment scheme'. This provides income stability for members of the Irish farming community.

3. To increase productivity

Impact on Ireland: CAP provides an opportunity for Irish farmers to increase productivity. By providing grants for investment in new technology and farm improvements, agricultural productivity and efficiency has improved.

4. To stabilise markets and regulate prices

CAP stabilises agricultural markets and regulates prices so that farmers can be assured that there will not be huge fluctuations in the prices they receive for their output.

Impact on Ireland: Since joining the EU, Irish farmers have benefited from major funding from CAP.

5. To ensure reasonable prices for consumers

Impact on Ireland: Irish consumers have a regular supply and choice of high-quality products at reasonable prices, produced to the highest food safety and traceability standards.

6. To provide access to a large EU market

Thanks to the CAP, Irish farmers have open access to one of the largest markets in the world. Agriculture makes a big contribution to Ireland's overall exports.

Impact on Ireland: Access to EU markets has brought a lot of sales and profits to Irish farmers.

7. To preserve and restore rural infrastructure and villages

Impact on Ireland: This supports Ireland's tourism industry.

8. To benefit Irish agriculture using money from the structural funds.

Reform of the Common Agricultural Policy

Why reform?

The EU's Common Agricultural Policy (CAP) is a dynamic policy which, through successive reforms, has been **adapted to new challenges** faced by European agriculture.

These challenges include more sustainable use of natural resources, climate change, increased competition from global markets and the need to maintain thriving rural areas across the EU.

The CAP needs to continue to ensure viable food production and a stable food supply, while taking into account food safety, the rural economy, animal welfare, and social and environmental concerns.

The CAP reform

The new CAP covers the period from **2014 to 2020**. The reform is fully in line with the fundamental principles of the Common Agricultural Policy. These will continue to focus on providing sufficient high-quality, safe food at affordable prices to consumers in the EU and globally. At the same time, the reform fully respects EU rules on animal welfare and the environment and ensures a fair standard of living for European farmers. The reformed CAP includes:

1. The '**greening**' of farm payments, through the introduction of environmentally sound farming practices, such as crop diversification, and maintaining ecologically rich landscape features and a minimum area of permanent grassland.

2. More **equality** in the distribution of support in order to reduce the biggest differences in the levels of income support received by farmers across the EU, and a reduction in payments above a certain amount for the biggest farms.

3. **Better targeting of income support** to farmers most in need, particularly young farmers, farmers in low-income sectors and farmers in areas with natural constraints.

Common Fisheries Policy (CFP)

The Common Fisheries Policy is an EU policy covering all aspects of fishing in the EU. The main provisions of the policy are:

1. **To support the incomes of those involved in the fishing industry**
   CFP aims to achieve this by:

   - Reserving access to Irish coastal waters to fishermen from local ports to a distance of 12 miles offshore. This prevents foreign boats from fishing in these areas.
   - Setting the price of fish at the start of each year, which guarantees Irish fishermen a decent income.
   - Providing grants for the modernisation of fishing boats and improving technology, which helps to increase catches and improves sales and profit.

> **Impact on Ireland**: The restructuring of the fishing industry in the EU has ensured better prices for efficient Irish fishermen and improves their income.

2. **To promote the conservation of Irish fish stocks**
   This policy is designed to protect fish stocks from overfishing.
   CFP aims to achieve this by:

- Setting maximum quantities (quotas) of fish that can be caught each year.
- Regulating the mesh size of nets to limit the catching of small fish.
- Restricting fishing in certain areas to protect fish breeding grounds.

Impact on Ireland: CFP protects the marine environment and helps conserve and improve fish stocks.

3. **To promote the marketing of fisheries products**

CFP aims to achieve this by:

- Implementing a marketing fisheries policy designed to stabilise markets, guarantee a steady supply of quality fish products at reasonable prices to Irish consumers, and support Irish fishermen.

Impact on Ireland: This policy provides good-quality food for Irish and EU consumers.

4. **To monitor fishing activity**

The responsibility to ensure that all rules are applied rests with each member state (Ireland, in this case).

Impact on Ireland: The EU provides aid to Ireland for the purchase of fishery protection vessels and aircraft for the authorities.

Common Fisheries Policy reform (2014–20)

The Common Fisheries Policy (CFP) is a set of rules for managing European fishing fleets and for conserving fish stocks. Designed to manage a common resource, it gives all European fishing fleets equal access to EU waters and fishing grounds and allows fishermen to compete fairly.

The agreement included:

- A ban on the wasteful practice of discarding perfectly edible fish
- A legally binding commitment to fishing at sustainable levels
- Decentralised decision-making, taking place at regional rather than European level.

Competition Policy

The aim of the Competition Policy is to ensure that there is fair competition among businesses in the EU so that consumers get a choice of quality goods and services at reasonable prices (i.e. the existence of competition among suppliers).

It ensures that Irish businesses operate on a fair basis and that customers benefit.

The main areas of competition policy are:

1. **Cartels**

This restricts Irish businesses from forming anti-competitive cartels which:

- Fix prices or keep prices artificially high
- Divide up the market
- Prevent new firms entering the market

Impact on Ireland:

- Irish consumers are assured of better choice, quality and prices of goods and services.
- It is easier for new Irish firms to set up and compete in the market.

2. Dominant position

Firms in a dominant position in the market cannot abuse that position to charge excessively high prices, restrict smaller competitors, or drive firms out of the market. Example: A dominant firm selling at low cost with the aim of eliminating competitors or making market entry more difficult.

Impact on Ireland:

- Abuse of dominant position by firms is eliminated.
- Irish consumers are protected against firms that abuse their dominant position.
- Smaller Irish firms cannot be forced out of the market by larger businesses.

3. Mergers and takeovers

The European Commission has the power to control mergers and takeovers if it believes they would restrict competition or create a dominant position.

Example: In July 2010, Ryanair had their application to take over Aer Lingus blocked by the European Court of Justice. The Court said the takeover would give Ryanair a dominant position, which would represent a monopoly adversely affecting consumers.

Impact on Ireland: It protects consumers against mergers and takeovers that restrict competition or create a monopoly or dominant position.

4. Monopolies

All monopolies must be deregulated to allow firms into the market, which must be open to competition.

Examples: The electricity market in Ireland has been open for competition. Prior to this, ESB operated a state-owned monopoly. Independent suppliers such as Airtricity and Energia have gained a foothold in the Irish electricity market. The Irish telecommunications industry was also deregulated – the telecoms market was opened to competition.

Impact on Ireland:

- Many Irish consumers have switched their service provider to avail of cheaper prices.
- Competition in these sectors should ensure more choice, a better service and cheaper prices for consumers.

European Union Social Charter

The aim of the Social Charter is to protect the rights of workers in the European Union. It leads to better employment legislation, which improves workers' rights and protects them. The Social Charter proclaims the following rights:

1. **The right to freedom of movement/the right to work in the EU country of one's choice**

Impact on Ireland:

- Irish workers can live and work anywhere in the EU.
- Irish firms can recruit workers from other EU countries.

2. **The right to a fair wage**

Impact on Ireland:

- All Irish workers must be paid the minimum wage. This provides employees with a reasonable standard of living.
- Payment of the minimum wage increases business costs.

3. **The right to equal treatment for men and women**

Impact on Ireland: The policy has ensured greater equality of treatment for Irish men and women in the workplace.

4. **The right to health protection, safety at work and improved working conditions**

Impact on Ireland: The policy has improved working conditions for Irish workers through the introduction of a standard working week, holiday entitlements, health and safety protection of all employees at work.

5. **The right to consultation and participation for workers**

   The right to participate and be consulted in decision-making.

Impact on Ireland: Irish employers must consult their workers about issues of concern to them in relation to their employment.

6. The right to vocational training

Impact on Ireland: The European Social Fund provides finance to train workers who are unemployed in order to provide them with opportunities to rejoin the workforce.

Economic and Monetary Union (EMU)

The policy of the Economic and Monetary Union is designed to meet two objectives:

- The introduction of a single currency – the euro.
- The creation of a single monetary policy for the European Union to be implemented by the European Central Bank.

Benefits of EMU for Ireland

1. Reduced business costs

Irish firms will not have to pay bank charges for currency conversion when Irish firms deal with customers in eurozone countries.

2. No exchange rate risks in the eurozone

Irish firms exporting and importing within the eurozone don't have to worry about changes in the exchange rate as all transactions are in euro. This should lead to more trade between countries.

3. Price transparency

All goods and services are priced in euro. Price comparisons between different countries have become easier for Irish consumers to make.

4. Lower interest rates

The ECB sets interest rates in the eurozone. The ECB has kept interest rates low to reduce the cost of borrowing for individuals and businesses. This reduces costs and increases profit for businesses, and reduces loan and mortgage repayments for individuals.

5. Lower inflation

The primary objective of the European Central Bank is maintaining a regime of price stability and low inflation.

6. Tourism and travel

Travel within the eurozone is easier as people don't have to change currency when travelling within it.

Disadvantages of the EMU for Ireland

1. UK does not use the euro

The UK is not a member of the single currency, and has voted to leave the EU. A large part of Ireland's international trade is with the UK. Sterling may go up or down in value relative to the euro. Fluctuating exchange rates can lead to exchange rate losses for Irish firms.

2. Irish interest rates are set by the ECB

The ECB controls interest rates in the eurozone. The rates are set for Europe as a whole and do not always suit the Irish economy.

The Single European Market

The Single European Market removed barriers to trade among member states in order to provide full and open competition in both goods and labour within the EU.

Impact of the Single European Market on Irish business

1. Free trade between member states

The elimination of barriers or tariffs allows the free movement of goods/services throughout the European Union.

> **Impact on Irish Business**
> - Irish firms have free access to EU market for exports.
> - However, it puts pressure on Irish firms to become more competitive in order to compete with foreign goods coming into Ireland.

2. Free movement of capital

Firms can move capital from one country to another.

> **Impact on Irish Business**
> Individuals/businesses can invest in shares in companies throughout Europe.

3. Free movement of people

European citizens are allowed to move freely between member states.

> **Impact on Irish Business**
> - Free movement may lead to competition for local jobs by non-nationals.
> - It may lead to a scarcity of skilled staff in Ireland as workers may move to other countries.

4. Economies of Scale

A larger market could result in large-scale production, resulting in economies of scale and possible lowering of costs. Open borders allow firms to expand.

> **Impact on Irish Business**
> This should increase the competitiveness of Irish businesses.

5. Common external tariffs

The EU has a common system of barriers on goods imported from outside the EU.

Impact on Irish Business

Irish industry is protected from goods from outside the EU.

6. Public procurement

Governments are required to put public contracts up for tender to firms throughout the European Union.

Impact on Irish Business

This could result in the loss of large contracts for Irish firms.

7. Documentation simplified

The introduction of a single administration document has eliminated a vast number of administrative forms.

Impact on Irish Business

This has resulted in the lowering of administration costs for Irish businesses.

Opportunities and Challenges for Irish Business in the EU market

Opportunities in the EU market for Irish business

1. Free access to EU market for Irish exports

The EU market is the third-largest in the world.

Evaluation

Business risks are reduced because of reduced dependence on the Irish domestic market.

2. Free movement of services, labour and capital

There is free movement of services, labour and capital throughout the EU.

Evaluation

- The Irish construction sector benefited hugely from availability of Polish and other EU workers during the boom years.
- Businesses may source the best investment/borrowing opportunities in EU.

3. Economies of scale

Economies of scale are made possible by the creation of a huge EU market.

Evaluation

This should increase the competitiveness of Irish businesses when selling abroad.

4. EU financial assistance

Funds from the EU are available for infrastructural development – improved infrastructure in Ireland.

> **Evaluation**
> Improved infrastructure in Ireland. Better roads have benefited Irish business.

5. Lower transport/distribution costs

Free movement of goods and lower administration costs.

> **Evaluation**
> It has become easier and cheaper for Irish firms to do business in the EU.

6. Public procurement

Irish firms are eligible to tender for government contracts in EU states.

> **Evaluation**
> Irish companies can quote for government contracts in any EU member state.

Challenges in the EU market for Irish business

1. High distribution costs

Ireland is a small island on the periphery of Europe.

> **Evaluation**
> Distribution costs for exports are high, making Irish products less competitive.

2. Competition

Increased competition from other EU countries.

> **Evaluation**
> Some Irish firms may have difficulty surviving against foreign competition and imports from other EU countries.

3. Public procurement

EU companies are eligible to tender for Irish government contracts.

> **Evaluation**
> Irish firms are no longer guaranteed to get Irish government contracts.

4. High-cost base

Ireland has high labour costs.

Evaluation

Some multinationals have transferred production to lower-cost economies like Poland.

In June 2016 the people of the UK voted to leave the European Union. Discuss the possible consequences for Ireland of the UK leaving the European Union.

Suggested solution

1. Reduction in bilateral trade

Estimates suggest that when the UK leaves this could reduce trade flows between Ireland and the UK by 20% or more. The impact would differ significantly across sectors and products as some sectors and products of Irish firms are more dependent on the UK as an Irish export market than others.

2. Trade barriers

The agri-food sector is particularly dependent on UK exports and any trade barriers for these products would have a considerable impact on trade volumes.

The UK is also a very important source of imports for Irish firms and any trade barriers would increase the prices of UK imports to Ireland. Consumers will face higher prices for UK imports.

3. Drop in the value of the UK pound sterling against the euro

The Brexit vote led to an immediate drop in the value of the UK pound sterling against the euro. A weak UK pound has a negative effect on Irish exports to the UK. However, a weak UK pound makes many goods imported from the UK cheaper for Irish consumers. Currency fluctuations make it difficult for businesses to plan as their costs and selling prices fluctuate.

4. Foreign direct investment (FDI)

It is possible that a reduction in FDI into the UK would result in an economic boost for Ireland through additional FDI projects relocating from the UK.

5. Restriction on free movement of people

A UK exit from the EU opens up the possibility of restrictions on the free movement of people between Ireland and the UK for purposes of work, including border controls with Northern Ireland as the UK is an important destination for Irish emigrants, especially in times of high unemployment.

Should Ireland leave the European Union? Outline reasons for your answer.

(20 marks)

Suggested solution
No/yes/maybe

Reasons for staying in the EU
Possible responses include:

- The creation of the Single Market in 1993 eliminated trade barriers within the EU, allowing for the free movement of goods, services, labour and capital between member states.
- Bigger market for Irish companies leading to greater economies of scale.
- Farmers, under the Common Agricultural Policy (CAP), receive income support measures. Between1973 and 2008, Irish farmers received €44 billion from the (CAP).
- Structural funds of over €17 billion have been made available to Ireland from the European Regional Development Fund and the European Cohesion Fund helping improve roads and public transport infrastructure.
- As a member of the EU, with open access to the EU market, the Irish economy attracts foreign direct investment (FDI), thereby creating employment opportunities. The value of (FDI) in Ireland stands at over €30 billion today.
- The introduction of the single currency brought additional incentives for foreign investors to locate in Ireland, along with relative price stability. The euro has made life easier for Irish businesses trading in and travellers visiting the eurozone.

Other:

- Less bureaucracy involved for businesses.
- Directives such as environmental directives help protect the environment, etc.

Reasons for leaving the EU

- Extra regulations:
  - o The EU places extra regulations on business which will increase business costs. Example: Mobile operator Three is raising its monthly prices by up to €5, blaming costs and new roaming regulations.
- Loss of decision-making powers:
  - o Rules and regulations impose constraints.
  - o The national government will not have complete control over its decisions. They will be subject to regulations which are binding immediately and take precedence over national laws.
  - o Limits/restrictions placed on government budgetary decisions. (e.g. the payment received for AIB shares to be used to pay down the national debt.)

- Brexit:
  - Has created huge uncertainty for Ireland's economic future. May have huge consequences for Irish trade. Much of Ireland's agricultural exports go to UK currently and, if tariffs and quotas are placed on them, Ireland will have to look at other markets.
- Immigration:
  - Free movement of labour may cause overcrowding in large urban areas. This can push up house prices and lead to congestion on roads.
- Threats to Ireland's corporation tax:
  - A push towards harmonised tax rates: a consolidated tax base for Ireland may result in a fall in tax revenues. Multinational companies which locate in Ireland because of low corporation tax rates may move to other countries.
- Apple tax decision:
  - The European Commission has found that Ireland granted undue tax benefits to Apple worth €13bn.

This may cause multinationals like Apple, Facebook and Intel to leave Ireland and locate in other countries, which have a more favourable tax rate.

Marking scheme

Should Ireland leave the European Union?   2 marks
Outline reasons for your answer.   3 × 6 marks (3 + 3)

Examples of an EU Directive and a Regulation affecting Ireland

Waste Framework Directive 2008/98/EC requires member states to adopt waste management plans and waste prevention programmes.

Regulation (EU) No. I 169/2011, which came into effect on 14 December 2014, includes new requirements for the way in which allergen information must be displayed in restaurants, delis, canteens, takeaways, cafés and retail outlets.

Outline how EU directives and regulations are formulated and implemented.

(20 marks)

Source: 2015 Higher Level Section 3

Suggested solution

- The European Commission is the executive body of the EU. It is the body responsible for **proposing** legislation/drafting legislation.
- These proposals are then **discussed** in the European Parliament, where amendments to legislation can be put forward.
- **Decisions** are usually made by the Council of the European Union. It is the main decision-making body of the EU.

- Once legislation is passed by the Council of the European Union and Parliament (co-decision), it is the Commission's responsibility to ensure it is **implemented** through a series of directives and regulations.

EU Directive:

- It obliges member states to change their national laws to allow for EU rules, within a certain time limit.
- It is binding only as to the results to be achieved, leaving member states to choose, within prescribed limits, the means by which the rules and targets are to be attained.
- They are used to bring different national laws into line with each other and are common in matters affecting the operation of the Single Market (e.g. product safety standards, WEEE (Waste, Electrical and Electronic Equipment Directive, Safety and Health at Work Directive.)

EU Regulation:

- This is a legislative act of the EU, which becomes enforceable immediately as law in its entirety in all member states simultaneously.
- It takes precedence over national law. It is self-executing and does not require any implementing measures. EU institutions can enforce a regulation throughout the EU. Flight Compensation Regulation 261/2004 established common rules on compensation and assistance to airline passengers.

Marking scheme

Formulation	12 marks (4 × 3 marks)
Directives	4 marks
Regulations	4 marks

Describe the legislative process within the European Union.

(20 marks)

Source: 2014 Higher Level Section 3

Suggested solution

- The European Commission is the executive body of the EU. It is the body responsible for proposing legislation, etc.
- These proposals are then discussed in the European Parliament and amendments to legislation can be put forward. There is a democratic deficit, however, because the European Parliament neither initiates nor passes legislation on its own.
- Decisions are usually made by the Council of the European Union. It decides on legislation drafted by the European Commission and discussed by the European Parliament. It is the main decision-making body of the EU.

- Once legislation is passed by the Council of the European Union and Parliament, it is the Commission's responsibility to ensure it is implemented.

Regulations/Directives/Decisions

- Decisions/legislation can be adjudicated upon by the Court of Justice. The Court of Justice interprets EU law to make sure it is applied in the same way in all EU countries.

Marking scheme
3 × 4 marks (1 + 3) + 3 + 3 + 2

Evaluate the impact that any two of the following EU policies have on Irish businesses:

(i) European Monetary Union (EMU)

(ii) European Union Competition Policy

(iii) European Social Charter

(20 marks)

Source: 2014 Higher Level Section 3

Suggested solution

(i) European Monetary Union (EMU)

- The main perceived advantages of EMU are a reduction in transaction costs and an end to destabilising currency shifts within Europe. The elimination of these transaction costs benefit a country like Ireland, whose businesses export a considerable amount of its output to the European Union.
- A single currency highlights price differentials. Businesses sourcing raw materials and components can readily identify the best bargains throughout the EU.
- The ECB has a monetary policy that focuses on price stability. This includes setting interest rates for the eurozone. Record low interest rates set by the ECB of late facilitate business expansion and investment.
- Ireland's common currency is an attraction for FDI because trade within a large European market is less bureaucratic and relatively cheap. Increased FDI has positive spin-off effects for Irish indigenous industry.

European Union Competition Policy

- It ensures the best chance for the Irish consumer of getting quality goods and services through suppliers competing for the business, i.e. the existence of competition among suppliers.
- It restricts Irish businesses from forming anti-competitive cartels or keeping prices artificially high or preventing newcomers from entering the market.

It controls the growth of large mergers and takeovers and this ensures that Irish businesses operate on a fair basis and that consumers benefit.

- In doing business with smaller firms, large firms may not use their bargaining power to impose conditions which would make it difficult for their supplier to do business with the large firm's competitors.
- The European Commission can and does fine companies for any unfair practices.

European Social Charter

- The EU Social Charter sets out basic principles that impact on Irish businesses.
- Free movement of labour. Workers have the right to migrate freely, which benefits employers in terms of recruitment and selection.
- Employees have the right to a fair wage. The establishment of the minimum wage level has increased costs for business.
- A commitment to vocational training through grant aid directly to trainees has greatly upskilled the labour force benefiting Irish businesses.
- Health protection and safety at work elements to the Charter have forced employers to improve health and safety conditions in the workplace.

Evaluation required in each case

Marking scheme

(EU Policy statement, impact) 2 × 8 marks (4 + 4)

(Evaluation of each policy) 4 marks (2 + 2)

aims Be able to:

- Explain the role of global marketing in international business.
- Explain the role of information technology in globalisation.
- Describe the reasons for the development of transnational companies.

Global marketing

Global business

A global business sells the same product worldwide It sees the whole world as its market and produces a product for that market.

Examples: Toyota, Microsoft, Intel, Google, Nokia, Dell.

Global product

A global product is designed to appeal to consumers all over the world. It may have to be adapted to suit different markets.

Examples: Coca-Cola, Nike Runners.

Global marketing

Global marketing involves marketing a firm's products and identity throughout the world as if the world is one market.

A global firm must develop a global marketing mix in relation to the Four Ps (product, price, promotion, place). Global marketing uses either a standardised (same) marketing mix or an adapted marketing mix to take account of differences in markets.

Role of global marketing in international business

1. **Activities planned and organised on a global basis**

   Business decisions are based on what is happening in world markets rather than national markets.

2. **Product standardisation of brand and product**

   Global companies do not consider the differences between countries and culture as being important. They attempt to sell one product in the same way worldwide, focusing all the time on the similarities in the markets and attempting to satisfy the common desires of people everywhere.

3. **Reduction in costs and economies of scale**

Global marketing allows firms to expand globally, availing of the elimination of trade barriers, improvements in transport and advances in ICT, resulting in the achievement of economies of scale, reduction in costs and increasing profit.

4. **Facilities in many different locations**

Global companies set up assembly and manufacturing facilities in a number of different countries and export their products worldwide.

They seek out the most cost-effective locations and most cost-effective methods of production. They may manufacture the products in one country and assemble them in another country.

5. **Availability of high-quality products at lower prices**

Because of economies of scale, consumers get reliable, high-quality products at lower prices.

Transnational companies

(i) Explain the term 'global business'.

(ii) Discuss the effects of 'globalisation' on the Irish economy. Provide examples to illustrate your answer.

(20 marks)

Source: 2014 Higher Level Section 3

Suggested solution

(i) A global business sees the world as one giant market and production location. A global business provides the same, undifferentiated product worldwide. It uses a global marketing strategy, which involves the same or sometimes an adapted marketing mix (product, price, place, promotion) throughout the world to build a global brand.

Examples of global businesses include Coca-Cola, Dell, Nike, Toyota, Microsoft, Intel, HP, Google and Nokia.

(ii) Globalisation can be viewed as an opportunity for Irish businesses to sell goods and services abroad and grow and expand their operations. Companies get access to much wider markets, e.g. Kerry Group and Glanbia plc, leading to economic growth for the Irish economy.

Globalisation impacts on the labour market within the Irish economy. Having experienced net emigration for decades, Ireland now has significant immigration as global companies located here try to fill high-skill vacancies, for example, in the technology sector, where there is a skill shortage.

Global companies located in Ireland are a significant source of employment. It is estimated that American global companies alone directly employ 115,000 people.

Companies such as Dell, Microsoft, Google, Hibernian, Aviva, Palm Inc., Facebook and Intel have all made significant contributions to the success of Ireland's economy.

Consumers get a much wider variety of products to choose from and they get the product they want at more competitive prices. There is increased domestic demand leading to economic growth in the Irish economy.

The growth in globalisation and global firms, with their quality produce at cheap prices, are a competitive challenge for Irish exporters. Irish exporting firms will have to become more efficient and invest in R&D in order to provide products with a unique selling point (USP) to survive the competitive threat from global firms.

Globalisation can be viewed as a threat to the Irish economy because, if Ireland is uncompetitive, its domestic industries will decline in the face of cheaper imports of goods and services produced globally.

Repatriation of profits/closure of business/impact on Balance of Payments/economies of scale, etc.

Marking scheme
(i) 4 marks (2 + 2)
(ii) 2 × 8 marks (3 + 3 + 2)

Global marketing mix

When marketing a product to a global market, a global company will use a **standardised marketing mix** throughout the world – the product is promoted, priced, distributed and sold in exactly the same way in different markets.

However, because of social, cultural, legal and economic differences in some markets, it may have to adapt the marketing mix to suit those markets. This is called an **adapted marketing mix**.

Elements of the global marketing mix

Global product

Product is the element of the marketing that global firms try not to change.

The global business aims to sell the same product in all markets, to develop a unique selling point and global brand and to benefit from economies of scale.

However, the product may need to be adjusted to reflect technical/legal requirements (e.g. left-hand drive car, etc.).

Packaging may also need to be changed to cater for the needs of the local market (e.g. recyclable materials).

Global price

Global firms try to keep the price the same in all markets, but prices may vary in different countries due to different factors, such as:

- Cost of living/incomes in different countries
- Recognising costs of production and extra transport distribution and marketing costs

- Duties or tariffs that might have to be paid
- Local prices levels/competitors' prices

Global promotion

If a global business can use the same promotional mix globally, it will save money. However, promotion may change in different countries to take account of legislation, language and culture.

Slogans need to be checked to avoid confusion and misunderstanding.

In addition to promoting goods and services through the normal avenues for advertising and sales promotion, global firms may use other promotion methods, including:

- Attending trade fairs
- Participating in trade missions
- Using the internet

Global place

Global channels of distribution are necessary to implement a global marketing mix. Channels include:

- Selling directly to customers.
- Using an agent – an independent person who will act on behalf of the firm, generally receiving a commission on sales.
- Forming a strategic alliance with a foreign company to produce and/or market products. Both companies work together for mutual benefit.

Illustrate your understanding of the terms *standardised marketing mix* **and** *adapted marketing mix* in relation to global marketing.   (20 marks)

Source: 2015 Higher Level Section 3

Suggested solution

Standardised: (Undifferentiated approach to the Four Ps; consistent marketing mix). Global businesses with successful brands, like Nike and Levi's, aim to take the same, undifferentiated approach worldwide and use a standardised marketing mix. All products are targeted at similar groups locally. This leads to lower company costs and increased profitability.

Adapted marketing mix: (Some element(s) of the marketing mix (product, price promotion and place) are changed to reflect local customs, values and economic situations).

It is common for businesses to adapt the marketing mix to reflect regional differences, local language, cultural, geographic, or economic differences present in the market.

Global Product

The product may need to be adjusted to reflect technical, legal and language requirements, e.g. a left-hand drive car; packaging may need to be changed to cater for the needs of the local market.

Examples:

Starbucks adjusts its menu to fit local tastes. In Hong Kong, for example, they sell dragon dumplings. As a global buyer of coffee, the company has long had a reputation for engaging local cultures according to their needs.

McDonald's varies items on its menu according to local tastes. Customers in Mexico can order a green chili cheese burger; customers in many Arab countries can enjoy the McArabia: a grilled kofta sandwich on pitta bread.

Global Price

Global firms attempt to achieve a uniform price in each market; however, this objective is often affected by the following factors:

- The cost of living in different countries/disposable incomes
- Different tariffs, customs duties and VAT rates
- Local price levels and prices charged by competitors in the market/exchange rate fluctuations

Global Place

Global channels of distribution for physical goods tend to be longer, involving more intermediaries such as exporters and agents.

Examples of the various channels available include:

- Selling directly to customers online
- Use of agent/independent person who will act on behalf of the firm, generally receiving a commission on sales
- Forming a strategic alliance with a foreign company to produce and/or market products.

Global Promotion

Differences in legislation, language and culture need to be recognised in the choice of promotion such as advertising and publicity campaigns.

Example:

The language of television advertisements may have to be amended in different countries due to language barriers or the message could be considered offensive in some countries.

Marking scheme

Standardised marketing mix (Example required)	8 marks (4 + 4)
Adapted marketing mix in relation to global marketing (Example can apply to any **one** element: product, price, promotion or place)	12 marks (4 + 4 + 4)

Role of information and communication technology (ICT) in globalisation

Advances in ICT have greatly advanced the development of globalisation.
Applications such as email, videoconferencing and EDI allow global business to
function efficiently. ICT helps global firms in several ways.

1. **Communication**

   ICT allows global firms to transmit information to remote locations around the
   world (e.g. email).

2. **Videoconferencing**

   Managers meetings can take place in different locations around the world without
   the need for expensive and time-consuming travel. Face-to-face communication is
   no longer necessary.

3. **Decision-making**

   Management can access data from anywhere in the world, availing of up-to-date
   information for speedy decision-making.

4. **Responding to change**

   Management must respond quickly to changes in the global market. Advanced ICT
   allows firms to respond faster than competitors to avail of opportunities.

Outline **four** developments in technology that have facilitated the growth in
globalisation. (20 marks)

Source: 2012 Higher Level Section 3

Suggested solution

- **Design/CAD**

CAD (computer-aided design) has revolutionised the design process, making it
much easier and faster, and allowing companies to react quickly to changing
global market conditions.

- **Production/CAM**

Computer-aided manufacture (CAM), where all equipment can be computer
controlled, and computer-integrated manufacturing (CIM), which involves total
integrated control of the production from design to delivery, all add to the
efficiency of production and the ability of firms to locate anywhere in the world
and produce standardised products, irrespective of local labour skill sets.

- **Communication/mobile technology/EDI**

EDI (Electronic Data Interchange) greatly facilitates communication in a global
market. Document transfer, automated stock ordering, details of trading figures,
etc. can be transmitted globally in a matter of seconds.

- **Decision-making/ISDN**

ISDN (Integrated Services Digital Network) uses telephone lines to transmit and receive digital information. File transfer, teleworking, videoconferencing, email, etc. allow vital information to be transferred anywhere in the world. This greatly assists management planning, organising and control and facilitates effective decision-making.

- **Marketing/Internet/Social networking**

The internet, including social networking sites such as Facebook and business networks such as LinkedIn, have facilitated the global marketing of companies and the establishment of global brands. Network advertising, company websites and electronic payment have allowed global e-commerce to flourish.

- **Distribution/JIT**

Logistics, just-in-time delivery, container transport and the relevant computer software programs facilitate the global distribution of goods.

Marking scheme

4 × 5 marks (2 + 3)

Transnational companies

Transnational company (TNC)

A transnational company has its controlling headquarters in one country and branches in many other countries.

It operates on a worldwide scale.

A transnational produces and markets goods in many countries. It treats the world as a single marketplace and may move operations from one country to another in response to changing market conditions.

Examples: Ford, Intel, Nestlé, Coca-Cola, CRH.

Reason for the development of transnational companies in Ireland

- **Transport improvements**

The availability of faster and cheaper methods of air and sea travel has made it easier to supply markets worldwide.

- **Advances in communications technology**

Improvements in communication have made it easier and faster to send and receive information (e.g. videoconferencing allows managers in different locations to hold a meeting without having to travel).

- **Economies of scale**

Expanding abroad allows firms to achieve economies of scale, thereby lowering costs per unit. This enables them to compete more effectively with larger competitors.

- **Larger markets**

Many companies find that their home market is saturated and does not offer the necessary scope for expansion. By setting up operations overseas, they can maximise sales and spread business risk.

- **Removal of trade barriers**

The removal of trade barriers has opened up international markets. The World Trade Organisation (WTO) has facilitated agreements between countries, eliminating or reducing barriers and freeing up international trade. A transnational company can locate a branch in Ireland and sell products into the EU member states.

Positive impact of transnational companies on Ireland

Transnational companies **impact positively** on the Irish economy in the following ways:

1. **Employment**

   Transnational companies buy raw materials and services from local firms, creating local employment. They are also a major direct employer in many locations in the country.

2. **Balance of payments**

   They export much of their finished products. Also, the level of imports of manufacturing products is reduced. This has a positive effect on the balance of payments.

3. **Government revenue**

   Transnationals are a major source of revenue for the government through corporation tax on profits, VAT on purchases, and PAYE and PRSI paid by employees.

4. **Competition**

   Transnational companies create competition for indigenous Irish firms. This is good for the Irish consumer as it leads to reduced prices and increased efficiency, resulting in better quality goods and services.

Negative impact of transnational companies on Ireland

Transnational companies **impact negatively** on the Irish economy in the following ways:

1. **Possible closure**

   Transnational companies may close plants in Ireland and move abroad in an effort to cut costs and become more competitive (e.g. in 2010, Dell moved its manufacturing operation from Limerick to Poland with the loss of 1,900 jobs in Ireland).

2. **Repatriation of profits**

   Most of their profits are transferred to head office, so the profits made do not benefit the Irish economy.

3. **Size and impact**

   Because of their size, transnationals have been known to exert pressure on governments and may threaten to withdraw from a country if they do not get their own way on grants, taxes, etc.

Discuss reasons why multinational companies (MNCs) may choose to locate in Ireland. Provide examples to support your answer.

(20 marks)

Source: 2015 Higher Level Section 3

Suggested solution

- Corporation Tax Rate: MNCs pay 12.5% corporation tax on their profits. This low rate of corporation tax is a key government strategy in attracting FDI.
- Global companies such as Intel and Google have a major presence here and, as a result, it can be inferred that Ireland is a good place to do business. This international goodwill encourages other businesses to locate here. Internet companies such as Facebook, Skype and eBay have followed Google.
- IDA Ireland is responsible for the attraction and development of foreign direct investment in Ireland. Companies such as Apple, Microsoft and Facebook, etc., have all interacted with the IDA and approximately 150,000 people are directly employed by foreign multinationals in Ireland.
- The availability of a highly skilled and well-educated workforce:

  MNCs employ highly skilled graduates, right up to PhD level. Many of these graduates are engaged in R&D, an important area in multinational businesses. Google's European headquarters are in Dublin.
- The introduction of the single currency brought additional incentives for foreign investors to locate in Ireland, along with relative price stability. The euro has made life easier for MNCs and travelling business executives trading or visiting in the eurozone area.
- The creation of the Single Market eliminated trade barriers within the EU, allowing for the free movement of goods, services, labour and capital between member states. MNCs located in Ireland have access to a huge EU market of over 500 million people. Pharmaceutical companies use Ireland as a stepping stone to the large EU market.
- Ireland is an English-speaking country and English is the international business language. In addition, the growing number of people living in Ireland that speak different languages is a key factor in encouraging MNCs to locate here.

Marking scheme

Discuss the reasons why MNCs may choose to locate in Ireland.	2 × 7 marks (4 + 3)
Provide examples to support your answer.	1 × 6 marks (3 + 3)

Discuss the different channels of distribution that Irish businesses may consider when introducing their products to international markets.

(15 marks)

Source: 2017 Higher Level Section 3

Suggested solution

Direct Export

The business may **sell directly from the factory to customers from all over the world**. This allows the business to spread the costs of manufacturing and achieve economies of scale. The increased sales and productivity will increase profits. Use of e-commerce/internet/website to sell products.

Expansion of own facility in foreign market (organic growth).

Set up a manufacturing facility in another country to manufacture your products.

Licences/franchising

The business produces goods locally under licence, e.g. Nike.

Agency

An export agent is an independent person or firm who will sell the goods in the target market for you in return for a commission.

Trading House

A company buys goods in one country and then resells the goods at a profit in another country.

Joint Venture

The firm will set up a joint venture with a local firm to produce for a local market.

Marking scheme

7 marks (4 + 3) + 2 × 4 marks (2 + 2)

Discuss the **marketing** challenges an Irish business may face when trading globally, providing examples to support your answer.

(20 marks)

Source: 2016 Higher Level Section 3

Suggested solution

Product may have to be adapted to meet local requirements. Example: Irish electronic/electrical products would have to be adapted to suit electrical sockets in all other countries they are sold to outside of Ireland and the UK.

Price must take into account standard of living, transport costs, local competition, taxes, exchange rates, etc. Irish firms may charge a higher price in Ireland due to the standard of living in Ireland and high-cost base, but may charge a lower price in low-cost countries such as those in South America.

Longer channels of distribution (place) may result in firms setting up manufacturing plants in other countries or operating under licence to other companies – Glanbia have set up plants in various countries including Germany, Belgium, USA.

Language, culture and media are major factors for businesses to take into account before engaging in a promotion campaign. Tobacco products cannot be advertised in Ireland, but can be in other countries.

Marking scheme

4 × 5 marks (2 + 2 + 1)

Illustrate how foreign transnationals (i.e. foreign direct investment (FDI) companies) have impacted on the Irish economy.

Suggested solution

Direct employment: Approximately 150,000 people are directly employed by foreign multinationals in Ireland. It is estimated that FDI companies give rise to indirect employment of twice that amount.

They employ highly skilled graduates, right up to PhD level, which prevents a 'brain drain' from the country. Many of these graduates are engaged in R&D, an important area in multinational businesses.

Tax revenue for the government: Transnationals pay 12.5% corporation tax on their profits. This low rate of corporation tax is a key government strategy in attracting FDI.

Positive spin-off effects for the local economy and local indigenous firms. They source their inputs from domestic companies where possible, thereby increasing employment in those firms.

They will mentor Irish firms to bring this about. Local taxis, catering firms, cleaners, security firms, local pubs and restaurants all benefit from the presence of a transnational in their locality.

Enhance Ireland's reputation and act as a catalyst for further FDI. As companies such as Intel and Google have a major presence here, it can be inferred that Ireland is a good place to do business (international goodwill).

Bring a **knowledge base and a business expertise to Ireland** in terms of management systems and organisational culture. The latest technology is introduced based on research carried out in other countries, thereby requiring less Irish expenditure on R&D. Irish managers gain experience and learn from foreign business executives.

Excellent high-tech companies **have easy access to international markets**. Some FDI companies are considered footloose, having no loyalty to Ireland. They may leave immediately if operating costs are lower elsewhere. The DELL Limerick move to Poland resulted in thousands of job losses in the Limerick area.

Irish employees of foreign multinationals learn the best business practices and technologies. This makes it easy for 'would-be entrepreneurs' to set up their own businesses, thereby **promoting an entrepreneurial spirit**.

Repatriation of profits, which means wealth leaves the Irish economy.

Positive impact on the Balance of Trade: They bring their own business plans and ready-made export markets. Up to 80% of Irish exports come from foreign multinationals (about 50% from just five companies). Because of their substantial exports, Ireland hasn't had a Balance of Payments problem for many years.

Marking scheme

Illustrate the impact of foreign transnationals/
FDI companies on the Irish Economy   5 × 5 marks (1 + 2 + 2)

Applied Business Question (ABQ) (Higher Level)

Based on Units 5, 6 and 7

This is a compulsory question for Leaving Certificate 2023/2028

Galaxy Games Ltd

Galaxy Games Ltd is a small indigenous company, operating in the new gaming technology sector. It was founded by two college graduates, David Whelan and Jane Ward. David is a software engineer and a web architect, while Jane is a marketing graduate. Their design team recently identified some ideas for new games in action–adventure, music, and e-learning.

After reviewing the various ideas put forward, *Knights' Domain*, a new action–adventure game that involved building a fantasy kingdom, was chosen. The design team decided to use Irish music and cutting-edge graphics to set the game apart. Jane completed a business report, including a detailed break-even analysis, to determine the potential of *Knights' Domain*. Following on from this report, the design team introduced more challenging levels to the game and added more 3D graphics. The game was introduced to a group of transition year students from a local secondary school, who commented positively on the different levels and on its distinctive graphics. The product *Knights' Domain* was launched in various games stores with an advertising campaign accompanying the launch.

Social responsibility is a key element in Galaxy Games's corporate business plan. Funding was invested in supporting the development of a highly skilled customer service department. Galaxy Games Ltd attracts and retains high-quality, creative employees. A major European venture capital firm has invested €1.5 million in the company to date. Galaxy Games Ltd maintains good relationships with its suppliers, many of whom have continued a business relationship with the company since its establishment. When choosing a suitable business premises, David and Jane prioritised energy efficiency.

As a result of Ireland's growing international reputation in the gaming technology sector and Galaxy Games's successful company presentation at the 2012 Dublin Web Summit, the company became a target for acquisition. In January 2013 it was taken over by BizzBuzz, a US global gaming company and a market leader in the industry. BizzBuzz implements a global approach to marketing its games. All games are available in ten different languages. Prices per game are set taking account of competitor prices and various economies of scale. Recent developments in technology enable BizzBuzz to distribute its games worldwide through download from the internet to laptops, smartphones and tablets. BizzBuzz is a globally recognised brand name and uses the slogan 'A new game every day' on its website.

(A) Outline the stages involved in the product development process of *Knights' Domain* for Galaxy Games Ltd. **(30 marks)**

(B) Discuss the social responsibilities of Galaxy Games Ltd to its stakeholders. **(20 marks)**

(C) Evaluate the global marketing mix of BizzBuzz. **(30 marks)**

(80 marks)

Suggested solution

(A)

Idea Generation

- Initial ideas for the new product are thought up systematically. They can be internal or external.
- Ideas may be generated by brainstorming sessions, market research, staff suggestions, customer suggestions/feedback on existing products or services, competitors, R&D, etc.

  Link: *'Their design team recently identified some ideas for new games in action–adventure, music and e-learning.'*

Product Screening

- All ideas are vetted and the impractical and unworkable ideas are dropped, leaving the most viable ones for further examination and development.
- Careful screening helps businesses avoid huge expenses in developing ideas that are subsequently not marketable and ensures that good opportunities are not lost.

  Link: *'After reviewing the various ideas put forward,* Knights' Domain, *a new action–adventure game that involved building a fantasy kingdom, was chosen.'*

Concept Development

- This involves turning the idea into an actual product or service that will appeal to/ meet the needs of customers.
- A unique selling point (USP) is identified which will differentiate it from other products on the market.

  Link: *'The design team decided to use Irish music and cutting-edge graphics to set the game apart.'*

Feasibility Study

- This is carried out to assess if a product has potential. It looks at whether it can be produced technically (production feasibility) and if it will be profitable (financial feasibility).
- It seeks answers to questions such as: what demand will there be for the product? What will it cost to produce and can the business afford it?

  Link: *'Jane completed a business report, including a detailed break-even analysis, to determine the potential of* Knights' Domain.

Prototype Development

- This stage involves developing a sample or model of a product. It is produced to see what materials are required to make it and if it appeals to customers.
- It can be used to test the product to see if it conforms to certain standards and to determine what adjustments/improvements can be made before deciding to go into full production.

  Link: *'Following on from this report, the design team introduced more challenging levels to the game and added more 3D graphics.'*

Test Marketing/Product Testing

- It involves doing a small-scale trial to identify possible faults and to assess customer reaction.
- The product is tested on a sample of potential consumers before going into full production to determine customer satisfaction with the product.

  Link: *'The game was introduced to a group of transition year students from a local secondary school, who commented positively on the different levels and on its distinctive graphics.'*

Production and Launch/Commercialisation

- The product is put into full-scale production and introduced to the market.
- The business will select a suitable marketing strategy to persuade consumers to buy the product.

  Link: *'The product* Knights' Domain *was launched in various games stores with an advertising campaign accompanying the launch.'*

Marking scheme

(A)	The stages involved in the product development process	5 stages @ 6 marks each (2 + 2 + 2)	30 marks

(B)
Social Responsibilities to Shareholders/Investors

- To act in accordance with its Constitution
- To provide a fair return on the investment by shareholders
- To avoid excessive payments to senior management
- To present a true and fair view of the financial performance and standing of the business and maintain a proper set of accounts.

  Link: *'A major European venture capital firm has invested €1.5 million in the company to date.'*

Social Responsibility to Customers

- Fair and honest advertising of its product
- Abide by health and safety regulations: products must be safe.
- Goods must be of merchantable quality, match their description, fit for purpose, etc.

- Uphold the right of the customer to complain and to investigate such complaints
- Good after-sales service
- Charge a fair price.

  Link: *'Funding was invested in supporting the development of a highly skilled customer service department.'*

Social Responsibility to Employees

- Adhere to employment law, health and safety regulations, etc.
- Pay a fair wage to all employees
- Provide a safe working environment
- Treat employees with dignity and respect/no discrimination
- Provide equal opportunities for promotion, pay, etc. to all employees.

  Link: *'Galaxy Games Ltd attracts and retains high quality, creative employees.'*

Social Responsibility to General Public/Community

- To be environmentally conscious; to implement environmentally friendly business practices
- Co-operate with government offices e.g. EPA
- Openness and transparency
- Recyclable packaging, clean manufacturing, sustainable development.

  Link: *'When choosing a suitable business premises, David and Jane prioritised energy efficiency.'*

Social Responsibility to Suppliers

- Follow tendering procedures where applicable; treat all suppliers fairly
- Pay amounts agreed within timeframe agreed.

  Link: *'Galaxy Games Ltd maintains good relationships with its suppliers, many of whom have continued a business relationship with the company since its establishment.'*

Marking scheme

(B)	Social responsibilities of Galaxy Games Ltd to its stakeholders	4 stakeholders @ 5 marks (1 + 3 + 1)	20 marks

(C)
Global Product

- This is the element of the marketing mix that companies try not to change.
- Global businesses aim to sell an undifferentiated product in all markets. They aim to develop a unique selling point for their products and a global brand name.
- However, the product may need to be adjusted to reflect technical, legal and language requirements, e.g. a left-hand drive car; packaging may need to be changed to cater for the needs of the local market.

  Link: *'All games are available in ten different languages.'*

Global Price

Global firms attempt to achieve a uniform price in each market; however, this objective is often affected by the following factors:

- The cost of living in different countries.
- The cost of production, distribution, marketing, transportation in different countries.
- Different tariffs, customs duties and VAT rates.
- Local price levels and prices charged by competitors in the market.

  Link: *'Prices per game are set taking account of competitor prices and various economies of scale.'*

Global Place

Global channels of distribution for physical goods tend to be longer, involving more intermediaries such as exporters and agents. However, the nature of the BizzBuzz product portfolio together with rapid technological developments means that a direct channel of distribution is appropriate. Examples of the various channels available include:

- Selling directly to customers
- Use of agents – independent persons who will act on behalf of the firm, generally receiving a commission on sales
- Forming a strategic alliance with a foreign company to produce and/or market products. Partners work together for mutual benefit.

  Link: *'Recent developments in technology enable BizzBuzz to distribute its games worldwide through download from the internet to laptops, smartphones and tablets.'*

Global Promotion

- Differences in legislation, language and culture need to be recognised in the choice of promotion.
- Internet advertising on social media sites, TV and radio, advertising on the BizzBuzz website and international trade fairs would be suitable methods of promoting the BizzBuzz brand, logo and slogan globally.

  Link: *'BizzBuzz is a globally recognised brand name and uses the slogan "A new game every day" on its website.'*

Evaluation: Own judgement required

Evaluation of any two of the Four Ps separately **or** one evaluation of the overall global marketing mix.

Marking scheme

(C)	The global marketing mix	2 elements @ 7 marks each (2 + 3 (2 + 1) + 2) and	30 marks
	Evaluation	4 marks (2 + 2)	